INSIDE
HORSERACING

An Invaluable Guide
for Owners or Bettors

JOSEPH B. DAVIDSON, D.V.M.

New York

First Arco Edition, 1973

Published by Arco Publishing Company, Inc.
219 Park Avenue South, New York, N.Y. 10003

Copyright © 1971 by Dr. J. B. Davidson

Library of Congress Catalog Card Number 73-169097

ISBN 0-668-03332-0

Printed in United States of America

FOREWORD

All horse races are fixed. This has been true from horse-racings humble beginning several thousand years ago of one rider challenging another to a race. Even then, a time, a place, a distance, and a mutual decision on how to start put at least four qualified fixes on the simplest of races. It is impossible to have a horse race without some fixing.

As time went on and horse racing became more popular more conditions had to be added. All of these tend to pre-determine the winner or to the purest the fixing conditions meant giving every horse a chance to win. This element of chance, of course, inspired a competitive sport to blossom into a multi-billion dollar international business. When racing was a sport it was common practice to place the fastest horse a few paces back of the rest or stagger a field of horses back various distances and all start on a signal to provide a more thrilling or closer finish. When little or no money was involved a group could get together and decide on proper handicapping of their respective mounts. Honest handicapping and good racing prevailed because the dishonest element was simply not invited to compete a second time. Thus policing early racing was not the complicated problem as it is today.

Horses down through the ages have been a source of liveli-hood and great pleasure to man. It is natural that man would become very emotionally involved with his favorite steed. Wars have been fought over a single horse. Wars have ended with the challenge of one chieftain to another for a settle-ment of the booty by a horse race between the two or between some of their subordinates. Paul Revere likely saved America, as we know it, because of a horse race against time. Early settlers survived in the push westward, in many instances, only if their horses could outrun or outlast those of the Indians. A race for life! Now races are for fun and money.

This book should bring all of the self appointed experts on horses and racing up to date on the matter of fixed races—a matter all losers and some winners have long suspected existed. Some will most certainly be overwhelmed with the magnitude of factors that are involved in the fixing. Hopefully some new conversational reasons will appear on the scene to justify the less profitable hunches and misjudgements in betting the wrong horse.

A frank confession that one does not know all about horses is courting social disaster: you will be shunned and despised by everyone, especially the horses. The "in" crowd digs horses and the horse numbers are growing so fast constant vigil and frequent trips to the racetracks is the only means of preventing a rash of horse "dropouts"—unthinkable in decent society and a horrible fate if one choses indecent society. Racing is here to stay so join the "in" crowd.

This is not a new fad. The conditions have changed since early racing made the scene and those conditions and changes are precisely what this book is all about. I hope it will help you have more winners and better understand the losers.

J. B. Davidson, D.V.M.

CONTENTS

INTRODUCTION

No book would be a complete account of race fixing without a chapter explaining an intriguing game related to horse-racing that many trainers have developed into a very exact science, hereinafter called "fixing the owner". Most trainers either do not participate in this game or they keep their rank as amateurs by only fixing the owner now and again, as life gets boring with the routine of training and racing horses—or their money gets short. Either of these is an acceptable reason to race less and enjoy it more by starting a little game of "fix the owner". However, since this pastime does not envolve the majority of the professional trainers, to a degree of employing some of the better techniques of the game, lets discuss the real dyed-in-the-wool professional "fix the owner player". We will call him the FTO trainer-player to distinguish him from the many good hard working honest trainers that resemble normal human beings and are respected members of the racing fraternity.

There are very few rules to this game at the beginning as most of them have to be made up as progress is made in fixing the owner. In fact, about the only things standard are the participants which can vary somewhat in the number of owners and number of horses the trainer wants to take on in any one given game. There is no time limit officially set. The FTO trainer-player is declared winner only after the owner has conceded complete defeat—oh, yes, the trainer always wins; that is why we call it "fixing the owner."

To start this game, a very astute business man (or someone who inherited a bundle) decided he should own a race-horse (this is the way many large expensive stables start). It is necessary to know his motivation for this unfortunate decision because his reasons will likely determine just how long he will stay in the game—i.e. some owners are easier to fix than others (they have more money or more guts to begin with). It must be remembered that a hard headed business-man who made enough money to afford a horse does not concede complete defeat without putting up a real fight. It is well to remember, also, that in this case he has no opportunity

1

to choose the weapons or the battleground. All these little advantages are taken by the FTO trainer-player who feels a deep moral responsibility to fix the owner in question permanently. To do this properly he must take complete advantage of the entire situation, including the owner's good nature and sense of fairness (which he will have less of after the game is over).

Now, to get on with the game. We have found one essential player—the predetermined loser who is willing to invest in a horse.

It would be well to point out here that buying and selling horses is not trade, commerce, business, or anything sordid like that; it is a joke. If you are a sport you cheer for the friend that 'got' you on the deal. Hurrah for you if you 'did' him, especially if you used some sneaky tactics—it is his turn to be a sport.

But don't let that kind of joking get out of hand and seep into your other pleasures. All this applies to horses only. If, after a few successful deals in horse-flesh, you try a similar deal at bridge or golf, you may be asked to leave. All is fair in love and war—and horse dealing.

You have not purchased your first horse, so it is time you were up and doing (or being done) which our FTO trainer will personally guarantee.

If a prospective owner were not in the intriguing game of getting himself fixed he could whisper around the track that he had decided to buy a horse. A few seconds after doing this you will receive hundreds of sacrificial offers to buy wonderful, sound horses that can sprint, go the distance, trot, or pace. This future horse owner must possess the ability to pick out of a group of well qualified professional trainers the one least likely to succeed as a trainer. This is usually very easy, because the ones who talk the most make the best impression on a prospective owner, and they invariably know the least about training horses. They have other, hidden, qualities that make them super par excellent contenders for "fixing the owner". Basic dishonesty is all that would really be required, but most of the pro's have still other success inspiring attributes like drinking too much, heavy gambling, borrowing money from

2

every available lender. A really good FTO-trainer-player has picked up many other vices to serve him well in the contest coming up. He has cultivated a friendship with one or more of the few unscrupulous veterinarians around tracks that will give shots within the restricted 48 hour period before a race. This "vet" will also make excessive charges for his services and split the fee with the FTO trainer-player. This can be very helpful in winning this game of "fixing the owner". A well selected tack or harness man (one that gives kick backs), an unqualified groom (let me say here there are many good ones) along with any cooperative transient purveyors of horse products gives the trainer a few more advantages for the coming event. At any rate, you can get the picture of what started out to be a trainer against an owner has developed into an army of allies hidden in the background on the FTO trainer-players side. The FTO trainer-player feels lots of friends is a justifiable balance because the owner has lots of money and taking it in the name of his beloved horse is the primary objective in "fixing the owner".

We now have a hardworking (he must not have too much time to spend at the track) honest businessman and a dishonest trainer with lots of questionable associates. The stage is set to start fixing the owner. He is not an owner yet, but is more than willing to become one. This game like most is divided into units with a breather between each segment. Racing is split into races or heats. Baseball is divided into innings. Football and basketball are separated into quarters. "Fixing the owner" usually has several parts best described as treatments.

The first treatment comes with buying the horse. Being a sound businessman our new, excited prospective owner seeks the advice of his very vocal trainer in this matter of buying a horse. A good performing stable is being sold to settle an estate which seemed to the owner a good place to pick up a horse or two. He would like for his trainer to go with him to inspect them before the sale to select possible candidates and buy the one that has the best possibilities for the best price.

Basic instincts alert the trainer that this owner is going to be hard to deal with if allowed to pursue this kind of logical

3

course in the race business. He goes into an act of being completely horrified that a man thinking of going into racing would even toy with the idea of buying someone else's 'used up' horses. Our owner feebly counters that it is an estate settlement and not just a sale of cripples but concedes that maybe the trainer knows best (he should not have done that— ten points for the trainer). Of course secretly the trainer knows he has very little chance of getting much of a kick-back at this kind of sale and even though he needed some of those good horses it was not worth taking a chance on letting a prospective owner make a decision that could turn out to be profitable. Such a move could jeopardize the whole future of this game before it got started.

It was decided (by the trainer) how to better spend the owners money for a horse. They would go to the Fall Colt sales and buy a yearling with lots of potential. Another way of saying this is they will buy an unproven colt for a big price with odds against him ever getting to the races—especially under our present set-up. The prospective owner has been convinced, after lots of conversation, this is the best way to get into the horse racing business and the trainer is convinced he has the situation well in hand and will make this first treatment in "fixing the owner" a good one without taking his new owner completely out of the game. He now has a lot of homework to do. First he must determine how much money his new owner is willing to spend so he will not exceed this by more than a few thousand dollars when the bidding starts. Next, he must find a consignee at the sale that will split with him for bidding his horse up far beyond what it would normally bring. Then he must get together with some of his allies that are bringing prospective new owners to the sale. They will decide who is to buy which horses and where each is to stop bidding so his client can get the horse selected for the amount they are willing to pay. With this type of co-ordinated effort several games of "fixing the owner" can be started at the same time that will produce a lot of desirable side effects and the first treatments can be rather painless $50,000 to $100,000 affairs. Among the benefits are ecstatic auctioneers that put on a wonderful show with spirited bidding.

4

All time record dollar volume sales make good publicity for racing. When lower quality horses bring more money the better bred ones certainly are worth more so prices go up and up. All of this is good for any sale. Our new Owner gets a $10,000 horse (for only $60,000). According to the FTO-trainer this horse should have sold for at least a $100,000 but his trainer slipped in and stole him while the crowd (including the new owner) were out for a sandwich." Of course, "he did have to go a few dollars over the $50,000 limit set up by the owner, but we got a real bargain." Before any objections can be lodged the trainer points to the horse just coming into the ring and suggests here is another one that would make an excellent stable mate for the one he had been so lucky to get at such a bargain. That is to say, "he could buy another $40,000 colt with the money he had saved on the first one". All good professional "fix the owner" players know their owners think by logic and they must handle these delicate situations of overspending the bosses money with sound logic. It is very difficult, at times, for a mere spectator of this game to understand this kind of logic, but bear in mind we are at a sale that is pure unadulterated organized confusion that leaves any neophyte a bit shaky concerning the rapid turn of events. It attests to the truth of the adage, "that if you can keep your head when all of those about you are losing theirs, chances are you don't know what the issue is." Some call it auction fever—very contagious and expensive disease with few recoveries (many close heart attacks, but few deaths).

A quick review of the outstanding pedigree displayed in the sale catalogue and a reminder that the trainer had signed the sale slip as the new owners agent convinced him that he had bought a fine horse. After calling his banker to transfer another $10,000 to the newly established horse account and writing a check for the sixty grand this somewhat numb new horse owner did not somehow feel as happy as he had imagined he would upon buying his first horse. He could not derive much pleasure out of the game he had become a major participant in because he did not yet realize he was in the irreversible game of "fixing the owner".

Feeling certain he had chalked up a lot of points in this

first treatment and noticing some of the gaiety (and color from the owners face) had vanished, the trainer decided it was time to take the new owner on an elbow tour to see his new future champion.

While walking down the row of temporary box stalls this man-in-the-know was pointing out various horses and their selling prices knowing this would help to bring the owner out of shock. When they arrived at the newly acquired colts stall the trainer threw the gate open and exclaimed: "... just look at that; man what a bargain; a sure Kentucky Derby (Hambeltonion or Brown jug) winner; ... how could a man be so lucky on the first try; look at that intelligent expression; yes this colt shows determination in his eyes already—a sure winner." A quick glance reveals the owner is perking up a little. A review of anatomy might even bring a smile of approval so the trainer goes on, "did you ever see such legs; the feet are perfect—no foot no horse you know." "Oh, yes they are a little broken but the blacksmith can fix that easily (at $25 per trip plus a little padding)." "Notice the fetlocks and how straight the pasterns are". "No, the right foot does not turn out, it's just the way he is standing". "Boy, what hocks, I can hardly wait to start training this one." Admittedly, all yearlings look like champions and the owner is starting to feel that maybe he had made a sound investment. He noticed the nice halter and gingerly asked if it was included in the deal. "Yes sir" was the reply, "you get all of this horse and the halter."

Logic almost crept back into the mind of the new owner at this period when he caught himself estimating how much this "sure winner" had cost by the pound. A wave of sentiment gave him a guilty feeling for even thinking of such a thing—his color was returning and he had become a very proud owner of a horse born to win. Like a new father he was pointing out the intelligent look, straight pasterns, good feet and magnificent hocks to all passers-by.

The trainer was taking this all in, of course, and knowing his owner was making a remarkable come-back set his gamely talents for treatment number two.

Yes, this could develop into a classic case of "fixing the owner."

Treatment number two would conform to rules of the game and be a relatively light one to allow the owner to recover as completely as possible. Employed properly, this could be a long profitable game because this owner had clearly demonstrated he could take punishment in his wallet section and bounce back. The trainer noted too the straight forward way his client had simply called the bank and asked for $10,000 to be transferred to the horse account. There was no doubt this man had decided to go into the horse business to stay (of course there will be some moments of doubt and a few more surprises along the way). Now it was safe to leave the new owner to arrange transportation. He was in a newly found glory, of introducing his new 'steal' to all of the admiring first-timers that agreed he had gotten more than his money's worth and non-committal veterans that managed weak sympathetic smiles of approval with best wishes for success before turning away and shaking their heads in utter disbelief. Of course some came by to be sure they had not overlooked something special about this colt that sold so well. Most silently agreed they had not overlooked too much and maybe this new owner just wanted a bay colt with two white feet and a blaze in his face. Anyway we hear what we want to and enough people had told the owner he had gotten a bargain that he could tell everyone that already knew (because the stall numbers were still up and they had all sale prices marked in their catalogues) he had gotten this fine colt for a paltry sixty thousand. Naturally the more he said it the more he believed it.

This symptom of horse fever is very contagious. Little is known about the true cause of this malady. It is a known fact that close proximity to a horse does strange things to the very strongest men's thinking process. It may be the characteristic odor or the noble appearance. In any event, whether it be olifactory or optic the physical effects are devastating to man. Vision is blurred. Respiration is markedly increased. Rationalization replaces logic with optimism running rampant and reality becomes something that likely never really existed or at least never will again unless the smitten gets into a game of "fixing the owner". Even during these crucial moments of confidence building on the owner's part, the trainer-player is building up his box-score on treatment number two. He has found a friendly trucker that will be happy to van this horse from the sale to his stable and explain to the new owner that he is giving his trainer a special rate on half a load.

Informed of the special rate of one hundred dollars, the owner (now horseman) suppressed his desire to scream that this seemed a bit steep for hauling such a little horse such a short distance. However, logic came to his rescue in time to save any words of disagreement with the trucker's rate. He reasoned that one hundred dollars was not too much to pay for safe delivery of such a valuable animal with so much potential. Renting a trailer would be cheaper, but the colt might get hurt. "It's a deal," he commented, "anyway, what's a hundred dollars?" (In this case it was fifty for the trucker and fifty for the trainer-player.) You see, our trainer-player never forgets he is out to win this game of "fixing the owner," and the owner still doesn't even know he is in the game. No wonder it is so exciting for the outsider looking in. If you do not presently know an owner in this situation, by all means try to find one, and follow the rise and demise of a real sportsman who certainly unintentionally picked the wrong man and follows his advice because there are too few guidelines for the newcomer in the racing business.

The Absent Owner Treatment

The sale is over, everyone is concerned now with getting their precious cargo home. Our FTO trainer-player has built some confidence of his resourcefulness in the new owner by being out ahead of the crowd with his arrangements to ship. This bit of forward thinking will not only make our FTO player fifty dollars but, by building the owner's confidence, will enable him to rack up some real points in treatment number three. Sometime before the whistle blows to end this treatment our owner may suspect or even be well aware that he is in a rather costly game with lots of surprises. At this point he will concede defeat or find another trainer. Either will be a decided improvement that will save money and maybe the owner's health, if not his faith in humanity.

This treatment starts out with only the FTO-trainer in the game. The owner of the horse will be left out completely until after the horse has won his first race after many bad starts. The course of events is no accident. All actions are well thought out to exclude the owner from this one and make it appear like an oversight that he was not there for the festive occassion. For the first well planned torture climax, the FTO-trainer calls the owner collect to tell him his horse won the feature yesterday as planned (this is the first the owner even knew his horse was racing). The jubilant FTO-trainer allows, "It was really too bad the owner could not have been there to accept the trophy and congratulatory kiss from the County Bean Queen". Now you know wild horses could not have kept Mr. Owner away if he had the slightest idea his horse might have been entered.

The owner could no longer contain his fury and disappointment with such a negligent, inconsiderate, (censored) trainer that would not even tell him when his horse is racing. He starts violating a FTO—trainer rule of this game of "Fixing the Owner" by raising his voice. The sizzling telephone conversation went as follows:

Owner: "I am not psychic, how in the h – – – do I know my horse is racing if you don't tell me?"

FTO-trainer: "I meant to call, but could not find a telephone."

Owner: "For three days you can't find a phone. You d-- sure can find a telephone when you need to borrow some money or buy more equipment for the hayburner that has done nothing but cost me money. Now he wins and I don't even get to see the race. Why didn't you tell me you had entered the horse when I talked to you day before yesterday?"

FTO-trainer: "I forgot."

Owner: "Who paid the starting fee?"

FTO-trainer: "I did. That's what I needed the five hundred dollars for that you sent after our talk day before yesterday?"

Owner: "Why didn't you tell me what it was for then. I would have known my horse was being entered."

FTO-trainer: "You didn't ask."

Long pause.

FTO-trainer: "Are you there? Are you all right?" (this fellow is all heart; I didn't think he really cared what happened to his owner. Here is evidence he does have some concern).

Owner: "Yes, I am all right, but why couldn't you let me know just so I could have seen the race whether he won or not?"

FTO-trainer: "I am sorry about that".

Owner: "What did he pay?"

FTO-trainer: "One hundred twenty one to one and change." Longer pause.

FTO-trainer: "Are you still there?" "Wasn't that a terrific payoff?"

Owner: "I will take your questions in rotation, one at a time. I just took a look out the window and pinched myself to see if I was here at all." He was still furious that he was not informed of the race so he could have been there to get in on the bonanza. "If I had been there I would have bet a few bucks for you."

FTO-trainer: "Now don't fret about that. I figured he was the best and had him covered real well. Collected a bundle. You know boss, this is the first chance I have had to square things with the boys (meaning the ones that had been giving him tips and loaning him money all season) and they were real happy—we all did real good." Then sensing the owner was a lot less than happy about this whole fiasco quickly added, "The next time you can get down here they will fix us up with a good winner."

Owner: Completely numb, "O.K. and goodbye." After hanging up the owner remembered he forgot to ask how the horse came out of the race, but the trainer would have said something if all was not well (or would he?). He knew he had been fixed up pretty badly and quickly looked around as he hung up the phone to see if anyone had heard him say, "One hundred twenty to one—if he does this to me again I will kill him—so help me, I will kill him." If it had happened again real soon he might have done just that too, but FTO-trainers space these atomic blows strategically with time for the owners to recover somewhat. They well know one of the symptoms of horse fever is a partial loss of memory of past events. A blow by blow account of how real great the horse ran and what a future this horse had will lull the owner back into a false sense of security again.

A tack-room meeting must be called to plan some stategy for the next move. The FTO-trainer really knows what he will do next, but wants to talk to his cronies to get up courage to carry this next treatment out (could he be getting soft—never). Anyway the meeting is callled.

Tack Room Meeting

The FTO trainer told his friends that the boss is a little hot about being left out, but they all agreed, "You just can't trust an owner to come to the track and maybe bring a lot of his friends. They might bet on the race and run the odds away down. The owner has a lot of money invested in this horse and he just might try to get even—you know how funny these horse owners are about money." They all agree the owners are a pretty strange breed that can foul up the payoff on a fixed race. INTERESTING FACT—if all of their fixed races turned out the way they had them planned this meeting would be on the French Riviera and not in this musty tack room. In response to a question from the floor; our FTO-trainer did not think the old man was mad enough to take the horses away from him and give them to another trainer (secretly they were all hoping—you know, . . . no honor among thieves). To proceed, our shrewd FTO-trainer knew, however, this treatment would have to be altered a little in order to repeat it with any degree of safety.

Course number two must be instituted and when it follows the previous course some preparations must be made. First of all it will be necessary to regain the owners confidence. The best approach here would be to get the owner to bring his wife over next Saturday. He knew a horse in the last race that had a chance and the owner liked to bet on sure things. Knowing he would need considerable time to thaw the situation, the FTO-trainer figured he would have them come early and look over the stable first. This meant he would have to get the horses and the stable cleaned up better to make a good impression,

11

but he would make the sacrifice—staying there to see that the groom worked and missing one day's golf was better than losing a good horse that could be exploited still further. He would make club house reservations so they could eat after looking the horses over and have lots of time to talk about how wonderful the horse looked in the last race. He might even apologize again for not being certain the owner was there to see the great effort. He would not bring up the matter, but if the owner mentioned it he would apologize again and with the Mrs. there the owner could not get too violent, especially while in the clubhouse. There would be a few tense moments when they first arrived but he could handle that with the scare technique.

Even amateur FTO-trainers know the owner lives in constant fear that something will happen to his precious horse. After all he has been purposely conditioned to this fright by horror tales from the FTO-trainer concerning other great horses that would have made it big except one of the hundreds of things that can wind up a race horse's career stepped in and declared the horse, "all done".

All good FTO-trainers remember to bring up a few of these scarey episodes every time the trainer shows up for three reasons. 1. It bolsters their worth in the owner's eye, as long as the horse involved is kept sound. 2. It prepares the owner for the worst and convinces him the trainer is not at fault if misfortune takes over (and one can't be too careful in this area when most of the trainer's time is spent on the golf course). 3. There is always a possibility that by previous conditioning a real scare thrown at an owner that can shift the owners attention to the horse's welfare and forget everything else that was on his mind. To be more specific the situation that is coming up.

Timing is everything in a situation like this. To have effective split second timing requires planning, so our FTO-trainer starts planning. He will know when his owner arrives because he has always forgotten (purposely) to give the owner his stable gate pass. This required the owner to wait at the gate while the FTO-trainer then goes to the gate and gets the owner admitted (such a system keeps the owner from making surprise visits to the stable before a few things can be put in order). It, also, makes unauthorized, undesirable people get a sticker or come in with someone that has a sticker, but that is another story.

Anyway he would call the owner and tell him about the winner in the last race next Saturday. He would also tell him the rest of the plans for the day. It would be just great if they could arrive early to see the stable and look over the future champion. The way this horse ran the other day leaves no doubt about being able to go all the way. Realizing he probably should not have mentioned that race the FTO-trainer talks faster, "Now you just come to the stable gate and have them call me and I will be right over." "Oh, yes, remind me to give you your stable area sticker" . . . "(if he does I will think of something— some way to avoid giving it to him until this meet is over.)" He can then put it on the windshield with the others I saved until the meets were over. This way his friends know he is a privileged horse owner. The owner sounded a little excited in his acceptance of this generous gesture by the FTO—trainer. The Mrs. would be glad to accompany him and they would be there (at the stable gate) at eleven o'clock.

With this part of the plan confirmed and out of the way, the FTO-trainer begins concentrating on the finer details of future relations with this owner. He must not forget to ask who has a chance in the last race next Saturday, but right now attention must be given the upcoming scare that is going to make the owner forget he was not told about the last race. Knowing the owner the way our FTO-trainer does, he is certain the owner will come right out with his objections about this loosely phrased "oversight" when he gets there. This being the case, it will be best to send the groom to the gate to bring in the owner to get the most out of this scare. The FTO-trainer will extemporaneously tell the groom (when he hears his name called over the P.A. system) that the owners horse showed a slight soreness at the morning workout. He believes it would be best for him to do the leg up and for the groom to go to the gate and tell the watchman to let the owner in. Prior to the eleven o'clock call they will, of course, get the tack in A-1 shape, the stalls bedded twice as deep as necessary and the front of the stable raked out and watered down to give it a clean look (better get rid of the empty beer cans, too). He will time the owners arrival from the gate to coincide with his last wrap of the stable bandage

13

on the right leg of the owners pride and joy. He will jump up, wipe the excess liniment, the owner could smell all the way from the gate, on his trousers and pump the owners hand with sincerity fiting the return of the prodigal's son. He will look straight at the eyes of the owner which are glued on the bandaged leg. "Yes, this will do it." The owner won't even say hello. His horrified remark will be, "What happened to my horse's leg?"

The ensuing dialogue assured him, "nothing really—he turned up a little lame afer the last race. We will get some x-rays the first of the week to determine if any bones are broken. In the meantime we are keeping him bandaged and under close observation. We took him to the track this morning and he did not seem too bad." The shock had been effective, but our FTO-trainer's trained eye could see the owner staring to relax a little so this was the place to stop building confidence and give him another jolt. The FTO-trainer stimulated the owners adrenals a little more by casually remarking, "he hoped it was not a broken sesmoid, cracked navicular, or fractured splint bone." The sympathetic tones coming from this hardened trainer's throat, as he talked about these three terrorizing possibilities, sent a wave of chills up and down the spine of the owner. While he remained speechless the FTO-trainer turned on his best brand of charm and welcomed Mrs. Owner to the races. She smiled but could not hide the obvious concern for her husband. "If this horse is finished that will be almost too much" she thought trying to think of some consoling words. She looked back at the FTO-trainer for help, who by all rules should never be sympathetic in a game of fixing the owner. For her sake he said, "It might not even be that bad," and for the egotistical icing added, "I have brought a lot of bad ones through." Feeling his purpose had been throughly successful and having convinced the owner his services were needed, as never before, he suggested they go eat. The owner wondered who could possibly eat at a time like this, but they really did not know yet that the leg was broken in three places and he would need all the strength he could muster to withstand the ordeal if his future prospect was out of it, so "let's go". He was not at all hungry, but a triple martini might uncongeal his blood and get circula-

14

tion going again. He would have a few drinks and try not to worry about that leg until the facts were known. As they got in the car to go to the clubhouse his, something less than helpful, wife reminded him that he looked a little pale—he felt pale. I doubt that it would have helped him to know he was in a losing game of fix the owner.

Most owners like to see their horses win now and again. Not only does winning help defray the rather heavy burden of expense connected with this sport of kings, but being able to cash a winning ticket on their own horse is a reward far in excess of its monetary value. The inexperienced owner with a FTO-trainer relys on the word of his first-in-command for the proper race for their horse to be a sure winner—(I told you races are fixed). This sets the stage for the real painful treatment in our game of fix the owner. I might add, while this is not the end of the game (no such luck) it is usually the beginning of the end. In fact the shock of this treatment may leave the owner requiring months of therapy on the couch before being able to talk or move his arms and legs freely again. Let me explain how such a traumatic experience can result from a simple desire of wanting to see his horse win and collect a little bet (or a big bet).

Here might be the appropriate place to point out some advantages of any prospective horse owner getting a complete physical examination (and maybe line up a psychiatrist) before getting into the racing business if you are going to get involved with an FTO player. You may have decided by now that these trainers are tough, but you haven't seen anything yet. One of the most important reasons for the physical is to be sure your blood pressure is under control. There will be many occasions when it will shoot up considerably in response to surprise moves by your FTO opponent. Remember, he is a dedicated man, and a real pro with an enviable knowledge of horse terms, psychology of human weaknesses, arrangement mathematics—and knows all of the short cuts in every treatment of "fixing the owner" (these are the printable things he is).

The next reason for this check-up is to be sure the heart is in good shape. There are a number of reasons for this precaution. First of all, you will have to work harder to get things organized at the office to get a few moments at the track. Secondly, every FTO worthy of the name knows he must remove unnoticed portions of his opponent's heart until he has none left, to have a complete victory. In his fraternity anything less would be frowned upon. Even the amateurs do pretty well in the heart department. Some of them leave the owners pretty heart-sick, to say the least. A further reason for needing a sound heart in the racing business is on the off-chance your horse makes it to the races. The thrill of seeing him break out of the gate ahead of the pack could be a little too much for someone not up to that kind of excitement. On the other hand, if he failed to leave the gate, as sometimes happens in the first race, this could be a lot too much for a weak ticker (with all your friends sitting in your box holding fifty-dollar win tickets). Horses have a strange reverse affect on human emotional response. In a situation like this, when you have been hurt and shocked—any place except at a race track, these friends would be more than sympathetic. At the race track they will be downright hostile. The fact that you took them there as guests, just to see if your new horse would make a good showing matters not. The fact that it was his first race matters not. He should have won—and some of them will never speak to you again. Here you lose the first portion of your heart, in the name of horseracing, by not caring whether they are ever speak or not if they are that shallow. You suddenly realize that horse took a small chunk of your heart, too, when, on the second look you see him still glued to the starting gate while the field is making a cloud of dust on the backstretch turn. You must agree by now that this is not the business for the faint hearted soul.

Assuming you have made the grade with the cardiac specialist, there is another part of your anatomy that must really be fuctioning perfectly to jump headlong into as formidable business as horse racing. I refer to the entire nervous system, and question whether the neurology experts have devised tests to parallel the shocks to the system that will be forthcoming. Get the best check you can on your ability to withstand nerve shattering experiences. I can promise that they will come in explosive groups from 3-D and stero angles with psychedelic coloring. Your recovery rate must be exceptional, too, because

16

our FTO-trainer-player will have a well planned campaign to provide you with a number of consecutive jolts during a few of your treatments. This lowers a horseman's desire to come around to see what's going on with his stable. Sometimes it's better just not to know how bad the situation really is. Having had a lot of experience with previous owners, our FTO-trainer-player realizes a man can stand only so much and he will capitalize (that is the right word) on this to the Nth degree. Do you feel a little unnerved at the callousness of this future associate-opponent? If so, chess is a delightful game involving horses to a much safer level.

O.K. so you have nerves of steel and are determined to accept the challenge with positive thinking. You have a good heart, lots of money, great physical stamina, intestinal fortitude, unflinching nerves, patience of Job, a great sense of humor, boundless determination and advice from a trainer that certainly seems to know what he's talking about—you will never make it. There was a ray of hope until this last unsurmountable obstacle came into focus. This FTO-trainer-player is honor bound to win this game and defeat you. He has had a few games that wound up in a tie, but he has never lost a contest of his wits against somebody else's money. In the dead heat endings, most of them result when the owner finds out he is in the right game, but wrong league.

In the more fortunate cases where an owner has survived a full game of "fixing the owner" and finds a good quiet reliable trainer (as most of them are) to carry on his stable many changes are soon evident. Blood pressure drops, hollow cheeks fill and they regain healthy bloom. The stable starts to win its share of the races. A little more time restores the spring in the owners step, the sun begins to shine again and the birds suddenly recall their role in life and sing sweeter than ever before. Some old friends start speaking again. The price of horses, tack, veterinary services, moving and an assortment of other incidentals goes down reducing the drain on the old bank account. The wife becomes easier to get along with and is finally convinced you may not have completely flipped your lid. She will never know how hard you tried to win the first one nor the odds you were up against. Our FTO-trainer-player

17

never even slowed down to catch his breath because someone else needed his services right away so treatment number one was already under way on the new victim.

Life as a horseman can be beautiful with a good stable, a good trainer and an experience that only hurts when you think about it. You muse that in this competitive business there just is not much way to eliminate all of the fakers. They thrive on starry-eyed novices that think it would be such fun to have his own horse. It is, if a few disagreeable elements are avoided.

To the future horse owner a word of advice. Use the same good judgment in this business as in your vocation. When things just don't seem right chances are they are not right. Never let sentiment or dazzling words sway you in a decision to buy, sell or keep a horse. Properly bought, trained and raced they will keep you and you will have more pride of ownership. In short do not get in a game of "fixing the owner"—you can't win, the game is fixed!

Fix Your Own Races

There is a lot of good to be derived from owning a race horse, so this next part is for the underprivileged—for those men and women who have been deprived of the pleasure and thrill of owning a horse and going to the winners circle. If you have ever wanted to own a horse and be a participant in the sport I now want to encourage you by pointing out how this can be a reality and a pleasant experience if a few rules are followed. This probably can be done with much less difficulty than you imagine.

Then to the man or woman about to respond to the age-old chant, "Get a horse!" a vista of wonderful possibilities spreads across the horizon. The rewards of owning a race horse are many and varied. There is the unparalelled thrill of working and training the horse for the big race. There are the joys of victory, of near-misses and waiting for the judges to examine the photograph, of seeing a horse come to its peak form, of standing in the winners circle, and perhaps, if you are among the lucky ones, of seeing your animal flirt with or actually attain equine greatness.

It is not easy; no easier, sometimes, than raising a son or daughter, but the rewards are within reach, if you care to undertake the challenge. It is a wonderful hobby or an exciting business, whichever you choose to make it. It can be both.

For those that are considering getting a horse, what should they think about first. We will assume you know, especially after finishing this book, that speed, heart, breeding, conformation, and soundness are criterion for judging a horse. You know that a good trainer is a man who can estimate, select, combine, and develop these attributes into a polished racing machine that you will be proud to own.

You also know which trainers, or trainer-drivers you like best. You know that there is a racing secretary who is probably the best informed and best acquainted man in the equine end of the track operation. You know that there is a stable superintendent who, likewise, knows the trainers and drivers.

Knowing all this and possibly having acquaintances among owners and others to help guide you, the first thing to do is decide upon a trainer. Arrange for introductions thru the racing secretary, stable superintendent or one of your acquaintances. The trainer will be the whole key to your success.

A responsible, experienced trainer can be of inestimable value in helping you select and acquire the type of racing stock that is most likely to get you off on the right foot.

It might be best to talk to more than one prospect before making your decision on a trainer. You and the trainer must be able to get along, to understand each other, and to be as open toward each other as possible.

Basic to your decision is a knowledge of a trainer's charges and just what they cover. Where he trains in winter and where he intends to race are the other factors of vital interest to you. If you expect to race colts, check your prospective trainer's success in that department. He may be a great trainer otherwise, but just not have the patience or understanding it takes with young stock.

Advised of the amount you can comfortably invest in horse ownership, your trainer can steer you in the direction of the horses most likely available at your price. He will know if the horse can be picked up by private purchase or at an auction of racing stock or yearlings.

Having reached your decision on a trainer, you are in position to give him a green light for bargaining; or, if you choose, to go with him and decide together at a sale. This latter method is far better as you will learn a lot and it will build your confidence in your trainer. If you both were there it also takes him a little off the spot should the horse fail to live up to expectations.

Now for the horse—how much and what kind? You can pay from $50 to $50,000 or more for a thoroughbred or standard-bred. The question of cost thus starts with your inclination and, logically, with your ability to afford.

Entering into the decision on initial outlay is the question of whether you buy an aged horse, which probably has raced or a yearling which will race the first time, at the earliest, late in the Spring of the following year.

Perhaps you will decide on a young, "green horse" which is ready to race but has not yet done so.

In any event, keep in mind that attrition is high in racing and many horses never quite make the grade. Horses are atheletes and can be compared to your high school days—only a small number of the boys in school made the football team and fewer yet were very outstanding.

There must be a decision made on gait and sex which is a matter of individual preference. With thoroughbreds this is no problem unless you happen to prefer a sprinter, distance horse, or a turf horse. With a great deal of added money for locally owned horses, you may want to select one bred in your state to be eligible for these richer purses. As for standardbreds, there are a few more decisions. Trotters in general require more patience and skill to train than pacers, but earning opportunities are higher for good ones. Fillies in general cannot beat colts, but they do have plentiful opportunities to race each other and provide the basis for later breeding operations or sell better for breed stock if they go lame or for any other reason do not make it to the races. Geldings have little value if they can not race.

Now that you have decided what you want in the way of a horse let's go to the auction. Every year thousands of race horses and yearlings are sold at many auctions held all over the country. Catalogues are obtainable and a look through back issues of the horse journals will reveal the prices paid. Yearlings run, on an average, from two to ten thousand dollars. These auction averages indicate what a purchase price may be only. It is important to note, however, that many, many horses change hands as a result of private transactions with only buyer and seller knowing the actual purchase price.

Then there are the claiming races. Once you own a horse, a new avenue opens for you to acquire others. That is by "claiming". There is a rapidly increasing number of claiming races thru which a starter can be obtained, or disposed of, at a predetermined price.

The existence of claiming races might lead a prospective owner, new to the sport, to the erroneous belief that this is a channel thru which he may procure his first horse, but this is not usually the case. Generally, to be eligible to claim an owner must have programmed at least one horse to start.

In some states, however, notably Illinois, open claiming prevails and any reputable person may claim any horse from a claiming race.

Basically, a claiming race is a means of classifying horses by price, not of selling them, but the possibility of buying and selling thru claiming races does exist and is used.

There are a few rules that should be kept in mind when buying horses. Don't try to work miracles with a cast-off, lame, or bad mannered horse. If others have not succeeded, you are not likely to. An aged, experienced horse is the best to learn with if you expect to work around the horse yourself and have not had a lot of experience. Check the horse out completely. The Year Book lists all horses that have raced in any given year, show all races and gives money and races won by the horse. These books cost very little or most horse owners have one you could likely borrow to look up a horse. Select a horse that is well bred. Pedigrees pay off. They are not everything, but if you get one with breeding, you may get something good. If you select one without good ancestors, you can lay odds against getting a winner. Have your trainer check the horse and if at all possible have a veterinarian check too. The fee he will charge may be the best money you will spend as he will know where to look for future trouble and how to treat it if he feels it is a condition that can be remedied. If the horse is racing, see him race, or at least see him train. The "sharpie" will have some excuse for not taking him out on the track—forget it until he can, even if you have driven a long way to see that horse.

Everyone wants a good horse so we should discuss what good horses cost. There is no sure formula. Some of the sports happiest success stories illustrate why.

Two fine pacers, the brothers Stephan Smith and Irving Paul, cost $2,500 as a pair when they were youngsters. Their owner later sold Irving Paul for $35,000 and kept Stephan Smith, who retired with earnings of $335,110, Irving Paul did even better, and the total earnings of the pair exceeded $879,000.

Belle Acton, who proved to be a great pacing mare, cost $2,600 as a yearling and earned $353,063. Duke Rodney, purchased as a yearling for $7,000 won over $637,000 trotting in the next six years.

Stymie was claimed for $1,500 and made over $900,000. There are cases every year where a cheap horse goes on to greatness and big winnings.

On the other hand, high-priced yearlings have paid off handsomely too. Bret Hanover, probably the greatest pacer of all time, sold for $50,000 as a yearling, but won $514,274 his first two seasons of racing and went on to make it a million the next year before being retired to stud. These champions are syndicated for more millions after they are through racing. Older horses have been bought and gone on to much greater things too. It is all up to the individual. With some luck anyone can hit the jackpot. If there was any sure way of predetermining the horses potential the average man would not ever have a chance to get the better horses.

What about the horse's earning power? It is frequently said that the proper price to pay for a horse is what he can win in one year. The question is, what year? Presumably, the one most recently raced. Remember, however, that not all horses have equal earning opportunities and where the horse raced as well as where you plan to race him is a mighty important consideration.

You may want to keep him close to home where you can always have the pleasure of seeing him race, but that may not always provide maximum earning power.

In these matters, your own desire and your trainer's advice will have to be the controlling factors. Your ambitions and hopes (and what your pocket can stand) will shape your final decision.

What are the costs of training and racing? Just as cost vary greatly in initial outlay, they vary in training and racing. To the owner who is situated and has the ability to perform most of the tasks himself, costs may amount to less than a thousand dollars a year. To the owner who must use, as the great majority do, a "public Trainer" for the entire year, costs may range from $3,500 to $10,000 or more per horse, depending upon where the animal is being trained and raced.

On all levels, staking (paying advance fees to enter specific races of significant value) can add materially to the cost. Also, involved, as a horse starts earning, is a ten percent driving or jockey fee. There are exceptions, but this is the rule. That is, the driver or jockey gets ten per cent of what the horse wins.

Where horses are trained in the South in Winter months, or raced in widely separated areas, costs rise appreciably.

At smaller raceways, where minimum purses are under a thousand dollars, one can expect to spend from $3,500 to $5,000 a year per horse for training and racing in a public stable.

At the larger metropolitan tracks, full year expenses are likely to run from $5,000 to $10,000, depending on how extensively a horse is staked and shipped. Both of these figures include normally anticipated expenses: feed, care, training, shoeing, and preventative veterinary care. They do not include initial or replacement equipment costs, driver's percentage, transportation or staking.

To determine how trainers charge would take an entire book as there are so many different ways and their methods of billing vary considerably. Some charge by the day ($10 to $20) for training, grooming and feeding plus billing at cost for other items like shoeing and equipment. This is likely the best for all concerned. The 10% item is one which owners are delighted to pay for winnings, because they are getting nine times that and accomplishing what they set out to do.

So far we have only discussed costs (there will be times when a new owner thinks that is all there is), but balanced against these costs are purse earnings, which may vary from a few dollars for an entire season's efforts to hundreds of thousands of dollars earned every year by the sport's top stars. Purses, like the sport itself, are zooming upwards year after year and earning opportunities have never been greater. Nearly any horse that can race can find a place to do some good. Total purses for standardbreds last year were nearing $55,000,000. This went to around 25,000 starters. Your chances of getting a $100,000 winner the first time around are rather remote. However, with any kind of good judgment and luck your prospects of getting a horse that pays his way and shows a profit are good and increase every racing day.

With purses climbing steadily, three or four victories can go a long way toward contributing to a solid successful season. If you happen to be measuring by aesthetic, rather than financial standards, that many wins can send you halfway to heaven.

Horses can be leased, like many other major possessions. If leasing interests you, you may be able to reach an agreement with an owner who wants to retain a horse for breeding purposes later on but doesn't want to race him himself right now. Or you may be able to work out lease arrangements with option to buy with small breeders or other individual owners.

Leasing horses offers the same advantages as leasing other items of substantial value: possession without large capital outlay. It, also, involves the same risks: be sure you can afford to train and race the horse.

Lease arrangements are not standardized; they depend on agreement between two or more individuals. A frequent basis is for the person who is granted the lease to pay all expenses of training and racing and retain a stipulated percentage of earnings—ranging ordinarily from 50% to 80% with an average of around 70%. The remainder goes to the owner with no expense other than his original investment. Regardless of terms, a copy of the lease must be filed with the United States Trotting Association (for Standardbreds) before racing eligibility papers will be issued and then the horse must race in the name of the person granted the lease.

Assuming we have made some money there is that matter of taxes. This happy situation should be handled with the same tax expert who helps the owner with his personal income tax statement. Horses are capital investments. They produce profits or loses, they are subject to depreciation, and they are subject to capital gains and capital loss taxes. Special rules cover some situations. It is too complex, as are most tax matters, to cover in this book with the allotted space.

Like all other valuable property, horses can be insured against loss by fire, accident or other disaster. Annual premiums run around four or five percent of the amount of insurance, and the policies cover loss of the horse, not injury or incapacitation. It is a life insurance policy on the horse, payable on death.

Many owners and trainers believe wholeheartedly in insurance for their horses; others are highly selective in which horses they insure. This decision, like many you will have to make in racing, is one for you to reach after careful thought and study on your individual stable situation.

There is the matter of names. Unless you get into the breeding end of the sport and raise your own colts and fillies, your horse almost always will have a name when you buy it, even if it is a yearling.

You can change the name if you wish by paying a fee. It costs a great deal more to do this after the horse has raced. There are numerous rules governing permissible names. The principal ones limit the name to 16 letters and three words, rule out names already in use and names of former outstanding horses, govern farm names and prohibit use of names of living persons without written permission of those persons.

As for stable and farm names, you may race your horses under such names providing you register the name with the Association.

25

After you have bought a horse and really are in the business you will have to get an owners license at the track you intend to race. You will likely want to join various associations (some are mandatory) and subscribe to one of the many magazines that covers your choice of racing.

If you select harness horses you can help drive as they need miles of jogging in addition to their training. One of the greatest of all pleasures of harness horse ownership—and one that sets it apart from nearly all other racing sports—is that you can participate actively and help drive your horse.

A person is hardly ever too old and never too young to take a turn on the training cart. This is the true joy of owning trotters and pacers, and one of the principal reasons that the appeal of the sport has mushroomed so tremendously.

Whether you are banker or lawyer, doctor or merchant, laborer or technician, man or woman, young or old, you can help jog your horse and get to know intimately and first hand, the incomparable thrill of gliding along behind a smart-stepping trotter or smooth-gaited pacer. This is one of life's memorable experiences.

If you are really serious about driving, you first need to learn to train and handle a horse competently. You can learn this only by working with a knowledgeable horseman, and you will need at least a year's full-time training experience before you will be able to drive in a race of any kind. Most applicants have two or three years behind them.

By full-time experience we mean working with horses exclusively and working with a stable where you will gain experience in every phase of caring for and racing horses. Intermittent and part-time training requires a longer period of time.

There are no comprehensive books available on the subject and no substitute for experience. Many drivers—and nearly all good ones—learned first by grooming, then by assisting in training and finally by beginning to drive at the county fairs and matinee meetings without purses. That is the soundest route, and even then the USTA will decide when you're qualified and ready to make the next big step of driving in races where money is involved.

You're now equipped with some of the information you need

to start, but not with all you will need. Racing is far too fascinating, once you have gotten into it, to be casual about it ever again.

That's another fascinating thing about racing: there's always another question to be asked and usually a clear answer in prospect. The horse can usually answer these if observed closely enough. Hoping you get the answers—and lots of luck with them. You are extended a warm welcome as a member (or prospective member) of the wonderful world of horse owners. You can now start doing your part in fixing races. Good Luck.

Are Horseraces Fixed?

If you are in any way associated with the racing industry, most likely many people have ask, "Don't you think the races are fixed?" If you like the sport (most like it better if they are not recent losers) and know all of the complicated control measures, you immediately quell their suspicions with a very positive, "Certainly not—how could they be fixed?"

This is not true. Indeed all races are fixed with many people getting into the act of fixing them. In fact, it is impossible to have a horserace without a great deal of fixing taking place. The basic ingredients of a horserace has to be; a fixed time, a fixed place, a fixed distance, fixed conditions and a number of other predetermined elements including post position, weight, equipment and the selected participating horses.

About the only cases of unfixed races in this country were the chance meeting of a band of Indians with a lone frontiersman. The insuing chase to get his scalp did not allow for much fixing. This situation does not fit into the category of wholesome sport nor were there any two dollar windows around to get a quick bet on the outcome. The frontiersmen won enough of these contests to get our country settled down to where racetracks could be built and we could start fixing races.

Back to the issue, before we are accused of evading the question of long standing concerning irregularities in the horse racing business. Whether the horses in a race are 'doped' or the assortment of misdeeds people have been accused of to alter

27

the outcome, and in fact, predetermine the final results are factors in racing is debatable. Without doubt, this book will be completed without covering many of them, as there are many, many connecting subjects. An attempt will be made to present as many of the legal and illegal fixes as possible. While it is ridiculous to overlook the many attempts to fix races, illegally, it has been my experience that this is virtually impossible to accomplish, even in isolated cases. For the most part, horse-races are very honest efforts and the public generally gets a good show for their money, whether they win, lose, or draw.

Further, all of this fixing (that is, the legal fixing) is done for the benefit of the bettor. If the racing fan will study all of the facets of this great sport and use a certain amount of restraint, it can be a very enjoyable and even profitable pastime. Indeed the odds are much against anyone becoming a winner that attempts to bet every race. To be successful one must be selective because horseraces are fixed—and success depends upon how well the bettor knows how and why they are fixed. Such information will, also, enable this person to dispell this myth that illegal fixing is prevalent in the horseracing business.

Thus the first few chapters here will be devoted to trying to point out how fixing is accomplished and how knowing this procedure can be helpful to the racing public.

The dates are fixed by the various State Racing Commissions. They allot each track in their respective states a given number of racing days. Usually the entire racing season is divided among the licensed track operating organizations with only one or two operating concurrently. These commissions are, for the most part, appointed by the governor of their state. They have almost dictatorial power over the entire industry. Being political this arrangement can leave a lot to be desired. Ohio even passed a law that anyone associated with racing could not serve on the commission. While this was done to eliminate conflict of interest, it in reality prevents the best qualified from top authority. Time and events may prove this to be a poor policy. It always takes a few people that know what they are doing to run and organization efficiently. Be that as it may, the Commissioners start the big fix by fixing the dates a track can race. After the dates are set most of the race fixing is up to the racing secretary as far as the racing program is concerned.

For the racing secretary to have any horses to select and choose from someone has to selectively breed prospects and the trainers have to take these potential champions and mold them into useful products for the racing card.

There are a lot of steps in the process that call for a lot of talent, precise operating procedure and always lots of luck. Every movement along the way leaves room for the outcome of any given race to be altered, so to be well informed on the subject of fixing races it is necessary to know all of the changeable facets connected with the great sport of horseracing. It is necessary not only to know the procedure, but all of the variations and who can possibly be in position to make changes in the proper chain of events that lead up to bringing a group of horses to post that will normally end up with one winner. The trainer can work his heart out to get his horses in perfect condition for the race and have a jockey give the horse a bad ride, intentionally or otherwise and all of his efforts go down the drain for that race. There is also a measure of protection from questionable practices with this human element having a hand in the outcome of the races.

Therefore we will procede without indicting anyone until all of the facts are in and we can take a comprehensive look at the entire racing picture from an objective standpoint without sentiment entering in to cloud the image.

Present horse racing is a far cry from its inception as a sport. About the only remaining factors the two have in common are that horses are still used and it is still competitive. A great imagination is necessary to classify horse racing as a true sport. It is big business. It is, in fact, a very complex business employing hundreds of specialized skills to insure its future first place in the sporting world. To name a few; these skills include grooms, trainers, breeders, farm managers, track and lighting engineers, caterers, judges, stewards, parking attendants, ticket salesmen, electronic experts, handicappers, horseshoers, veterinarians, jockeys and drivers, photographers, hot walkers, exercise boys, pony boys, newspaper reporters, public relation experts, security guards, grounds maintenance crews, saddlery men, telephone operators, bookkeepers, racing secretaries, saliva, blood and urine chemists, biological laboratories, hay and grain dealers, and on and on.

All of these have a hand in determining the outcome of any given race. They all help "fix the races. Because so many and varied skills go into a single race the possibility of having any giving race completely fixed—that is, illegally fixed is nearly impossible. Therefore, it may logically be concluded that the very complexity of racing insures honesty and a fair chance for all participants whether they be owners, trainers, or the bettor.

Whether the horse has been "doped" by some means or the assortment of people that could predetermine the end results of a race are a factor in racing, is a broad subject and, without doubt, this book will be completed without covering many of them. Many attempts have been made to illegally fix races. These are rare, not generally very effective and are soon discovered as horse racing is the best policed sport in the world. Basically, I must say my experience has been that most races are very honest efforts. The public generally gets a good show with lots of thrills for their money.

Further, if they will study all of the facets of horse racing and use restraint, racing can be a profitable pastime. However, little can be learned about racing, as a business and the things that make it tick, in the grandstand or clubhouse. Most participants in the sport of racing, especially the bettors, have little idea what goes on in the barn area. A better understanding of what goes on where the horses are being preped to run should greatly increase ones chances of being successful at the windows. There is nothing mysterious about what goes on in the stable area. Mostly it is methodical, dedicated work by organized teams of various skills that brings the horses to the post for the public's enjoyment. For the most part they all think they are going to win this race. There is usually a valid reason for the ones that lose. A better understanding of the training and other factors that go into the making and maintaining of a racehorse certainly should be very useful information for the average racing enthusiast.

This book is an attempt to point out the factors that affect racing, both good and bad. Dishonest racing on a wide scale would prevent anyone from becoming very proficient at picking winners. It must be plain to most turf fans that since there are skillful handicappers, most of the results depend on the ability of the horses. It would be a great waste of time and money to even go to the track if fraudulent practices were permitted to exist. Therefore, the habitual or even the casual loser should not try to cover his lack of knowledge or poor judgment by a blanket condemnation of racing. In the past there were a lot of questionable practices and even today an occasional crook turns up to promote the conviction of some that racing is all bad news. There are crooks in every trade, business, or profession where millions of dollars change hands. Racing does not have any more than its share.

Every fan that has studied the past performance charts at great length and made selections based on his judgment then gone to the track and watched his selections trail the field is likely to question racing in general. Instead of accepting the fact that he probably did not know enough about those races and the participants, he is more likely to salve his ego by insisting the owners, trainers, and jockey's conspired to take him down the dirty road of ruin and destruciton. His feelings do not alter the facts. If he would bother to learn more about how racing is fixed he could become more successful which is the reason this book is dedicated to the losers.

The time honored axiom of bettors is that you can beat a race, but you can't beat the races. Simply expressed, this means you can win a race or a few races, but if you insist on betting on every race at the track, the odds are you will wind up loser. In other words you must be selective in the races you bet on because the races are fixed. You had better know what, how, and why they are fixed if you plan to be on the winning side.

Playing the races and making a profit at the track are two different things. To rise above the ordinary horse player takes training, skill, and ability. There are a lot of systems, but memorizing a few rules of mathematics adapted to horse racing and playing the horses is a costly way to have a good time at the track. There are too many other factors to consider. Hopefully most of them will be covered in the next few chapters.

A logical place to start would be with the selection of the

sire and dam of a prospective race horse, but so many things can happen along the way that we might never get to the track. It seems like a better plan to start with the make-up of a race and then get into other factors that will affect the racing card or an individual horse.

Anatomy Of A Race

A broader look into the anatomy of a race card might be appropriate at this time. To conserve time we will assume the horses at the track have been here for a few weeks so that most have raced a time or two at this track.

This is a very important point in the initial fixing of a race. The racing secretary, who must make up the racing card has to know all of the horses on the grounds and what each is capable of doing under a variety of conditions of distance, weight, etc. He is the chief fixer and must know what he has to work with.

Racing secretaries are great people that must be a combination of genius, displomat, and salesman with ability to look into the future. Horses that get rich, go lame, or move to another track all becomes his problems to put on the required number of daily races.

It has been estimated that a two month racing meet will require well over 1000 horses to fill all the races. The racing secretary must know all these horses' abilities, their physical condition, with most of their owners and trainer's whims in order to provided daily programs of good racing that will satisfy the public and the horse owners.

The public likes a varied racing card which must be made up from horses on the grounds that are ready to run (the chapter on training will explain what it takes to get a horse ready to run). If there are not different types and classes of races the public would get very bored.

There are four main types of races:

1. Stakes race where the owner pays a fee to nominate, to enter, and to start with some stakes there are periodic fees to keep the horse eligible. All of this money goes to the purse along with added money from the track, in many cases.

2. Handicaps are races where the racing secretary tries to get horses of nearly equal ability then he assigns each horse different weights to further equalize the race. The weight assignments are based on his judgment considering various horses past performances and workout times. There is a general rule of "weight-for-age-scale" which is based on different ages with varying distances and the time of the year. Since all horses have a birthday on January 1, two year olds might only be a little over a year old. This is the reason two year olds racing against three year olds would be assigned less weight early in the Spring than later in the year when they would be more mature. The weight we are discussing consists of the jockey's weight along with his saddle and pads. When weight is added, it is in the form of lead strips placed in the pad or weight bag under the saddle. The jockeys must weigh in with their saddle after each race.

Handicapping is truly an art. The perfectly handicapped race would find all horses at the wire in a deadheat (if this happened the racing secretary would probably drop dead or retire). This is what they strive for, but with all of their fixing there is usually just one winner, because of all of the other factors that fix a race.

Next we go to: 3. Allowance races that are about the same as handicap races. The main difference is that a base weight is set as a standard for that race using the weight-for-age-scale. Horses that have been doing poorly carry less than the base while those with more recent wins are assigned more weight to slow them down.

4. Claiming races make up the largest number of races and is the most useful tool in the racing secretary's bag of "fixing" tricks. Horses run in claiming races are actually put up for sale at the price of the Claiming race. Any eligible buyer (usually a person with other horses on the grounds) can put in a Claim fifteen minutes or so before the start of the races. When the race begins he owns that horse (sound, lame, dead, or alive). The Claimer or "halter man" puts a claiming slip in the Claim box at the racing secretary's office. After the race the previous owner gets anything the horse may have won in the race and the "halter man" takes the horse to his stable. If there is more

than one claim for the same horse there is a drawing to determine who gets the horse with all of the others money being returned to them. This keeps racing honest and exciting. A good horse with stakes ability is not going to be run in a cheap Claiming race (at least not more than once). This has been done, of course, but there is always someone watching ready to claim any horse put in too cheap. This is a good way to buy horses for a good trainer. It is, also, a good way to sell unwanted horses that have gone lame or for any other reason need to be weeded out of the stable—just keep dropping the price and someone will claim them. Stymie was claimed for $1,500 and went on to make over $900,000. There are many other varied conditions tied to allowance and claiming races that the racing secretary must make up ahead of time.

Between races the racing secretary must read another chapter on "How to Win Friends and Influence People" and maybe something like "I Don't Have to be Right—I Am the Boss" because the owners that get top weight seldom ever like it and usually find their way to the racing secretary's office to question his judgment, if not his motives for, "trying to break down his horse and come in dead last." Like the baseball umpires, though, he has good reasons and generally wins all such contested decisions with the finish of the race attesting as to whether he was right or wrong (then it is too late). In most cases the owner or trainer could scratch his horse if he thought he was really being mistreated. Sometimes they do just that, especially if their horse is a big drawing card and the weight is completely out of line. However, usually the trainers know and respect the secretary.

There are many other factors for the racing secretary to contend with, but let's see him at work on a hypothetical race to see how he goes about fixing it.

With some knowledge of the few hundred horses he has to work with the secretary selects a distance to be raced, determines whether it will be on the dirt or turf. He must decide whether it will be a claimer which, again, permits the owners and trainers to handicap their own horses, for the most part, or whether it will be a conditioned race with a great many factors for him to put his fix on.

34

Likely he will start with age. Ideally two year olds would race only with horses of their own age, three year olds with three year olds and so on, but many times this is impractical as there are not enough of the same ages of the same class to make a fair race.

Next, he will decide whether sex will be a limiting factor. Generally speaking, horses or geldings (males) race slightly better than mares or fillies (females). If they are put in the same race with equal ability the females should normally have some weight or position advantage to equalize the race. In the case of claiming races this is accomplished with claiming price allowances.

We now have a race fixed in one of several ways. 1. All male two year olds carrying the same weight, 2. All males of different ages carring different weights as per the weight-for-age-scale, or 3. A mixed race of males and females properly handicapped as to age and sex. The only obvious advantage, if they all have equal ability, is the post position. This is determined by a drawing before the race and, of course, is in the program. The number one horse should win, but does he? Only slightly more often than the others. There must be other variable factors or advantages. Perhaps the jockeys "fixed" this one and all bet on the number eight horse because they know he would have the best odds.

"Why did number eight win?"

One reason could be that this was a short race of five furlongs and number eight is a fast, short-distance sprinter. This means he can travel faster than the rest for short distances. There are other horses in the field that have more endurance and in a longer race can beat this horse every time. Another factor could be the horses ability to start out of the starting gate. In older horses with more starts this becomes less of a factor than with the inexperienced youngsters. Ability of jockeys to rate their mounts is another important factor. A good jockey or driver knows what his mount can do and should know what the others are capable of doing. He plans his race from start to finish. With all of the planning in the world there is always lady luck (who sometimes is no lady) to contend with and here is one of the greatest fixers of races.

35

The judges must determine whether luck or foul play is involved in every race. They do an exceptional job with a film recording for almost instant rerun of every race. Any jockey that gets out of line is called to account. Any time there is any indication of abuse of the rigid set of rules governing every race, that jockey will be fined or not allowed to ride for a period of time depending on how serious the rule infraction may have been.

Thus, the judges do their share of fixing the races. They insure the race being run according to the rules—all designed to give the betting public a good race for their money.

About 90 per cent of the people who own race horses use them as a means of making a living. The other 10 per cent are more monied people that just like the sport or want to contribute something worthwhile to the breed or sport. To protect the sport and the public these people have set down rigid sets of rules covering all foreseeable situations. Every racing enthusiast should acquaint himself with these rules for a clearer overall picture of racing.

THE AMERICAN STUD BOOK

Principal Rules and Regulations

Registration Rules and Requirements:

1A. Stallion Reports:

Every stallion owner must report all thoroughbred mares bred to his stallion during the year. The reports must be filed promptly at the end of the breeding season, but not later than September 1st.

A separate report must be made for each stallion each year.

All thoroughbred mares bred (not just those in foal) must be listed, with the names of the owners of the mares and *all* dates of service.

The report must be signed by the owner of the stallion or his authorized agent. The address of the owner or agent should be included.

The stallion owner should give a completed, signed service certificate giving *all* dates of service to the owner of each mare bred.

Certificates of Registration for foals will not be issued unless both the stallion report and the service certificate are on file in the Registry Office. The dates and signatures on the two documents must correspond.

If a mare is covered by more than one stallion during a breeding season, service certificates giving dates of service by both stallions must be furnished.

Starting with the 1966 breeding season (foals of 1967), if a mare is covered by more than one stallion during the *same heat period* the foal is not eligible for registration.

Every stallion must be identified when it first enters the stud and each time it changes ownership. The new owner should identify the stallion by giving all the information requested on the back of the form for reporting mares bred.

When a stallion is pasture bred to a mare, the stallion owner is required to furnish a notarized statement certifying that there was no other stallion in the vicinity which could have covered the mare and giving the date the mare was placed in the pasture with the stallion as well as the date they were separated.

When a stallion is leased, a copy of the lease must be filed with The Jockey Club, along with the name of the party who is responsible for signing the reports required by the Registry Office.

A foal is not eligible for registration unless it is begotten by natural service, although it is permitted to reinforce at once the natural service by artificial insemination with semen from the stallion performing the natural service on the mare that has just been covered.

2A. Registration of Foals:

1. Registration Fee:

The fee is register a foal is $30.00, but this amount *must* be paid by September 30 of the year of the foal's birth.

After September 30 of the year of birth the fees increase as follows:

From October 1 to December 31 of the year of birth—$60.00.

From January 1 to December 31 of the yearling year—$150.00.

From January 1 to December 31 of the two year old year—$300.00; with an additional penalty of $50.00 to name, a total of $350.00.

A foal is *not* eligible for registration after January 1 of its three year old year.

2. Application for Registration:

Application blanks will be mailed without charge promptly upon request.

One application blank must be filed out, in ink or on the typewriter, for each foal. *All* information asked for must be given, including a complete written description of the foal's markings.

If a mare was bred to two or more stallions, the names of all stallions must be given as the sire of the resulting foal.

Snapshots should be furnished with every application.

In the case of twin foals, each foal should be registered separately and the fee for each must be paid. If one twin dies and the other lives and is registered, the fact that it is a twin must be noted on the application for registration.

Mares must be identified when they first enter the stud and each time they change ownership. The new owner should identify the mare by giving the information requested on the front of the application blank in the spaces designated for that purpose.

Names may be claimed on the application for registration or at a later date. However, names must be claimed by January 1 of the two year old year. After that date a $50.00 penalty goes into effect.

If, for any valid reason, the application blank cannot be completed by September 30 of the year of the foal's birth, temporary application may be made by paying the registration fee and giving the color, sex, sire and dam of the foal. Completed application blanks must follow promptly.

3. Service Certificate:

A service certificate must be mailed to the Registry Office with the completed application. This service certificate must be signed by the owner of the stallion or by his authorized agent, and must give *all* dates of service (month, day and year) the year previous to the birth of the foal.

Service certificates should *not* be stapled to the application. Please use a paper clip or pin.

4. Delayed Registration Requirements:

If application is made to register a foal after December 31 of the year of birth, the following additional requirements must be furnished:

A set of snapshots of both the foal and its dam, clearly showing the face, both sides of the body and the legs of each, including the heels.

A notarized affidavit signed by the person who owned the dam at the time the foal was dropped, stating that he (or she) did own the mare at that time, giving the exact date of foaling and the color, sex and markings of the foal.

38

3A. Names:

A foal may be named without charge if name is claimed prior to January 1 of the two year old year. After that date a $50.00 penalty goes into effect. If the name claimed prior to January 1 is not eligible the penalty does not apply and additional names may be claimed after January 1 without charge.

It is not necessary to have the Certificate of Registration in order to claim a name.

Names may not be claimed by telephone or telegraph. It is required that all names be claimed in writing for specific foals, giving color, sex, age, sire and dam. All claims for names must be signed by the applicant.

Names cannot be claimed for unregistered foals.

When a foreign words or names are submitted a translation must be furnished.

When "coined" or "made-up" names which have no meaning are submitted, an explanation must be funished.

Names Not Eligible:

Names currently in use. (See Rule 67 (b) of the Rules of Racing on p. 19.)

Names consisting of more than eighteen (18) letters. Spaces and punctuation marks count as letters.

Names of living persons, unless their written permission to use the name is filed with The Jockey Club.

Initials (such as C.O.D., F.O.B., etc.)

Names consisting entirely of numbers, such as ONE SIX, TWO FOUR EIGHT, etc.

Names which are recorded "assumed names" or "stable names" used for racing purposes.

Names of race tracks and/or stakes races.

Names of stallions whose daughters are in the stud.

Names of famous horses.

Names similar in spelling or pronunciation to names already in use.

Names of famous or notorious people.

Trade names, names claimed for advertising purposes, or names with any commerical significance.

Copyrighted names, such as titles of books, plays, moving pictures, popular songs, magazines, etc.

Names which are suggestive, or which have a vulgar or obscene meaning.

2nd, 3rd, etc. even though spelled out, cannot be used in naming horses. These designations are used only for horses imported into the United States from a foreign country whose names are the same as names already in use.

Identical prefixes or suffixes may not be used by any owner in naming horses bred or owned by him.

When application is made to register a foal by an unnamed stallion or out of an unnamed mare, the stallion or mare must be named before the registration of the foal can be completed. In a case of this kind there is no charge to name the stallion or mare, but such stallion or mare may not race under the name.

A name may be changed prior to January 1 of the two year old year for a fee of $10.00. After that date the fee is $100.00 and permission of the Stewards of The Jockey Club is required. No change of name will be permitted after a horse has started.

4A. Transfers: Purchase and Sale of Thoroughbreds:

When a thoroughbred is bought or sold the registration certificate which was issued for the horse must be given free of charge to the new owner at the time of purchase.

It is advisable that no one complete the purchase of a thoroughbred until the registration certificate has been received from the previous owner.

The new owner should check the description on the certificate with the actual markings of the horse before completing the sale.

The space for transfer on the back of the certificate should be filled out and signed by the former owner, giving the name and address of the new owner, and the date of transfer.

The Jockey Club does not execute or record transfers of ownership. Certificates of registration must be preserved and transferred to the new owner without charge. Possession and presentation of the certificate is a requirement to race the horse.

5A. Duplicate Certificates:

A duplicate certificate will not be issued as long as the original certificate is still in existence.

The requirements for a duplicate certificate are:

1. The fee of $50.00.

2. A notarized statement as to the loss or destruction of the original certificate. This statement must be made by the party who had the original certificate and who lost or destroyed it.

3. Identification of the animal: name, age, color, sex, sire, dam, the tattoo number on the inside of the upper lip; a history of the former ownership; and pictures clearly showing all markings.

4. A bill of sale or other satisfactory proof of ownership.

If the original certificate is located after a duplicate has been issued, the *original* must be returned to the Registry office for cancellation.

6A. Corrected Certificates:

If the Certificate of Registration does not accurately describe all the markings of the horse for which it was issued, a corrected certificate should be applied for.

The requirements for a corrected certificate are:

1. The fee of $5.00.

2. The return of the original certificate.

3. A set of snapshots clearly showing all of the markings, or absence of markings.

4. A notarized affidavit made by the breeder of the horse, certifying that this horse was bred by him, requesting correction, and describing the color and markings of the horse as they now appear.

7A. Imported Horses:

The requirements to register a horse foaled outside the United States or its possessions, Canada or Cuba, are:

1. The original Stud Book Certificate or Export Certificate issued by the Stud Book authorities of the country in which the horse was born.

2. A veterinary's certificate of identification, made after importation. This must give name, age, color, sex, sire, dam, an outline of all markings and a complete written description of the markings.

40

3. Pictures, taken after importation, clearly showing face, both sides of body and the legs, as well as the heels, of each horse.

4. A certified copy of the horse's complete racing record in all countries, stating the date, the type race, distance, and the amount of money won in each race.

5. The exact date of arrival.

6. The registration fee: $30.00 if paid within sixty (60) days after arrival. After 60 days and until the horse has been in the country for six months: $100.00; after six months and up to one year: $200.00; after one year and up to two years: $400.00.

An imported horse may not be registered after it has been in the country more than two years. (See Rule 69, pp. 20 and 21.)

8A. Export Certificates:

The Jockey Club Certificates of Registration are for use only within the American Stud Book jurisdiction. When a horse is sent to another country a Certificate of Exportation must be applied for.

The requirements are:

1. The fee of $5.00.

2. The Certificate of Registration properly transferred to the new owner.

3. The country of destination, name of owner at time of shipment, date of shipment and the name of the boat or airline on which shipment is to be made.

4. If a broodmare, in foal, is exported, the name of the stallion or stallions to which she was bred must be furnished, with the dates of covering.

9A. Sold Without Pedigree:

A horse sold or disposed of as without pedigree must be reported promptly and the Certificate of Registration must be surrendered for cancellation. A horse so disposed of, and whose registration is cancelled, cannot be reinstated and is no longer considered thoroughbred for racing or breeding.

All requests to have horses recorded as **Sold Without Pedigree** must be signed by the actual owner of the horse at the time the request is made and must give the date on which the horse was so disposed of. Such requests may not be made retroactive.

10A. Tabulated Pedigree:

Tabulated pedigree, showing five crosses, will be furnished upon payment of the fee of $5.00.

Certified tabulated pedigree, showing five crosses, will be furnished upon payment of the fee of $10.00 and satisfactory identification of the animal.

11A. Altering Certificates:

Any person who alters a registration certificate or who wilfully gives misinformation in the registration of a horse shall be reported by the Registrar to the Stewards of The Jockey Club for action under the rules covering corrupt practices.

12A. Arabians:

Arab and Anglo-Arab horses are no longer eligible for registration for any purpose whatsoever.

41

13A. Breeder—Leases:

The breeder of an animal, for the purposes of registration, is the owner of the dam at the time of foaling, and when held under a lease, bred on shares or in partnership, only such lease or partnership will be recognized for such purposes which is filed in the Office of The Jockey Club.

Leases of mares must be filed with The Jockey Club not later than the time application is made to register the foal. Leases may mot be made retroactive.

The fee to file a lease is $1.00 per year for each mare.

14A. Mare Reports:

The breeding status of all mares must be reported each year. If a mare has no living foal the report must state whether she was barren, slipped her foal, had a dead foal, was not covered the previous year, or just exactly what the status was.

15A. Death Reports:

All deaths should be reported giving the date of death. Registration certificates for animals which are dead should be returned to the Registry Office for cancellation.

Registration fees may not be refunded unless the foal dies and the deathe is reported prior to October 1st of the year of birth, and provided the Registration Certificate has not been issued.

Dead animals cannot be registered.

16A. Gelding Reports:

All geldings must be reported, giving the date of castration.

17A. Horses which have been domiciled in Hungary, Germany or Austria, if imported into the United States, will not be considered for registration except in those instances where they have been theretofore accepted, with proper credentials, into the Stud Book of England, France or Italy. Such credentials must accompany the animals.

18A. Indentification Requirements:

Indentification consists of the name, age, color, sex, sire, dam, the tattoo number on the inside of the upper lip; a history of the former ownership; and pictures clearly showing all markings or a diagram accurately outlining all markings.

Rules from Rules of Racing:

4. A horse is "bred" at the place of his birth.

5. The age of a horse is reckoned as beginning on the first of January in the year in which he is foaled.

22. The "Breeder" of a horse is the owner of his dam at the time of foaling.

59(a). Except as provided in section (b) of this Rule, no horse may start in any race unless duly registered in the Registry Office and duly named.

(b) If for any reason ineligible for registration, or pending inquiry as to eligibility, a horse foaled outside the United States or its possessions, Canada or Cuba and imported into the United States may be submitted by the owner for approval solely for racing purposes if the application is accompained by such information as the Stewards of The Jockey Club shall require; whereupon if said Stewards shall consider that the horse has an outstanding racing record and that the application and accompanying information meet the requirements prescribed by said Stewards, they may direct the Executive Secretary or other person authorized by them to issue a permit granting racing privileges only for such horse.

Application for such a permit for such a horse must be made to The Jockey Club within thirty days of the original arrival of the horse in the United States—the application to be accompanied by a fee of $50, which will include the permit if granted. In case of failure to apply for a permit within the thirty-day period, and upon proof that failure to do so was unintentional or accidental, application for such a permit may be made within three months after original arrival. Such application shall be accompanied by a fee of $200, which will include the permit if granted.

60. The Registry Office, which is the office of The Jockey Club, is established for the identification of all race horses, whether foaled in the United States or its possessions or in other countries, and for the certification of their pedigrees.

61. Except as provided in Rule 65, horses foaled in the United States or its possessions, Canada or Cuba must be registered with the Registry Office before October 1st of the year in which they are foaled.

62(a). The registration shall comprise the name, if any; the color and marks, if any; whether a horse, mare or gelding; and the names of its sire and dam. If the mare was covered by more than one stallion, the names or descriptions in full must be stated. However, if a mare is covered by more than one stallion during a single heat period, any resulting foal is not eligible for registration.

(b) In any case of doubt regarding the true parentage or identification of an animal, blood tests may be required, and, taking into consideration the results of such tests and/or such other information as may be available, the Stewards may authorize such corrections in the records as may be determined to be necessary or appropriate.

63. Only those horses are eligible for registry which authentically trace, in all of their lines to animals recorded in The American Stud Book or in a Stud Book of another country recognized by The Jockey Club, and which are eligible under the rules and regulations from time to time adopted by the Stewards of The Jockey Club. A horse born in the United States or its possesions, Canada or Cuba may not be registered unless both its sire and dam have been previously registered in The American Stud Book. The only exception to this rule is a foal imported in utero whose dam is properly registered in The American Stud Book after importation and whose sire was not imported but is properly recorded in the Stud Book of a country recognized by The Jockey Club.

65. Upon failure to register a horse before October 1st of the year of his birth, he may be registered prior to January 1st of his three-year-old year by special permission of the Stewards of The Jockey Club, but not thereafter. If the application to register be made prior to the January 1st next following his birth, the payment of a fee of $60 will be required; if made after that date and prior to January 1st of his two-year-old year the required fee will be $150; and if made after that date and prior to January 1st of his three-year-old year $300.

66. A name for each horse may be claimed gratis through the Registry Offlice before January 1st of his two-year-old year. On or after that date, a horse may

43

be named upon payment of a fee of $50 and then only if the name is claimed and allowed at least two days before the date of his first start.

67(a). All names are subject to approval or disapproval by the Stewards of The Jockey Club.

(b) No name that has been used during the previous fifteen years, either in the stud or on the turf, shall be duplicated, and no name may be claimed for any unregistered horse.

68. By special permission of the Stewards of The Jockey Club a name may be changed but only upon the payment of a fee of $100, except that when a horse's name is changed before January 1st of his two-year-old year, permission is not necessary and the fee is only $10. However, no change of name will be permitted after a horse has started.

69(a). No horse foaled out of the United States or its possessions, Canada or Cuba shall be registered until the owner has filed in the Registry Office a certificate stating age, color, sex, distinguishing marks, if any, and pedigree as recorded in the recognized Stud Book of its native country or of that country from which it is exported; or unless, in respect of the age and identity of the horse, the owner has otherwise satisfied the Stewards of The Jockey Club. In both cases there must be filed after importation a veterinarian's certificate of identification.

(b) All such applications must be accompanied by a certified copy of the horse's complete racing record in all countries; such record to state date, the type race, distance and the amount of money won in each race.

(c) This registration must be made at the Registry Office within sixty days after the horse's original landing in the United States or its possessions, Canada or Cuba, and the registration fee shall be $30 for each horse, which will include certificate of registration.

(d) If it be proved to the satisfaction of the Stewards of The Jockey Club that the failure to apply for the registration of a horse within the 60-day period provided for in paragraph (c) of this Rule was the result of excusable inadvertence, such registration may be permitted thereafter, provided, however, that the Stewards are furnished with such other authenticated information, in respect of the age and identity of the horse and other relevant matters, as they may require and, provided, further, that no application for registration will be accepted if made more than two years after original arrival of the horse in the United States or its possessions, Canada or Cuba, unless the Stewards find that its acceptance is necessary to avoid clear injustice or hardship.

It the application to register be made within six months after original arrival, the fee will be $100 for each horse; if made within one year after original arrival, the fee will be $200; and if made after such time, the fee will be $400.

82. Upon any change of name of a horse which has run in any country, his old name as well as his new name must be given in every entry until he has run three times under his new name over the course of an Association.

Color Guide

BAY: This varies from a light yellowish tan to a dark rich auburn shade. A bay always has a black mane and tail and black on legs. (Black points.)

DARK BAY OR BROWN: Used to describe animals whose color is marginal, as well as those which are brown.

BLACK: The body, head, muzzle, flanks and legs are composed of uniform black hairs.

CHESTNUT: This varies from light washy yellow to dark liver in color. Never has black mane, tail or legs, but may have black hairs in mane and tail. May also have a flaxen mane and tail.

GRAY: This is a mixture of white and black hairs.

ROAN: This is a mixture of white and red hairs.

In borderline cases, the predominant color is the color of the horse.
Example: If the head is covered with red and white hairs and the rest of the body with white and black hairs, the horse is called a gray.
(The individual designations "dark bay" and "brown" have been dropped)

The American Stud Book

This invaluable record published by The Jockey Club should be in the hands of every Breeder and Owner of thoroughbreds.
Priced as follows:

Volumes II, III and IV	$15.00 each
Volumes XI, XII and XIII	$20.00 each
Volumes VIII, IX, XV and XVI	$25.00 each
Volumes VII, XIV and XVII	$30.00 each
Volumes XVIII and XIX	$35.00 each
Volume XX	$45.00 each
Volume XXI	$55.00 each
Volume XXII, listing the foals of 1954,1955,1956, and 1957	
Leather binding to match set	$55.00 each
Buchram binding	$50.00 each
Volume XXIII, listing the foals of 1958,1959,1960 and 1961	
Leather binding	$85.00 each
Buckram binding	$75.00 each

Volumes I, V, VI and X are out of print and not available.
Supplements are published annually, for the then two-year-olds.
Supplements listing foals of 1958,1959,1960,1961,1962 and 1963 are $27.50 per copy.

Rules And Regulations Of The United States Trotting Association

Rule 1.—Mandate.

Section 1. The following Rules and Regulations, having been duly enacted, are hereby declared to be the Official Rules and Regulations of The United States Trotting Association which shall apply to and govern the Registration of Standard Bred Horses and the conduct of all racing by Members and upon Member Tracks.

All published conditions and programs of Member Tracks shall state that said races shall be conducted under and governed by the Rules and Regulations of The United States Trotting Association, with only such exceptions stated as are specifically authorized and permitted.

§ 2. In the event there is a conflict between the rules of The United States Trotting Association and the rules or conditions promulgated by any of its members, the rules of The United States Trotting Association shall govern.

§ 3. In the event USTA denies membership to any person for failure to meet the requirements of the By-Laws relative to membership, and in the event a State Racing Commission determines that such person fully meets its requirements and licenses such person to participate at meetings under the jurisdiction of such Commission, USTA will issue an eligibility certificate and/or a drivers license limited to such meetings and keep performance records on such person and his horses while racing at such meetings in the same manner and for the same fee as for members.

Rule 2.—Authorities And Terms.

Section 1. The term "President" or "Executive Vice-President" in these Rules refers to the President or Executive Vice-President of The United States Trotting Association. "Board of Review" refers to the Board comprised of the Directors from the Association District where the matter originated. The term "Association" when used in these rules refers to The United States Trotting Association.

Rule 3.—Violations.

Section 1. Any Member of this Association violating any of its Rules or Regulations, shall be liable upon conviction, to a fine not exceeding One Thousand Dollars ($1,000.00) or suspension, or both, or expulsion from the Association, unless otherwise limited in the rules.

The conviction of any Corporate Member of this Association of a violation of any of its rules or regulations may also subject the Officers of the said corporation to a penalty not exceeding that which is hereinabove provided.

§ 2. Any attempt to violate any of the Rules and Regulations of this Association falling short of actual accomplishment, shall constitute an offense, and, upon conviction, shall be punishable as hereinabove provided.

Rule 4.—Definitions.

Section 1. **Added Money Early Closing Event.**—an event closing in the same year in which it is to be contested in which all entrance and declaration fees received are added to the purse.

§ 2. **Age, How Reckoned.**—The age of a horse shall be reckoned from the first day of January of the year of foaling.

§ 3. **Appeal.**—A request for the Board of Review to investigate, consider, and review any decisions or rulings of Judges or officials of a meeting. The appeal may deal with placings, penalties, interpretations of the rules or other questions dealing with the conduct of races.

§ 4. **Claiming Race.**—One in which any horse starting therein may be claimed for a designated amount in conformance with the rules.

§ 5. **Classified Race.**—A race regardless of the eligibility of horses, entries being selected on the basis of ability or performance.

§ 6. **Conditioned Race.**—An overnight event to which eligibility is determined according to specified qualifications. Such qualifications may be based upon:

(a) Horses' money winnings in a specified number of previous races or during a specified previous time.

(b) A horses' finishing position in a specified number of previous races or during a specified period of time.

(c) Age.

(d) Sex.

(e) Number of starts during a specified period of time.

(f) Or any one or more combinations of the qualifications herein listed.

(g) Use of records or time bars as a condition is prohibited.

§ 7. **Dash.**—A race decided in a single trial. Dashes may be given in a series of two or three governed by one entry fee for the series, in which event a horse must start in all dashes. Positions may be drawn for each dash. The number of premiums awarded shall not exceed the number of starters in the dash.

§ 8. **Declarations.**—Declarations shall be taken not more than three days in advance for all races except those for which qualifying dashes are provided.

§ 9. **Disqualification.**—It shall be contrued to mean that the person disqualified is debarred from acting as an official or from starting or driving a horse in a race, or in the case of a disqualified horse, it shall not be allowed to start.

§ 10. **Early Closing Race.**—A race for a definite amount to which entries close at least six weeks preceding the race. The entrance fee may be on the installment plan or otherwise, and all payments are forfeits.

§ 11. **Elimination Heats.**—Heats of a race split according to Rule 13, Sections 2 and 3, to qualify the contestants for a final heat.

47

§ 12. **Entry.**–Two or more horses starting in a race when owned or trained by the same person, or trained in the same stable or by the same management.

§ 13. **Expulsion.**–Whenever the penalty of expulsion is prescribed in these rules, it shall be construed to mean unconditional exclusion and disqualification from any participation, either directly or indirectly, in the privileges and uses of the course and grounds of a member.

§ 14. **Extended Pari-Mutuel Meetings.**–An extended pari-mutuel meeting is a meeting or meetings, at which no agricultural fair is in progress with an annual total of more than ten days duration with pari-mutuel wagering.

§ 15. **Futurity.**–A stake in which the dam of the competing animal is nominated either when in foal or during the year of foaling.

§ 16. **Green Horse.**–One that has never trotted or paced in a race or against time, either double or single.

§ 17. **Guaranteed Stake.**–Same as a stake, with a guarantee by the party opening it that the sum shall not be less than the amount named.

§ 18. **Handicap.**–A race in which performance, sex or distance allowance is made. Post positions for a handicap may be assigned by the Racing Secretary. Post positions in a handicap claiming race may be determined by claiming price.

§ 19. **Heat.**–A single trial in a race two in three, or three heat plan.

§ 20. **In Harness.**–When a race is made to go "in harness" it shall be construed to mean that the performance shall be to a sulky.

§ 21. **Late Closing Race.**–A race for a fixed amount to which entries close less than six weeks and more than three days before the race is to be contested.

§ 22. **Length of Race and Number of Heats.**–Races or dashes shall be given at a stated distance in units not shorter than a sixteenth of a mile. The length of a race and the number of heats shall be stated in the conditions. If no distance or number of heats are specified all races shall be a single mile dash except at fairs and meetings of a duration of 10 days or less, where the race will be conducted in two dashes at one mile distance.

§ 23. **Maiden.**–A stallion, mare or gelding that has never won a heat or race at the gait at which it is entered to start and for which a purse is offered. Races or purse money awarded to a horse after the "official sign" has been posted shall not be considered winning performance or affects status as a maiden.

§ 24. **Match Race.**–A race which has been arranged and the conditions thereof agreed upon between the contestants.

§ 25. **Matinee Race.**–A race with no entrance fee and where the premiums, if any, are other than money.

§ 26. **Overnight Event.**–A race for which entries close not more than three days (omitting Sundays) or less before such race is to be contested. In the absence of conditions or notice to the contrary, all entries in overnight events must close not later than 12 noon the day preceding the race.

§ 27. **Protest.**–An objection, properly sworn to, charging that a horse is ineligible to a race, alleging improper entry or declaration, or citing any act of an owner, driver, or official prohibited by the rules, and which, if true, should exclude the horse or driver from the race.

§ 28. **Record.**–The fastest time made by a horse in a heat or dash which he won. A standard record is a record of 2:20 or faster for two-year-olds and 2:15 or faster for all other ages.

§ 29. **Stake.**–A race which will be contested in a year subsequent to its closing in which the money given by the track conducting the same is added to the money contributed by the nominators, all of which except deductions for the cost of promotion, breeders or nominators awards belongs to the winner or winners. In any event, all of the money contributed in nominating, sustaining, and starting payments must be paid to the winner or winners.

§ 30. **Two in Three.**—In a two in three race a horse must win two heats to be entitled to first money.

§ 31. **Two Year-Olds.**—No two-year-old shall be permitted to start in a dash or heat exceeding one mile in distance. Except where elimination heats are required, two-year-olds may start only in races conditioned not to exceed two dashes or in a two in three race which shall terminate in three heats. Starting a two-year-old in violation of this rule shall subject the member track to a fine of not less than $25.00 and the winnings of such two-year-old shall be declared unlawful. In two year old races any colt may default the end of the second heat or dash and the remaining colt shall be declared the winner. Any colt withdrawing under this rule shall forfeit all right to the race winner's share of the purse or to the award of the trophy. Any arrangement between contestants for sharing purse money shall be a violation of Rule 5 Section 3 (Hippodroming). In the event all eligibles withdraw, the sponsor may retain the ten per cent and the trophy.

§ 32. **Walk Over.**—When only horses in the same interest start, it constitutes a walk over. In a "stake race" a "walk over" is entitled to all the stake money and forfeits unless otherwise provided in the published conditions. To claim the purse the entry must start and go once over the course.

§ 33. **Winner.**—The horse whose nose reaches the wire first. If there is a dead heat for first, both horses shall be considered winners. Where two horses are tied in the summary, the winner of the longer dash or heat shall be entitled to the trophy. Where the dashes or heats are of the same distance and the horses are tied in the summary, the winner of the faster dash or heat shall be entitled to the trophy. **Where the dashes or heats are of the same distance and the horses are tied in the summary and the time, both horses shall be considered winners.**

§ 34. **Wire.**—The wire is a real or imaginary line from the center of the judge's stand to a point immediately across, and at right angles to the track.

§ 35 **Contract Track.**—A pari-mutuel track, not a member of this Association, which receives data and services pursuant to Article VII, Section 7 (c) of the Association's By-Laws.

Rule 5.—Track Members.

Section 1. Whenever races are conducted each member track shall display its certificate of membership in this Association for the current year and specified dates. Horses racing after January 1, 1940, upon due notice to members on tracks which are not in contract or which are not in membership with The United States Trotting Association or the Canadian Trotting Association, or racing on tracks in membership with the Association on dates that have not been sanctioned by the Association shall from the date of the first such race be ineligible to race in anything but a free-for-all, and he is barred from classified and claiming and conditioned races and no eligibility certificate will be issued on that horse in the future. In the event of a bona fide sale of the horse to an innocent party or upon satisfactory proof that the owner of such horse was deceived as to the absence of contract with such track, the non-membership of such track or failure to be sanctioned for such dates, the penalty hereinbefore provided may be limited in the discretion of the Board of Review. Such horse may be restored to eligibility and may be admitted to classified, claiming and conditioned races and may receive USTA eligibility certificate upon the payment of the sum of $10 per start with a maximum of $50 for any one meeting to cover the cost of establishing and verifying the racing performances of that horse on such non-member or non-contract track.

§ 2. **Location of Judges' Stand.**—The Judges' stand shall be so located and constructed as to afford to the officials an unobstructed view of the entire track and no obstruction shall be permitted upon the track, or the centerfield which shall obscure the officials' vision of any portion of the track during the race. Any violation of this section shall subject the member to a fine not exceeding $500 and immediate suspension from membership by the President or Executive Vice-President, subject to appeal.

§ 3. **Hippodroming Ban.**—All races conducted by Member tracks shall be bona fide contests with the winner receiving the largest share of the purse and the balance of the purse distribution made according to the order of finish. No hippodroming or other arrangement for equal distribution of the purse money among the contestants is permitted. Violation of this rule will subject the track member, officials in charge, and the owners and drivers to fine, suspension, or expulsion.

§ 4. **Default in Payment of Purses.**—Any member that defaults in the payment of a premium that has been raced for, shall stand suspended, together with its officers. No deduction, voluntary or involuntary, may be made from any purse or stake, or futurity other than for payments to be made to the owners, nominators, or breeders of money winning horses and clerical, printing, postage and surety bond expenses specifically related to such purse, stake or futurity.

§ 5. **Time to File Claims for Unpaid Purses.**—Unless claims for unpaid premiums shall be filed with this Association within sixty days after the date the race is contested the Association may release any performance bond that had been required.

§ 6. If at a meeting of a member a race is contested which has been promoted by another party or parties, and the promoters thereof default in the payment of the amount raced for, the same liability shall attach to the members as if the race had been offered by the member.

§ 7. **Dishonored Checks.**—Any member who shall pay any purse, or charges due The United States Trotting Association, or a refund of entrance fees by draft, check, order or other paper, which upon presentation is protested, payment refused, or otherwise dishonored, shall by order of the Executive Vice-President be subjected to a fine not exceeding the amount of said draft, check or order and shall be suspended from membership until the dishonored amount and fine are paid to the Executive Vice-President.

§ 8. **Minimum Advertised Purse or Schedule of Purses.**—When any member track advertises minimum purses or purses for a class and conducts any race for that class for less than said advertised minimum or class purse, such track member shall be fined by the Executive Vice-President the difference between the advertised minimum or advertised purse and the lesser purse for which such race was conducted unless there is a contract with a horsemen's association concerning purse distributions.

§ 9. **Removal of Horses From the Grounds.**—No horse shall be ordered off the grounds without at least 72 hours notice (excluding Sunday) to the person in charge of the horse.

§ 10. **Driver Awards.**—Except as herein stated, no member track in the United States shall advertise to pay or pay any awards other than to the Owners, Nominators, or Breeders of money winning horses. Awards may be made to drivers of horses breaking or equaling track or world records, or to leading drivers at meetings.

§ 11. **Paddock Rules.**—Every extended pari-mutuel track shall:

(1) Provide a paddock or receiving barn.

(2) The paddock or receiving barn must be completely enclosed with a man-tight fence and all openings through said fence shall be policed so as to exclude unauthorized personnel therefrom.

(3) Horses must be in the paddock at the time prescribed by the Presiding Judge, but in any event at least one hour prior to post time of the race in which the horse is to compete. Except for warm-up trips, no horse shall leave the paddock until called to the post.

(4) Persons entitled to admission to the paddock:

    (a) Owners of horses competing on the date of the race.

    (b) Trainers of horses competing on the date of the race.

    (c) Drivers of horses competing on the date of the race.

    (d) Grooms and caretakers of horses competing on the date of the race.

    (e) Officials whose duties require their presence in the paddock or or receiving barn.

(5) No driver, trainer, groom, or caretaker, once admitted to the paddock or receiving barn, shall leave the same other than to warm up said horse until such race, or races, for which he was admitted is contested.

(6) No person except an owner, who has another horse racing in a later race, or an official, shall return to the paddock until all races of that program shall have been completed.

(7) No more than two members of a registered stable, other than the driver, shall be entitled to admission to the paddock on any one racing day.

(8) During racing hours each track shall provide the services of a blacksmith within the paddock.

(9) During racing hours each track shall provide suitable extra equipment as may be necessary for the conduct of racing without unnecessary delay.

(10) Each track shall see that the provisions of this rule are rigidly enforced and a fine not to exceed $500.00 for each violation of this rule may be imposed.

§ 12. **Photo Finish, Head Numbers—Starting Gate.**—At all member tracks where pari-mutuel wagering is allowed, a photo finish, head numbers, and starting gate must be used. Whenever the Judges use a photo to determine the order of finish, it shall be posted for public inspection. Photo finish equipment whall not be acceptable unless a spinner or target is used therewith.

§ 13. **Payment of Dues.**—If a member fails to pay the dues prescribed by the By-Laws of the Association within thirty (30) days of notice of the amount due, the member together with its officers and directors may be suspended from membership in the Association.

§ 14. **Driver Insurance.**—Each member conducting an extended pari-mutuel meeting shall prepare a prominently display, in the Race Secretary's office, a statement giving the name of the company with which they carry driver insurance.

§ 15. **Supervision of Meeting.**—Although members have the obligation of general supervision of their meeting, interference with the proper performance of duties of any official is hereby prohibited.

Rule 6.—Race Officials.

Section 1. **Officials Required.**—In every race over the track of a member, the Manager shall appoint or authorize the appointment of three men familiar with the rules to act as Judges, one of whom shall be designated as Presiding Judge, who shall be in charge of the stand. He shall also appoint a licensed Starter, three Timers, and a competent person to act as Clerk of the Course.

At all matinees there shall be at least one licensed official in the Judges' stand.

§ 2. No license shall be granted to any person not in membership with this Association.

§ 3. Any member track permitting an unlicensed person to officiate when a license is required shall be fined not exceeding $100 for each day such unlicensed person officiates. Any person officiating without being licensed as required by these rules or acting as an official at any meeting not in membership with this Association, or the Canadian Trotting Association, shall be fined not exceeding $100 for each day he acts as such an official; PROVIDED HOWEVER, that nothing herein contained shall prevent any person from officiating at a contract track.

§ 4. **Officials at Extended Meetings.**—No presiding Judge, Starter or Race Secretary shall be qualified to serve as such at an extended pari-mutuel harness race meeting or a grand circuit meeting without a license valid for pari-mutuel meetings or grand circuit meetings. An Associate Judge, Barrier Judge, Patrol Judge, Clerk of the Course, or Paddock Judge who serves at an extended pari-mutuel meeting or at pari-mutuel meetings totaling more than ten days during a race season must have a license valid for pari-mutuel meetings. Starters, Presiding Judges and Race Secretaries holding pari-mutuel licenses are authorized to officiate at all meetings, and Associate Judges holding pari-mutuel licenses are authorized to serve as Presiding Judges at pari-mutuel meetings of ten days or less and at non pari-mutuel meetings. No person shall serve as an Associate Judge at any pari-mutuel meeting in the United States unless he is a member of the USTA. The Executive Vice-President may permit an exchange of license in the various capacities above, upon proper application. The fee for each such license shall be $25.00 for all categories with the exception of the Patrol Judge and Clerk of the Course which shall be $15.00, which includes an active membership in this Association. The applicant for such license must satisfy the Executive Vice-President that he possesses the necessary qualifications, both mental and physical, to perform the duties required. Elements to be considered among others shall be character, reputation, temperament, experience, and knowledge of the rules and of the duties of a racing official. No official acting as Judge at a pari-mutuel meeting shall serve as a Race Secretary or Clerk of the Course at such meeting. No licensed official shall be qualified to act as such at any pari-mutuel meeting where he is the owner or otherwise interested in the ownership of any horse participating at such meeting. Any refusal to grant this license to a person who had been so licensed in the past may be reviewed by the Board of Appeals as provided in Article IX of the By-Laws.

§ 5. **Disqualification to Act as Official.**—A person under suspension, expulsion, or other disqualification, or who has any interest in or any bet on a race or has an interest in any of the horses engaged therein, is disqualified from acting in any official capacity in that race. In the event of such disqualification the management shall be notified by the disqualified person and shall appoint a substitute. Any person who violates this restriction shall be fined, suspended or expelled.

§ 6. **Suspension or Revocation of Official's License.**—An official may be fined, suspended, or his license may be revoked or denied at any time by the President or Executive Vice-President for incompetence, failure to follow or enforce the rules, or any conduct detrimental to the sport including drinking within 4 hours prior to the time he starts work as an official. Such license may be reinstated by the President or Executive Vice-President in his discretion upon such terms as he may prescribe. Any revocation or suspension of license hereunder may be reviewed by the Board of Appeals as provided in Article IX of the By-Laws.

Breath Analyzer Test.—Any officials, when directed by a representative of this Association, shall submit to a breath analyzer test, and if the results thereof show a reading of more than .05 per cent of alcohol in the blood, a report shall be made to the respective State Racing Commissions and The United States Trotting Association for appropriate action.

§ 7. **Ban on Owning or Dealing in Horses.**—No employee of any pari-mutuel track whose duties include the classification of horses shall directly or indirectly be the owner of any horse racing at such meeting, nor shall he participate financially directly or indirectly in the purchase or sale of any horse racing at such meeting. Any person violating this rule shall be suspended by the Executive Vice-President.

§ 8. **Judges' Stand Occupants.**—None but the Judges, the Clerk of the Course, the Secretary, Starter and Timers, Official Announcer, and Officers, Officials, and Directors of this Association, and the State Racing Commission having jurisdiction shall be allowed in the Judges' stand during a race. Any association violating this rule shall be fined not to exceed $100.

§ 9. **Improper Acts by an Official.**—If any person acting as Judge or an official shall be guilty of using insulting language from the stand to an owner, driver, or other person, or be guilty of other improper conduct, he shall be fined not exceeding $500, or be expelled.

§ 10. **Presiding Judge.**—No person shall act as Presiding Judge where purses are raced for unless he is a member of and holds a license for the current year from this Association.

A Presiding Judge's license shall be issued by the Executive Vice-President upon payment of an annual fee of $25.00 which includes an active membership, when the applicant therefor has established that his character and reputation, knowledge of the rules, harness horse experience, temperament and qualifications to perform the duties required are satisfactory. Such application must be accompanied by the written approval of at least one Director of this Association from the district in which the applicant resides. However, a license limited to one public race meeting not exceeding five days in duration may be issued for $5.00 but no Judge shall receive more than one such limited license a year.

(a) The Presiding Judge shall have supervision over:

1) Associate Judges   5) Finish Wire Judge
2) Patrol Judges   6) Clerk of the Course
3) Starters   7) Timers
4) Paddock Judge

53

(b) Shall examine the official track license issued by the Association and if the license is not produced shall make public announcement that the meeting shall not proceed.

(c) Notify owners and drivers of penalties imposed.

(d) Report in writing to the Executive Vice-President violations of the rules by a member, its officers or race officials giving detailed information.

(e) Make such other reports as required by the Executive Vice President.

(f) Sign each sheet of the judges' book verifying the correctness of the record.

(g) Be responsible for the maintenance of the records of the meeting and the forwarding thereof to The United States Trotting Association except in cases of a contract track in which the contract provides otherwise.

Services of the Presiding Judge shall be paid for by the track employing him and he shall not act as a Starter, announcer or an officer at any meeting at which he officiates as Presiding Judge.

§ 11. The Judges shall have authority while presiding to:

(a) Inflict fines and penalties, as prescribed by these rules.

(b) Determine all questions of fact relating to the race.

(c) Decide any differences between parties to the race, or any contingent matter which shall arise, such as are not otherwise provided for in these rules.

(d) Declare pools and bets "off" in case of fraud, no appeal to be allowed from their decision in that respect. All pools and bets follow the decision of the Judges. Such a decision in respect to pools and bets shall be made at the conclusion of the race upon the observations of the judges and upon such facts as an immediate investigation shall develop. A reversal or change of decision after the official placing at the conclusion of the heat or dash shall not affect the distribution of betting pools made upon such official placing. When pools and bets are declared off for fraud, the guilty parties shall be fined, suspended or expelled.

(e) Control the horses, drivers, and assistants and punish by a fine not exceeding $100.00 or by suspension or expulsion, any such person who shall fail to obey their orders or the rules. In no case shall there be any compromise or change on the part of the Judges or members of punishment prescribed in the rules, but the same shall be strictly enforced. Members shall not remove or modify any fine imposed by the Judges of a race, review any order of suspension, expulsion, or interfere with the Judges performing their duties.

(f) Examine under oath all parties connected with a race as to any wrong or complaint. Any person required to appear before the Judges for a hearing or examination who shall fail to appear after due notice in writing shall be penalized as provided in (e) above.

(g) Consider complaints of foul from the patrols, owners, or drivers in the race and no others.

§ 12. It shall be the duty of the Judges to:

(a) Exclude from the race any horse that in their opinion is improperly equipped, dangerous, or unfit to race, which shall include sick, weak, and extremely lame horses. No horse shall race with a tube in its throat.

(b) Investigate any apparent or possible interference, or other violation of Rule 18, Section 1, whether or not complaint has been made by the driver.

(c) Investigate any act of cruelty seen by them or reported to them, by any member towards a race horse during a meeting at which they officiate. If the Judges find that such an act has been committed, they shall suspend or fine the offending member not to exceed $500.00.

(d) Immediately thereafter or on the day of the race conduct an investigation of any accidents to determine the cause thereof, and the judges shall completely fill out an accident report and mail to the Association office.

(e) Observe closely performance of the drivers and the horses to ascertain if there are any violations of Rule 18; particularly, interference, helping, or inconsistent racing, and exhaust all means possible to safeguard the contestants and the public.

(f) Grant a hearing at a designated time before a penalty may be imposed upon any party. All three Judges should be present if possible, and at least the Presiding Judge and one Associate Judge must be present at all Judges' hearings. The Judges may inflict the penalties prescribed by these rules.

In the event the Judges believe that a person has committed a rule violation other than a racing violation and has left the grounds and they are unable to contact him, and hold a hearing thereon, they may make an investigation and send a detailed written report to the Executive Vice-President of this Association. The Executive Vice-President may impose a penalty not to exceed 10 days without a hearing based upon the report of the Judges. No penalty in excess of 10 days shall be imposed before a hearing is granted.

It shall be the duty of the Judges to submit in writing, a complete list of all witnesses questioned by them at any hearing, which list of witnesses, along with the testimony of such witnesses, shall be forwarded to the Executive Vice-President along with the reports required in Rule 6, Section 10.

The testimony of all witnesses questioned by the Judges shall be recorded by one of the following methods: written, signed statements, tape recorders or court reporter's transcript. At all extended pari-mutuel tracks Judges shall use tape recorders to record their hearings.

No decision shall be made by the Judges in such cases until all of the witnesses called by the Judges and the person so required to appear before the Judges have given their testimony. Any person charged with a rule violation shall be given at least until 12:00 noon of the following day to prepare his defense if he so requests.

(g) It shall be the duty of the Judges to declare a dash or heat of a race no contest in the event the track is thrown into darkness during the progress of a race by failure of electricity.

§ 13. It shall be the procedure of the Judges to:

(a) Be in the stand fifteen minutes before the first race and remain in the stand for ten minutes after the last race, and at all times when the horses are upon the track.

(b) Observe the preliminary warming up of horses and scoring, noting behavior of horses, lameness, equipment, conduct of the drivers, changes in odds at pari-mutuel meetings, and any unusual incidents pertaining to horses or drivers participating in races.

(c) Have the bell rung or give other notice, at least ten minutes before the race or heat. Any driver failing to obey this summons may be punished by a fine not exceeding $100.00 and his horse may be ruled out by the Judges and considered drawn.

(d) Designate one of their members to lock the pari-mutuel machines immediately upon the horses reaching the official starting point. The Presiding Judge shall designate the post time for each race and the horses will be called at such time as to preclude excessive delay after the completion of two scores.

(e) Be in communication with the Patrol Judges, by use of patrol phones,

55

from the time the Starter picks up the horses until the finish of the race. Any violation or near violation of the rules shall be reported by the Patrol Judge witnessing the incident and a written record made of same. At least one Judge shall observe the drivers throughout the stretch specifically noting changing course, interference, improper use of whips, breaks, and failure to contest the race to the finish.

(f) Post the objection sign, or inquiry sign, on the odds board in the case of a complaint or possible rule violation, and immediately notify the announcer of the objection and the horse or horses involved. As soon as the Judges have made a decision, the objection sign shall be removed, the correct placing displayed, and the "Official" sign flashed. In all instances the Judges shall post the order of finish and the "Official" sign as soon as they have made their decision.

(g) Display the photo sign if the order of finish among the contending horses is less than half-length or a contending horse is on a break at the finish. After the photo has been examined and a decision made, a copy or copies shall be made, checked by the Presiding Judge, and posted for public inspection.

§ 14. **Patrol Judges.**—At the discretion of the Judges, patrol may be appointed by the member, but such patrols shall be approved by the Presiding Judge and work under his direction. At extended pari-mutuel meetings and at other meetings conducting one or more races with a purse value of $5,000 or over, at least two (2) Patrol Judges shall be employed. It shall be their duty to phone or repair to the Judge's stand and report all fouls and improper conduct. The result of a heat or dash shall not be announced until sufficient time has elapsed to receive the reports of the patrols. Where there is a Patrol car, only one Patrol Judge shall be required.

§ 15. **Emergency Appointment of Official.**—If any licensed official is absent or incapacitated, the member or director, or officer of the association, may appoint a substitute at such meeting, or until another licensed official can be procured. If such official acts for more than three days, he shall apply for a license in that capacity. Notice of any temporary appointment shall be wired immediately to the main office of this Association. This power may only be used in case of unavoidable emergencies. Any Director of this Association, in an emergency, may exercise any or all of the functions of any official or licensee.

§ 16. **Starter.**—No person shall be permitted to start horses on a track in membership with this Association unless he holds a Starter's license for the current year. An application for such license must be accompanied by the written approval of at least one Director of this Association from the district in which the applicant resides. Upon sufficient information as to good character, knowledge of these rules and ability to do the work, a license to start horses may be issued by the Executive Vice-President upon payment of an annual fee of $25.00. However, a license limited to start horses in matinee races, or at one public race meeting not exceeding five days in duration may be issued to members upon payment of an annual fee of $5.00, but no starter shall receive more than one such license in any one year.

§ 17. The Starter shall be in the stand or starting gate fifteen minutes before the first race. The Starter, prior to starting any race at a meeting, shall examine the official track license issued by this Association and in the event the same is not produced, shall make public announcement that the meeting shall not proceed. He shall have control over the horses and authority to assess fines and/or suspend drivers for any violation of the rules from the formation of the parade until the word "go" is given. He may assist in placing the horses when requested by the Judges to do so. He shall notify the Judges and the drivers of penalties imposed by him. He shall report violations of the rules by a member or its officers, giving detailed information. His services shall be paid for by the member employing him. An Assistant Starter may be employed when an association deems it necessary. At all meetings at which the premiums do not exceed three thousand dollars, the Starter may also act as an Associate Judge.

§ 18. **Clerk of Course.**—The Clerk of the Course shall:

(a) At request of Judges assist in drawing positions.

(b) Keep the Judges' Book provided by the U.S.T.A. and record therein:

(1) All horses entered and their eligibility certificate numbers.

(2) Names of owners and drivers and drivers' license numbers.

(3) **The charted lines at non-fair pari-mutuel meetings. At fairs, the position of the horses at the finish. At all race meetings, the money won by the horse at that track.**

(4) Note drawn or ruled out horses.

(5) Record time in minutes, seconds and fifths of seconds.

(6) Check eligibility certificates before the race and after the race shall enter all information provided for thereon, including the horse's position in the race if it was charted.

(7) **Verifying the correctness of the Judge's Book including race time, placing and money winnings, reasons for disqualification, if any, and** see that the book is properly signed.

(8) Forward the Judges' Book, **charts and marked programs** from all extended pari-mutuel meetings the day following each racing day and from fairs and other meetings not later than the last day of the meeting.

(9) Notify owners and drivers of penalties assessed by the officials.

(c) Upon request may assist Judges in placing horses.

(d) After the race, return the eligibility certificate to owner of the horse or his representative when requested.

Failure to comply with any part of this rule and make the above listed entries legible, clear and accurate, may subject either the Clerk or the Member, or both, to a fine of not to exceed $50.00 for each violation.

§ 19. **Timers.**—At each race there shall be three Timers in the Judges' or Timers' stand except when an electric timing device approved by the Executive Vice-President of the Association, is used, in which event there shall be one Timer. The chief timer shall sign the Judges' Book for each race verifying the correctness of the record. All times shall be announced and recorded in fifths of seconds. An approved electronic or electric timing device must be used where horses are started from a chute.

The Timers shall be in the stand fifteen minutes before the first heat or dash is to be contested. They shall start their watches when the first horse leaves the point from which the distance of the race is measured. The time of the leading horse at the quarter, half, three-quarters, and the finish shall be taken.

§ 20. **Paddock Judge.**—Under the direction and supervision of the Presiding Judge, the Paddock Judge will have complete charge of all paddock activities as outlined in Rule 5 Section 10. The Paddock Judge is responsible for:

(a) Getting the fields on the track for post parades in accordance with the schedule given to him by the Presiding Judge.

(b) Inspection of horses for changes in equipment, broken or faulty equipment, head numbers or saddle pads.

57

(c) Supervision of paddock gate men.

(d) Proper check in and check out of horses and drivers.

Check the identification of all horses coming into the Paddock including the tattoo number if he does not personally recognize the horse.

(e) Direction of the activities of the paddock blacksmith.

(f) The Paddock Judge will immediately notify the Presiding Judge of anything that could in any way change, delay or otherwise affect the racing program.

The Paddock Judge will report any cruelty to any horse that he observes to the Presiding Judge.

(g) The Paddock Judge shall see that only properly authorized persons are permitted in the paddock and any violation of this rule may result in a fine, suspension or expulsion.

§ 21. **Program Director.**—Each extended pari-mutuel track shall designate a Program Director.

(a) It shall be the responsibility of the Program Director to furnish the public complete and accurate past performance information as required by Rule 7, Section 2.

(b) No person shall act as a Program Director at an extended pari-mutuel meeting unless he has secured a license from this Association. A license may be granted to any person who, by reason of his knowledge, experience and industry, is capable of furnishing accurate and complete past performance information to the general public.

(c) The annual fee for such license shall be $25.00 which includes an active membership.

§ 22. **Duties of Patrol Judges.**—The Patrol Judges shall observe all activity on the race track in their area at all times during the racing program. They shall immediately report to the Presiding Judge:

(a) Any action on the track which could improperly affect the result of a race.

(b) Every violation of the racing rules.

(c) Every violation of the rules of decorum.

(d) The lameness or unfitness of any horse.

(e) Any lack of proper racing equipment.

The Patrol Judges shall, furthermore:

(a) Be in constant communication with the Judges during the course of every race and shall immediately advise the Judges of every rule violation, improper act or unusual happening which occurs at their station.

(b) Submit individual daily reports of their observations of the racing to the Presiding Judge.

(c) When directed by the Presiding Judge shall attend hearings or inquiries on violations and testify thereat under oath.

§ 23. **Licensed Charter.**—The charting of races shall be done only by a licensed charter and he shall be responsible for providing a complete and accurate chart. A license may be granted only to a person who has the knowledge, training and industry to accomplish this. The annual fee for such a license shall be $15.00 which includes an active membership.

Rule 7.—Identification of Horses.

Section 1. **Bona Fide Owner or Lessee.**—Horses not under lease must race in the name of the bona fide owner. Horses under lease must race in the name of the lessee and a copy of the lease must be recorded with this Association. Persons violating this rule may be fined, suspended or expelled.

§ 2. **Program Information.**—A printed program shall be available to the public at all meetings where purses are raced for. All programs shall furnish:

(a) Horse's name and sex.

(b) Color and age.

(c) Sire and dam.

(d) Owner's name.

(e) Driver's name and colors.

At extended pari-mutuel meetings the following additional information shall be furnished:

(f) In claiming races the price for which the horse is entered to be claimed must be indicated.

(g) At least the last six (6) performance and accurate chart lines. (See Rule 14, Section 2, Sub-Section (d).) An accurate chart line shall include: Date of race, place, size of track if other than a half-mile track, symbol for free-legged pacers, track condition, type of race, distance, the fractional times of the leading horse including race time, post position, position at one quarter, one half, three quarters, stretch with lengths behind leader, finish with lengths behind leader, individual time of the horse, closing dollar odds, name of the driver, names of the horses placed first, second and third by the Judges. The standard symbols for breaks and park-outs shall be used, where applicable.

(h) Indicate drivers racing with a provisional license.

(i) Indicate pacers that are racing without hopples.

(j) Summary of starts in purse races, earnings, and best win time for current and preceding year. A horse's best win time may be earned in either a purse or non-purse race.

(k) The name of the trainer.

(l) The consolidated line shall carry date, place, time, driver, finish, track condition and distance, if race is not at one mile.

§ 3. **Failure to Furnish Reliable Program Information.**—May subject the track and/or Program Director to a fine not to exceed $500.00 and/or the track and/or the Program Director may be suspended until arrangements are made to provide reliable program information.

§ 4. **Inaccurate Information.**—Owners, drivers, or others found guilty of providing inaccurate information on a horse's performance, or of attempting to have misleading information given on a program may be fined, suspended, or expelled.

§ 5. **Check on Identity of Horse.**—Any track official, officer of this Association, owner or driver, or any member of this Association may call for information concerning the identity and eligibility of any horse on the grounds of a member, and may demand an opportunity to examine such horse or his eligibility certificate with a view to establish his identity or eligibility. If the owner or party controlling such horse shall refuse to afford such information, or to allow such examination, or fail to give satisfactory identification, he horse and the said owner or party may be barred by the member, and suspended or expelled by the President or Executive Vice-President.

§ 6. **False Chart Lines.**—Any Official, clerk, or person who enters a chart line on an eligibility certificate when the race has not been charted by a licensed charter may be fined, suspended, or expelled.

§ 7. **Frivolous Demand for Identification.**—Any person demanding the identification of a horse without cause, or merely with the intent to embarrass a race, shall be punished by a fine not exceeding $100 or by suspension, or expulsion.

§ 8. **Tattoo Requirements.**—No horse will be permitted to start at an extended pari-mutuel meeting that has not been tattooed unless the permission of the Presiding Judge is obtained and arrangements are made to have the horse tattooed.

§ 9. **Withholding Eligibility Certificate.**—Any person withholding an eligibility certificate from the owner of a horse, after proper demand has been made for the return thereof, may be suspended until such time as the certificate is returned.

Rule 8.—Racing, Farm, or Stable Name.

Section 1. Racing, farm, corporate, or stable names may be used by owners or lessees if registered with this Association giving the names of all persons who are interested in the stable or will use the name. The fee for such registration is $100.00. **All stockholders of a corporation formed after April 1, 1962 and racing a horse must be members of the Association.** The Executive-Vice-President shall be notified immediately if additional persons become interested in a registered stable or if some person listed in a registration disassociates himself from the stable. Failure to do so will place the stable in violation of Rule 12, Section 2. Two stables cannot be registered under the same name and the Executive Vice-President may reject an application for a name that is confusing to the public, unbecoming to the sport, or exceeds 25 letters. All owners and persons listed in a registered stable, whether incorporated or not, shall be liable for entry fees and penalties against the registered stable. In the event one of the owners or persons listed in a registered stable is suspended, all the horses shall be included in accordance with Rule 22, Section 6. When a stable name is not in active use for a period of three consecutive years it will be placed on the inactive list.

§ 2. **Signature on Transfers and Other Documents Relating to Racing, Farm, Corporate and Stable Names.**—Only the signature of the corresponding officer of a racing, farm, corporate or stable name will be recognized on transfers and other documents pertaining to such organizations. Documents bearing the signature of the stable by the corresponding officer will be considered binding upon the members thereof.

Each member of a registered farm, corporate or stable should sign a document designating the name and address of the corresponding officer thereof—for future applications only.

Rule 9.—Eligibility and Classification.

Section 1. **Eligibility Certificate.**—There shall be an automatic fine of $10.00 on the owner if a horse is declared in without an eligibility certificate first being presented for the current year at the gait the horse is declared to race. The track member shall automatically be fined $5.00 for accepting a declaration without an eligibility certificate for the proper gait and a track member may refuse to accept any declaration without the eligibility certificate for the proper gait first being presented. Telegraphic or telephone declarations may be sent and accepted without penalty, provided the declarer furnishes adequate program information but the eligibility certificate must be presented when the horse arrives at the track and before he races, or the above fines will be imposed.

The Race Secretary or where the meeting is held at a contract track, the Association's authorized representative shall check each certificate and certify to the judges as to the eligibility of all the horses.

§ 2. **Fee for Eligibility Certificate and Replacement Certificate.**—The fee for an eligibility certificate shall be $5.00. In the event of the loss or destruction of an eligibility certificate, a replacement certificate may be issued to the same owner for $10.00 when the application therefor is accompanied by satisfactory information on the starts together with all qualifying races and matinee races made by the horse during the current year.

Applications for eligibility certificates must state the name and address of the owner, and the color, sex, age and breeding of the horse.

§ 3. **Issuance of Eligibility Certificate.**

(a) An eligibility certificate shall be issued only to an active member of this Association in good standing and shall not be issued to an owner or horse under penalty except as provided in Rule 1, Section 3.

(b) **Joint Ownership.**—When a horse is owned jointly by two or more parties, all owners must be members in good standing in this Association before an eligibility certificate will be issued.

(c) **Sale or Lease During Current Year.**—When a horse is sold or leased after an eligibility certificate is issued for the current year, the seller or his authorized agent duly authorized in writing shall endorse the eligibility certificate for the new owner or lessee who may use it providing he is a member for that year and providing he immediately sends the registration certificate in for a transfer or sends a copy of the lease, the eligibility certificate following the horse. If the new owner or lessee is not a member of this Association, he shall immediately apply for membership.

Failure to forward the registration certificate within 20 days after purchase of an animal which is racing, will subject the buyer to a fine not to exceed $100.00

(d) **Leased Horses.**—Any horse on lease must race in the name of the lessee. No eligibility certificate will be issued to a horse under lease unless a copy of the lease is filed with the Association.

(e) **Procedure Where Eligibility Certificate Is Not Endorsed.**—If the eligibiligy certificate is not endorsed to him, the new owner or lessee must apply for an eligibility certificate, pay the regular fee, send satisfactory information on the starts made by the horse during the current year.

(f) **Information Required From Horses Racing at Canadian Tracks.**— Prior to declarations, owners of horses **having Canadian eligibility certificates** who are not in membership with the USTA shall furnish the Racing Secretary with a Canadian eligibility certificate completely filled out for the current year, which has a certificate of validation attached thereto. **Residents of Canada under Canadian Trotting Association jurisdiction holding eligibility certificates** who are members of this Association may obtain a validation certificate by filing an application with this Association. **Residents of the United States and the Maritime Provinces holding Canadian eligibility certificates and who are members of this Association must have the horse registered in current ownership in The United States Trotting Association register before a validation certificate can be obtained by filing an application with this Assocation.** The fee shall be the same as

61

that for an eligibiligy certificate. This validation certificate may then be attached to the Canadian eligibility certificate and used at tracks in membership with this Association.

(g) **Tampering With Eligibility Certificates.**—Persons tampering with eligibility certificates may be fined, suspended or expelled and winnings after such tampering may be ordered forfeited.

(h) **Corrections On Eligibility Certificates.**—Corrections on eligibility certificates may be made only by a representative of this Association or a licensed official who shall place on the certificate his initial and date.

(i) **Withholding Eligibility Certificates On Horses Not Tattooed.**—An eligibility certificate may be denied to any person refusing to permit his horses to be tattooed.

§ 4. Information Required On Horses That Have Raced In A Country Other Than Canada.—No eligibility certificate will be issued on a horse coming from a country other than Canada unless the following information, certified by the Trotting Association or governing body of that country from which the horse comes, is furnished:

(a) The number of starts during the preceding year, together with the number of firsts, seconds and thirds for each horse, and the total amount of money won during this period.

(b) The number of races in which the horse has started during the current year, together with the number of firsts, seconds and thirds for each horse and the money won during this period.

(c) A detailed list of the last six starts giving the date, place, track condition, post position or handicap, if it was a handicap race, distance of the race, his position at the finish, the time of the race, the driver's name, and the first three horses in the race.

§ 5. (a) Registration of Standard and Non-Standard Bred Horses.— All foals of 1937 and thereafter shall be registered in current ownership either as Standard or Non-Standard. If registration is properly applied for and all fees paid, an eligibility certificate for one year may be issued and marked "registration applied for."

(b) **Horses 15 Years of Age or Older.**—No eligibility certificate shall be issued to any horse that is fifteen years of age or older to perform in any race except in a matinee.

(c) **Matinee Races Prior to April 1st.**—Permission may be given for horses and drivers to participate in matinees prior to April 1st in each year without having an eligibility certificate or drivers' licenses, respectively.

(d) **Use of Eligibility Certificates During the Month of January.**— Authorization may be granted to use eligibility certificates from the previous year during the month of January.

(e) **Bar On Racing Of Yearlings.**—No eligibility certificate will be issued on any horse under two years of age.

§ 6. Eligibility Certificates for Corporations.—Eligibility Certificates will be issued to a corporation only when the corporation is recorded with the Association to show the officers, directors, and any person owning more than 10 per cent of the capital stock.

No corporation or partnership or registered stable of more than 10 persons formed after April 1, 1962 will be acceptable either to race or **to lease** horses for racing purposes.

§ 7. **Eligibility.**—For purposes of eligibility, a racing season or racing year shall be the calendar year.

§ 8. **Time Bars Prohibited.**—No time records or bars shall be used as an element of eligibility.

§ 9. **Date When Eligibility Is Determined.**—Horses must be eligible when entries close but winnings on closing date of eligibility shall not be considered.

In mixed races, trotting and pacing, a horse must be eligible to the class at the gait at which it is stated in the entry the horse will perform.

§ 10. **Conflicting Conditions.**—In the event there are conflicting published conditions and neither is withdrawn by the member, the more favorable to the nominator shall govern.

§ 11. **Standards for Overnight Events.**—The Race Secretary should prescribe standards to determine whether a horse is qualified to race in overnight events at a meeting.

§ 12. **Posting of Overnight Conditions.**—Conditions for overnight events must be posted at least 18 hours before entries close at meetings other than extended pari-mutuel meetings.

At extended pari-mutuel meetings, condition books will be prepared and races may be divided or substituted races may be used only where regularly scheduled races fail to fill, except where they race less than 5 days a week. Such books containing at least three days racing program will be available to horsemen at least 24 hours prior to closing declarations on any race program contained therein.

§ 13. **Types of Races to be Offered.**—In presenting a program of racing, the racing secretary shall use exclusively the following types of races:

1. Stakes and Futurities.
2. Early Closing and Late Closing Events.
3. Conditioned Races.
4. Claiming Races.
5. Preferred races limited to the fastest horses at the meeting. These may be Free-For-All Races, JFA, or Invitationals. Horses to be used in such races shall be posted in the Race Secretary's office and listed with the Presiding Judge. Horses so listed shall not be eligible for conditioned overnight races unless the conditions specifically include horses on the preferred list. Twelve such races may be conducted during a 6-day period of racing at tracks distributing more than $100,000 in overnight purses during such period and not more than 10 such races shall be conducted at other tracks during a 6-day period of racing, provided that at least two of these races are for three year olds, four year olds, or combined three and four year olds. At tracks which race less than 5 days per week, not more than ten such races may be conducted during a 6-day period. Purses offered for such races shall be at least 15% higher than the highest purse offered for a conditioned race programmed the same racing week.

No two-year-old, three-year-old, or four-year-old, will be eligible to be placed on the preferred list to race against older horses until it has won five races at that member track during the year or has won a life-time total of $15,000 unless requested by the owner or authorized agent.

Where a meeting is in progress in December and continues in January of the subsequent year, races and earnings won at that meeting may be computed in determining whether a horse may be placed on the preferred list.

§ 14. **Limitation on Conditions.**—Conditions shall not be written in such a way that any horse is deprived of an opportunity to race in normal preference cycle. Where the word "preferred" is used in a condition it shall not supersede date preference. Not more than three also eligible conditions shall be used in writing the conditions for any overnight event.

§ 15. **Dashes and Heats.**—Any dash or any heat shall be considered as a separate race for the purposes of conditioned racing.

§ 16. **Named Races.**—Named races are not permitted except for preferred races for the fastest horses at a meeting as set forth in Section 13 (5) above, and invitational two, three or four-year-old races with a purse at least 15% higher than the highest purse offered for a conditioned race programmed the same racing week.

§ 17. **Selection or Drawing of Horses.**—For all overnight events, starters and also eligibles shall be drawn by lot from those properly declared in, except that a Race Secretary must establish a preference system for races as provided for in Rule 14 Section 5. However, where necessary to fill a card, not more than one race per day may be divided into not more than two divisions after preference has been applied and the divisions may be selected by the Racing Secretary. For all other overnight races that are divided the division must be by lot unless the conditions provide for a division based on performance, earnings or sex.

§ 18. **Posting Requirements.**—Names of all horses at the track ready to race shall be posted by gait in the declaration room, together with all the pertinent information concerning such horse which may be required to determine eligibility of such horse to condition races offered at the track. There shall be a separate posting of two, three and four-year-olds.

Supplemental purse payments made by a track after the termination of a meeting will be charged and credited to the winnings of any horse at the end of the racing year in which they are distributed, and will appear on the eligibility certificate issued for the subsequent year. Such distribution shall not affect the current eligibility until placed on the next eligibility certificate by this Association.

§ 19. **Rejection of Declaration.**—

(a) The Racing Secretary may reject the declaration on any horse whose eligibility certificate was not in his possession on the date the condition book is published.

(b) The Racing Secretary may reject the declaration on any horse whose past performance indicates that he would be below the competitive level of other horses declared, provided the rejection does not result in a race being cancelled.

§ 20. **Substitute and Divided Races.**—Substitute races may be provided for each day's program and shall be so designated. Such substitute may be used as part of the next program. Entries in races not filling shall be posted. A substitute race or a race divided into two divisions shall be used only if regularly scheduled races fail to fill.

If a regular race fills it shall be raced on the day it was offered. However, if all regularly scheduled races fill, one division of a split overnight race may be carried over to the next racing day.

§ 21. **Opportunities to Race.**—A fair and reasonable racing opportunity shall be afforded both trotters and pacers in reasonable proportion from those available and qualified to race. Claiming races may be carded to the proportion of each week's racing program as the number of claiming authorizations on file with the Racing Secretary bears to the total number of horses on the grounds which are qualified and available for racing.

§ 22. **Qualifying Races.**—A horse winning a qualifying race shall not be deprived by reason of such performance of his right to start in an event limited to maidens.

§ 23. **Definition of "Start".**—The definition of the word "start" in any type of condition unless specifically so stated will include only those performances in a purse race. Qualifying and matinee races are excluded.

§ 24. **Sandwiching Races.**—Not more than five races may be sandwiched.

Rule 10.—Claiming Races.

Section 1. **Who May Claim.**—An owner who has declared a horse programmed to start **at that meeting.** An authorized agent may claim for a qualified owner.

§ 2. **Prohibitions.**—

(a) No person shall claim his own horse nor a horse trained by him.

(b) No person shall claim more than one horse in a race.

(c) No qualified owner or his agent shall claim a horse for another person.

(d) No owner shall cause his horse to be claimed directly or indirectly for his own account.

(e) No person shall offer, or enter into an agreement, to claim or not to claim, or attempt to prevent another person from claiming any horse in a claiming race.

(f) No person shall enter a horse against which there is a mortgage, bill of sale, or lien of any kind, unless the written consent of the holder thereof shall be filed with the Clerk of the Course of the Association conducting such claiming race.

(g) Any entry in a claiming race cannot declare for a subsequent race until after the claiming race has been contested.

§ 3. **Claiming Procedure.**—

(a) **Owner's Credit.**—The owner must have to his credit with the track giving the race an amount equivalent to the specified claiming price.

(b) **Owner's Consent.**—No declaration may be accepted unless written permission of the owner is filed with the Race Secretary at the time of declaration.

(c) **Program.**—The claiming price shall be printed on the program and all claims shall be for the amount so designated and any horse entered in a claiming race may be claimed for the designated amount.

(d) **Claim Box.**—All claims shall be in writing, sealed and deposited at least 15 minutes before the race in a locked box provided for this purpose by the Clerk of the Course.

(e) **Opening of Claim Box.**—No official shall open said box or give any information on claims filed until after the race. Immediately after the race, the claim box shall be opened and the claim, if any, examined by the Judges.

(f) **Multiple Claims on Same Horses.**—Should more than one claim be filed for the same horse, the owner shall be determined by lot by the Judges.

(g) **Delivery of Claimed Horse.**—A horse claimed shall be delivered immediately by the original owner or his trainer to the successful claimant upon authorization of the Presiding Judge.

(h) **Refusal to Deliver Claimed Horse.**—Any person who refuses to deliver a horse legally claimed out of a claiming race shall be suspended together with the horse until delivery is made.

(i) **Vesting of Title to Claimed Horse.**—Every horse claimed shall race in all heats or dashes of the event in the interest and for the account of the owner who declared it in the event, but title to the claimed horse shall be vested in the successful claimant from the time the word "go" is given in the first heat or dash, and said successful claimant shall become the owner of the horse, whether it be alive or dead or sound or unsound, or injured during the race or after it.

(j) **Affidavit by Claimant.**—The judges may require any person making a claim for a horse to make affidavit that he is claiming said horse for his own account or as authorized agent and not for any other person. Any person making such affidavit willfully and falsely shall be subject to punishment as hereinafter provided.

(k) **Penalty for Thirty Days.**—If a horse is claimed it shall not start in another claiming race until thirty days have elapsed unless such horse is entered for a claiming price at least twenty per cent greater than the price at which it was claimed. The day following the date of the claiming shall be the first day. If a horse is claimed no right, title or interest therein shall be sold or transferred except in a claiming race for a period of 30 days following the date of claiming.

(l) **Return of Claimed Horse to Owner or Stable.**—No horse claimed out of a claiming race shall be eligible to start in any race in the name or interest of the original owner for thirty days, nor shall such horse remain in the same stable or under the care or management of the first owner or trainer, or anyone connected therewith unless reclaimed out of another claiming race.

§ 4. **Claiming Price.**—The track shall pay the claiming price to the owner at the time the registration certificate is delivered for presentation to the successful claimant.

§ 5. **Claiming Conditions.**—Whenever possible claiming races shall be written to separate horses five years old and up from young horses and to separate males from females. If sexes are mixed, mares shall be given a price allowance.

Optional claiming races shall not be used unless limited to horses six years old and up.

§ 6. **Minimum Price.**—No claiming race shall be offered permitting claims for less than the minimum purse offered at that time during the same racing week.

§ 7. Any person violating any of the provisions of this rule, shall be fined, suspended, or expelled.

Rule 11.—Stakes and Futurities.

Section 1. All stake and futurity sponsors or presentors, except contract tracks:

(a) Shall be members of this Association.

(b) Shall make an annual application for approval containing:

(1) Satisfactory evidence of financial responsibility.

(2) Proposed conditions.

(3) Sums to be deducted for organization or promotion.

(4) **Bond.**—An agreement to file with the Association a surety bond in the amount of the fund condition on faithful performance of the conditions, including a guarantee that said stake or futurity will be raced as advertised in said conditions unless unanimous consent is obtained from owners of eligibles to transfer or change the date thereof, or unless

66

prevented by an act of God or conditions beyond the control of the sponsor, segregation of funds and making all payments. Any association may deposit in escrow negotiable government securities in the amount of the fund and this may be accepted by The United States Trotting Association in lieu of a surety bond.

State Agency.—Where funds are held by a state or an authorized agency thereof, this provision will not apply.

Trust Funds.—Collections resulting from the forfeiting of any bond will be paid to the contestants according to the order of finish, or in the event the race is not contested, will be divided equally among owners of eligibles on the date the breach of conditions occurs.

(5) **Waiver of Bond.**—The requirement of a bond may be waived by the President of the Association upon written request of a sponsor who is a track member and whose financial statement shows a net worth of five times the amount of trust funds received from payments in stakes and futurities. Where this is permitted, the sponsor will furnish a certified copy of the bank deposit in lieu of the bond.

(c) **Rejection of Application.**—May appeal the rejection of an application to the Executive Committee within 20 days after the mailing of the notice of rejection by registered mail.

(d) **List of Nominations.**—Shall mail list of nominations within 30 days after the date of closing to this Association.

(e) **Financial Statement.**—Shall furnish this Association with an annual financial statement of each stake or futurity and, within 30 days following day of race, submit to this Association a final financial statement which shall be published in Hoof Beats.

(f) **Failure to Fill.**—Shall notify all nominators and this Association within 20 days if the stake or futurity does not fill.

(g) **Lists of Eligibles.**—Shall mail within 20 days a complete list of all horses remaining eligible, to owners of all eligibles and to this Association, together with a list of any nominations transferred or substituted if such is permitted by the conditions.

(h) **Nominating and Sustaining Payment Dates.**—Shall set the nominating date and the dates for all sustaining payments except the starting fee on the fifteenth day of the month, **and there shall be no payments on yearlings except a nomination payment and such nomination payment shall be due not later than August 15th.** Before taking any sustaining payments during the year the race is to be contested, the date and place of the race shall be stated. No stake or futurity sustaining fee shall become due prior to January 15 of the year in which the colt becomes two years of age. **There shall be no conditions that call for payments in stakes or futurities to fall due after August 15th and before January 15th of the following year.**

(i) **Notice of Place and Date of Race.**—Shall, if possible, advertise the week and place the stake or futurity will be raced before taking nominations. Otherwise announcement of the week and place shall be made as soon as the stake or futurity is sold or awarded.

(j) **Forms.**—All nominations and entry forms, lists of nominations and lists of eligibles shall be on standard 8½ x 11 paper. Such lists shall list the owners alphabetically.

(k) **Estimated Purse.**—No estimated purse shall be advertised or published in excess of the actual purse paid or distributed during the previous year, unless

67

increased by guaranteed added money. No stake or futurity shall be raced for less than 75% of the average estimated purse.

§ 2. **Sponsor's Contribution.**—The sum contributed by a sponsor who is not a track member shall be considered forfeit and is to be included in the sum distributed in the event the stake or futurity is not raced.

Effective, with stakes and futurities opened in 1965 thereafter, no stake or futurity shall be approved for extended pari-mutuel meetings if the added money is not at least 20 per cent of the purse and for all other meetings at least 10 per cent of the purse shall be added.

In the event a stake or futurity is split into divisions, the added money for each division shall be at least 20% of all nomination, sustaining and starting fees paid into such stake or futurity.

§ 3. **Failure to Make Payment.**—Failure to make any payment required by the conditions constitutes an automatic withdrawal from the event.

§ 4. **Refund of Nomination Fee.**—In the event that a mare nominated to a futurity **fails to have a live foal,** the nominator **shall** receive a return of his payment **upon notification by December 1st of the year of not foaling, or if the conditions so provide, he may substitute.**

§ 5. If the sponsor has failed to comply with the provisions of the within rules, the Executive Vice-President shall be authorized to refuse renewals of such Stakes and Futurities.

Rule 12.—Entries.

Section 1. All entries must:

(a) Be made in writing.

(b) Be signed by the owner or his authorized agent except as provided in Rule 14, Section 1.

(c) Give name and address of both the bona fide owner and agent or registered stable name or lessee.

(d) Give name, color, sex, sire and dam of horse.

(e) Name the event or events in which the horse is to be entered.

(f) Entries in overnight events must also comply with the provisions of Rule 14, Section 1.

§ 2. **Penalties.**—The penalty for noncompliance with any of the above requirements is a fine of not less than $5.00 nor more than $50.00 for each offense. If the facts are falsely stated for the purpose of deception, the guilty party shall be fined and/or suspended or expelled.

§ 3. **Sale of Horse With Entrance Due.**—If any person shall sell a horse to be free and clear and it appears thereafter that payments were due or to become due in races of any description and for which suspension has been or is subsequently ordered, such seller shall be held for the amount due with the penalty on the same and fined an amount equal to the amount of suspension. Unless the horse has been suspended prior to a sale, a subsequent suspension for unpaid entry fee will have no effect as against a bona fide purchaser for value without notice.

§ 4. **Receipt of Entries for Early Closing Events, Late Closing Events, Stakes and Futurities.**—All entries not actually received at the hour of closing shall be ineligible, except entries by letter bearing postmark not later than the following day (omitting Sunday) or entries notified by telegraph, the telegram to be actually received at the office of sending at or before the hour of closing, such telegram to state the color, sex, and name of the horse, the class to be entered; also to give the name and residence of the owner and the party making entry. Whenever an entry or payment in a stake, futurity, or early closing race becomes payable on a Sunday or a legal holiday that falls on Saturday, such payment is to be due on the following Monday and if made by mail the envelope must be postmarked on or before the following Tuesday. If a payment falls on a Monday that is a legal holiday, such payment is due on Tuesday, and if made by mail must be postmarked on or before the following Wednesday.

Postage Meter.—Where an entry is received by letter bearing the postage meter date without any postmark placed thereon by the Post Office Department, such postage meter date shall be considered to be a postmark for the purposes of this rule if the letter is actually received within seven days following the closing date of the event. Receipt subsequent to this time of an entry by letter bearing the metered postmark date shall not be a valid entry or payment to any event. **The metered date,** of course, must fonform to the postmark **date as set forth** above in order to be valid.

§ 5. **Deviation from Published Conditions.**—All entries and payments not governed by published conditions shall be void and any proposed deviation from such published conditions shall be punished by a fine not to exceed $50 for each offense, and any nominator who is allowed privileges not in accordance with the published conditions of the race, or which are in conflict with these rules, shall be debarred from winning any portion of the purse, and the said nominator and the Secretary or other persons who allowed such privileges shall be deemed to have been parties to a fraud.

§ 6. **Where Ineligible Horse Races.**—A nominator is required to guarantee the identity and eligibility of his entries and declarations and if given incorrectly he may be fined, suspended, or expelled, and any winnings shall be forfeited and redistributed to eligible entries. A person obtaining a purse or money through fraud or error shall surrender or pay the same to this Association, if demanded by the Executive Vice-President, or he, together with the parties implicated in the wrong, and the horse or horses shall be suspended until such demand is complied with and such purse or money shall be awarded to the party justly entitled to the same. However, where any horse is ineligible as a result of the negligence of the Race Secretary, the track shall reimburse the owner for the resultant loss of winnings.

§ 7. **Transfer of Ineligible Horse.**—A horse entered in an event to which it is ineligible, may be transferred to any event to which he is eligible at the same gait.

§ 8. **Withholding Purse on Ineligible Horse.**—Members shall be warranted in withholding the premium of any horse, without a formal protest, if they shall receive information in their judgment tending to establish that the entry or declaration was fraudulent or ineligible. Premiums withheld under this rule shall be forthwith sent to The United States Trotting Association to await the result of an investigation by the member or by the District Board of Review, and if the eligibility of the horse is not established within thirty days he shall be barred from winning unless the case is appealed to the Board of Appeals.

§ 9. **Effect of Death on Future Payments.**—All engagements shall be void upon the decease of either party or horse, prior to the starting of the race, so far as they shall affect the deceased party or horse, except when assumed by the estate or where the proprietorship is in more than one person, and any survive.

§ 10. **Agreement to Race Under Rule.**—Every entry shall constitute an

69

agreement that the person making it, the owner, lessee, manager, agent, nominator, driver, or other person having control of the horse, and the horse shall be subject to these Rules and Regulations, and will submit all disputes and questions arising out of such entry to the authority and the judgment of this Association, whose decision shall be final.

§ 11. **Early Closing Events and Late Closing Races.**—

(a) **Date and Place.**—The sponsor shall state the place and day the event will be raced and no change in date, program, events, or conditions can be made after the nominations have been taken without the written consent of the owners or trainer of all horses eligible at the time the conditions are changed.

(b) **File Conditions.**—An entry blank shall be filed with the Executive Vice-President.

(c) **Payments on the Fifteenth of the Month.**—All nominations and payments other than starting fees in early closing events shall be advertised to fall on the fifteenth day of the month.

(d) **List of Nominations.**—A complete list of nominations to any late closing race or early closing event shall be published within twenty (20) days after the date of closing and mailed to each nominator and the Executive Vice-President.

(e) **Procedure If Event Does Not Fill.**—If the event does not fill, each nominator and the Executive Vice-President shall be notified within ten (10) days and refund of nomination fees shall accompany the notice.

(f) **Transfer Provisions—Change of Gait.**—Unless a track submits its early closing conditions to the USTA at least 30 days prior to the first publication and has such conditions approved the following provisions will govern transfers in the event of a change of gait. If conditions published for early closing events allow transfer for change of gait, such transfer shall be to the slowest class the horse is eligible to at the adopted gait, eligibility to be determined at time of closing of entries, the race to which transfer may be made must be the one nearest the date of the race originally entered.

Two-year-olds, three-year-olds, or four-year-olds, entered in classes for their age, may only tranfer to classes for same age group at the adopted gait to the race nearest the date of the event originally entered, entry fees to be adjusted.

§ 12. **Subsequent Payments—Lists of Eligibles.**—If subsequent payments are required, a complete list of those withdrawn or declared out shall be made within fifteen (15) days after the payment was due and the list mailed to each nominator and the Executive Vice-President.

§ 13. **Trust Funds.**—All fees paid in early closing events shall be segregated and held as trust funds until the event is contested.

§ 14. **Early Closing Events by New Member.**—No early closing events may be advertised or nominations taken therefor for a pari-mutuel meeting that has not had its application approved by the President, unless the track has been licensed for the preceding year. Members accepting nominations to Early Closing Races, Late Closing Races, Stakes and Futurities will give stable space to any horse nominated and eligible to such event the day before, the day of, and the day after such race.

§ 15. **Limitation on Conditions.**—Conditions of Early Closing Events or Late Closing Races that will eliminate horses nominated to an event or add horses that have not been nominated to an event by reason of the performance of such horses at an earlier meeting held the same season, are invalid. Early Closing Events and Late Closing Events shall have not more than two also eligible conditions.

§ 16. **Penalties.**—Any official or member who fails to comply with any provisions of this rule shall be fined, suspended or expelled, unless otherwise provided.

§ 17. **Excess Entry Fees.**—When entry fees exceed 85% of the advertised purse value, such excess entry fees shall be added to the purse. Where the race is split into divisions, each division shall have a purse value of not less than 75% of the advertised purse. However, entry fees in excess of the amount prescribed above may be used toward the amount that must be added. In all cases the sponsor shall add at least fifteen per cent (15%) to the advertised purse.

Rule 13.—Entries And Starters Required Split Races.

Section 1. An association must specify how many entries are required for overnight events and after the condition is fulfilled, the event must be contested except when declared off as provided in Rule 15.

In early closing events, or late closing events, if five or more horses are declared in to start, the race must be contested, except when declared off as provided in Rule 15. (Pari-mutuel meetings may require five interests to start.) Stakes and Futurities must be raced if one or more horses are declared in to start except when declared off as provided in Rule 15.

In an early closing event, if less horses are declared in than are required to start, and all declarers are immediately so notified, the horse or horses declared in and ready to race shall be entitled to all the entrance money and any forfeits from each horse named.

§ 2. **Elimination Heats or Two Divisions.**—

(a) In any race where the number of horses declared in to start exceeds 12 on a half-mile track or 16 on a **larger** track, the race, at the option of the track member conducting same stated before positions are drawn, may be raced in elimination heats. No more than two tiers of horses, allowing eight feet per horse, will be allowed to start in any race.

(b) Where the race is divided, each division must race for at least 75% of the advertised purse.

In an added money early closing event the race may be divided and raced in divisions and each division raced for an equal share of the total purse if the advertised conditions so provide, provided, however, extended meetings shall add an additional amount so that each division will race for 75 percent of the advertised added money. These provisions shall apply to any stake with a value of $20,000 or less.

(c) In any stake race or futurity, where the conditions state that the event shall be raced one dash on a race track of less than a mile at an extended parimutuel meeting, and where the number of horses declared in to start exceed twelve, the race, at the option of the racing association conducting the same, stated before positions are drawn, may be divided by lot and raced in two elimination divisions with all money winners from both divisions competing in the final. Each division shall race one elimination heat for 20% of the total purse. The remainder of the purse shall be distributed to the money winners in the final.

§ 3. **Elimination Plans.**—(a) Whenever elimination heats are required, or specified in the published conditions such race shall be raced in the following manner unless conducted under another section of this rule. That is, the field shall be divided by lot and the first division shall race a qualifying dash for 30

71

per cent of the purse, the second division shall race a qualifying dash for 30 per cent of the purse and the horses so qualified shall race in the main event for 40 per cent of the purse. The winner of the main event shall be the race winner.

In the event there are more horses declared to start than can be accommodated by the two elimination dashes, then there will be added enough elimination dashes to take care of the excess. The per cent of the purse raced for each elimination dash will be determined by dividing the number of elimination dashes into 60. The main event will race for 40 per cent of the purse. In event there are three (3) or more qualifying dashes, not more than three (3) horses will qualify for the final from each qualifying dash.

Unless the conditions provide otherwise, if twelve horses declare to start, only the first four horses in each elimination dash qualify to continue. If thirteen horses declare to start the first four horses in the division with six horses and the first five horses in the division with seven horses qualify. If fourteen or more declare to start, only the first five horses in each elimination dash qualify to continue.

The Judges shall draw the positions in which the horses are to start in the main event, i.e., they shall draw positions to determine which of the two dash winners shall have the pole, and which the second position; which of the two horses that have been second shall start in third position; and which in fourth, etc. All elimination dashes and the concluding heat must be programmed to be raced upon the same day or night, unless special provisions for earlier elimination dashes are set forth in the conditions.

In the event there are three separate heat or dash winners and they alone come back in order to determine the race winner according to the conditions, they will take post positions according to the order of their finish in the previous heat or dash.

(b) In any race where the number of horses declared in to start exceeds 12 on a half-mile track or 16 on a mile track, unless other numbers are specified in the conditions, the race, at the option of the track members conducting the same, stated before positions are drawn, may be divided by lot and raced in two divisions with all heat winners from both divisions competing in a final heat to determine the race winner. Each division shall race two heats for 20% of the purse each heat. The remaining 20% of the purse shall go to the winner of the final heat.

(c) Whenever elimination heats are required, or specified in the published conditions of a stake or futurity, such race may be raced on the three heat plan, irrespective of any provisions in the conditions to the contrary, unless such published conditions provide otherwise. That is, the field shall be divided by lot and the first division shall race for thirty per cent of the purse, the second division shall race for thirty per cent, and the horses qualifying in the first and second divisions shall race the third heat for thirty per cent of the purse. If, after the third heat, no horse has won two heats, a fourth heat shall be raced by only the heat winners. The race winner shall receive the remaining ten per cent of the purse. The number of horses qualifying to return after each elimination heat will be the same as set out in Section 3 (a) of this rule.

§ 4. **Overnight Events.**—Not more than eight horses shall be allowed to start on a half-mile track in overnight events and not more than ten horses on larger tracks at extended pari-mutuel meetings.

§ 5. **Qualifying Race for Stake, Etc.**—Where qualifying races are provided in the conditions of an early closing event, stake or futurity, such qualifying race must be held not more than five days prior to contesting to main event (excluding Sunday) and omitting the day of the race.

Rule 14.—Declaration To Start And Drawing Horses.

Section 1. **Declaration.**

(a) **At Extended Pari-Mutuel Meetings.**—Unless otherwise specified in the conditions, the declaration time at extended pari-mutuel meetings shall be 9:00 A.M.

(b) **Declaration Time at Other Meetings.**—At all other meetings starters must be declared in at 10:00 A.M. unless another time is specified in the conditions.

(c) **Time Used.**—In order to avoid confusion and misunderstanding, the time when declarations close will be considered to be standard time, except the time in use at an extended pari-mutuel meeting shall govern that meeting.

(d) **Declaration Box.**—The management shall provide a locked box with an aperture through which declarations shall be deposited.

(e) **Responsibility for Declaration Box.**—The declaration box shall be in charge of the Presiding Judge.

(f) **Search for Declarations by Presiding Judge Before Opening Box.**— Just prior to opening of the box at extended pari-mutuel meetings where futurities, stakes, early closing or late closing events are on the program, the Presiding Judge shall check with the Race Secretary to ascertain if any declarations by mail, telegraph, or otherwise, are in the office and not deposited in the entry box, and he shall see that they are declared and drawn in the proper event. At other meetings, the Presiding Judge shall ascertain if any such declarations have been received by the Superintendent of Speed or Secretary of the Fair, and he shall see that they are properly declared and drawn.

(g) **Opening of Declaration Box.**—At the time specified the Presiding Judge shall unlock the box, assort the declarations found therein and immediately draw the positions in the presence of such owners or their representatives, as may appear.

(h) **Entry Box and Drawing of Horses at Extended Pari-Mutuel Meetings.**—The entry box shall be opened by the Presiding Judge at the advertised time and the Presiding Judge will be responsible to see that at least one horseman or an official representative of the horsemen is present. No owner or agent for a horse with a declaration in the entry box shall be denied the privilege of being present. Under the supervision of the Presiding Judge, all entries shall be listed, the eligibility verified, preference ascertained, starters selected and post positions drawn. If it is necessary to reopen any race, public announcement shall be made at least twice and the box reopened to a definite time.

Upon receiving a request by the Racing Secretary, the Presiding Judge may open the entry box prior to the time of closing and give the Racing Secretary the opportunity to process declarations contained therein. Information as to names of horses declared shall not be given by the Racing Secretary or his assistants until after the time for declaration has passed.

(i) **Procedure in The Event of Absence or Incapacity of Presiding Judge.**—At non-extended meetings in the event of the absence or incapacity of the Presiding Judge, the functions enumerated above may be performed by a person designated by said Judge, for whose acts and conduct said Judge shall be wholly responsible. If a substitution is made as herein provided, the name

73

and address of the person so substituting shall be entered in the Judges' Book.

(j) **Drawing of Post Positions for Second Heat in Races of More Than One Dash or Heat at Pari-Mutuel Meetings.**—In races of a duration of more than one dash or heat at pari-mutuel meetings, the judges may draw post positions from the stand for succeeding dashes or heats.

(k) **Declarations by Mail, Telegraph or Telephone.**—Declarations by mail, telegraph, or telephone actually received and evidence of which is deposited in the box before the time specified to declare in, shall be drawn in the same manner as the others. Such drawings shall be final.

(l) **Effect of Failure to Declare on Time.**—When a member requires a horse to be declared at a stated time, failure to declare as required shall be considered a withdrawal from the event.

(m) **Drawing of Horses After Declaration.**—After declaration to start has been made no horse shall be drawn except by permission of the Judges. A fine, not to exceed $500, or suspension may be imposed for drawing a horse without permission, the penalty to apply to both the horse and the party who violates the regulation.

(n) **Procedure on Unauthorized Withdrawal Where There Is No Opportunity for Hearing.**—Where the person making the declaration fails to honor it and there is no opportunity for a hearing by the Judges, this penalty may be imposed by the Executive Vice-President.

(o) **Horses Omitted Through Error.**—Such drawings shall be final unless there is conclusive evidence that a horse properly declared, other than by telephone, was omitted from the race through the error of a track or its agent or employee in which event the horse may be added to this race but given the outside post position. This shall not apply at pari-mutuel meetings unless the error is discovered prior to the publication of the official program.

§ 2. **Qualifying Races.**—At all extended pari-mutuel meetings declarations for overnight events shall be governed by the following:

(a) Within two weeks of being declared in, a horse that has not raced previously at the gait chosen must go a qualifying race under the supervision of a Judge holding a Presiding or Associate Judge's license for pari-mutuel meetings and acquire at least one charted line by a licensed charter. In order to provide complete and accurate chart information on time and beaten lengths, a standard photo-finish shall be in use.

(b) A horse that does not show a charted line for the previous season, or a charted line within its last six starts, must go a qualifying race as set forth in (a). Uncharted races contested in heats or more than one dash and consolidated according to (d) will be considered one start.

(c) A horse that has not started at a charted meeting by August 1st of a season must go a qualifying race as set forth above in (a).

(d) When a horse has raced at a charted meeting during the current season, then gone to meetings where the races are not charted, the information from the uncharted races may be summarized, including each start, and consolidated in favor of charted lines and the requirements of Section (b) would then not apply.

The consolidated line shall carry date, place, time, driver, finish, track condition and distance if race is not at one mile.

(e) The Judges may require any horse that has been on the Steward's List to go a qualifying race. If a horse has raced in individual time not meeting the qualifying standards for that class of horse, he may be required to go a qualifying race.

(f) The Judges may permit a fast horse to qualify by means of a timed workout consistent with the time of the races in which he will compete in the event adequate competition is not available for a qualifying race.

(g) To enable a horse to qualify, qualifying races should be held at least one full week prior to the opening of any meeting that opens before July 1st of a season and shall be scheduled at least twice a week. Qualifying races shall also be scheduled twice a week during the meeting.

(h) Where a race is conducted for the purpose of qualifying drivers and not horses, the race need not be charted, timed or recorded. This section is not applicable to races qualifying both drivers and horses.

§ 3. **Entries.**—When the starters in a race include two or more horses owned or trained by the same person, or trained in the same stable or by the same management, they shall be coupled as an "entry." Where pari-mutuel wagering is conducted and a wager on one horse in the "entry" shall be a wager on all horses in the "entry." If the race is split in two or more divisions, horses in an "entry" seeded in separate divisions insofar as possible, but the divisions in which they compete and their post positions shall be drawn by lot. The above provision shall also apply to elimination heats.

The Presiding Judge shall be responsible for coupling horses. In addition to the foregoing, horses separately owned or trained may be coupled as an entry where it is necessary to do so to protect the public interest for the purpose of pari-mutuel wagering only. However, where this is done, entries may not be rejected.

§ 4. **Also Eligibles.**—Not more than two horses may be drawn as also eligibles for a race and their positions shall be drawn along with the starters in the race. Also eligibles shall be drawn from those horses having the least preference. In the event one or more horses are excused by the Judges, the also eligible horse or horses shall race and take the post position drawn by the horse that it replaces, except in handicap races. In handicap races the also eligible horse shall take the place of the horse that it replaces in the event that the handicap is the same. In the event the handicap is different, the also eligible horse shall take the position on the outside of horses with a similar handicap. No horse may be added to a race as an also eligible unless the horse was drawn as such at the time declarations closed. No horse may be barred from a race to which it is otherwise eligible by reason of its preference due to the fact that it has been drawn as an also eligible. A horse moved into the race from the also eligible list cannot be drawn except by permission of the Judges, but the owner or trainer of such a horse shall be notified that the horse is to race and it shall be posted at the Race Secretary's office. All horses on the also eligible list and not moved in to race by 9:00 A.M. on the day of the race shall be released.

§ 5. **Preference.**—Preference shall be given in all overnight events according to a horse's last previous purse race during the current year. The preference date on a horse that has drawn to race and been scratched is the date of the race from which he was scratched.

When a horse is racing the first time in the current year, the date of the first declaration shall be considered its last race date, and preference applied accordingly.

This rule relating to preference is not applicable for any meeting at which an agricultural fair is in progress. All horses granted stalls and eligible must be given an opportunity to compete at these meetings.

§ 6. **Steward's List.**—(a) A horse that is unfit to race because he is dangerous, unmanageable, sick, lame, unable to show a performance to qualify for races at the meeting, or otherwise unfit to race at the meeting may be placed on a "Steward's list" by the Presiding Judge and declarations on said horse shall be refused, but the owner or trainer shall be notified in writing of such action and the reason as set forth above shall be clearly stated on the notice. When any horse is placed on the Steward's list, the Clerk of the Course shall make a note on the Eligibility Certificate of such horse, showing the date the horse was put on the Steward's list, the reason therefor and the date of removal if the horse has been removed.

(b) No Presiding Judge or other official at a nonextended meeting shall have the power to remove from the Steward's List and accept as an entry any horse which has been placed on a Steward's List and not subsequently removed therefrom for the reason that he is a dangerous or unmanageable horse. Such meetings may refuse declarations on any horse that has been placed on the Steward's List and has not been removed therefrom.

§ 7. **Driver.**—Declarations shall state who shall drive the horse and give the driver's colors. Drivers may be changed until 9:00 A.M. of the day preceding the race, after which no driver may be changed without permission of the judges and for good cause. When a nominator starts two or more horses, the Judges shall approve or disapprove the second and third drivers.

§ 8. It shall be the duty of the Presiding Judge to call a meeting of all horsemen on the grounds before the opening of an extended pari-mutuel meeting for the purpose of their electing a member and an alternate to represent them on matters relating to the withdrawal of horses due to bad track or weather conditions.

§ 9. In case of questionable track conditions due to weather, the Presiding Judge shall call a meeting consisting of an agent of the track member, the duly elected representative of the horesemen and himself.

§ 10. Upon unanimous decision by this committee of three, that track conditions are safe for racing, no unpermitted withdrawals may be made.

§ 11. (a) Any decision other than unanimous by this committee will allow any entrant to scratch his horse or horses after posting ten per cent of the purse to be raced for. In the event sufficient withdrawals are received to cause the field to be less than six, then the track member shall have the right of postponement of an early closing event or stake and cancellation of an overnight event.

(b) Said money posted shall be forwarded to The United States Trotting Association and shall be retained as a fine, or refunded to the individual upon the decision of the District Board hearing the case at its next meeting as to whether the withdrawal was for good cause.

THE ABOVE PROCEDURE APPLIES ONLY TO THE WITHDRAWAL OF HORSES THAT HAVE BEEN PROPERLY DECLARED IN AND DOES NOT RELATE TO POSTPONEMENT WHICH IS COVERED ELSEWHERE.

Rule 15.—Postponement.

Section 1. In case of unfavorable weather, or other unavoidable cause, members with the consent of the Judges shall postpone races in the following manner.

(a) Early Closing Races, Stakes, and Futurities. All shall be postponed to a definite hour the next fair day and good track.

(b) Any LATE CLOSING RACE, EARLY CLOSING RACE, and STAKE OR FUTURITY (except as provided in (d) and (e) below) that cannot be raced during the scheduled meeting shall be declared off and the entrance money and forfeits shall be divided equally among the nominators who have horses declared in and eligible to start.

(c) Any Late Closing Race or Early Closing Race that has been started and remains unfinished on the last day of the scheduled meeting shall be declared ended and the full purse divided according to the summary. Any such race that has been started but postponed by rain earlier in the meeting may be declared ended and the full purse divided according to the summary.

(d) Stakes and Futurities should be raced where advertised and the meeting may be extended to accomplish this. Any stake or futurity that has been started and remains unfinished on the last day of the scheduled meeting shall be declared ended and the full purse divided according to the summary except where the track elects to extend the meeting to complete the race.

(e) Unless otherwise provided in the conditions, in order to transfer stakes and futurities to another meeting unanimous consent must be obtained from the member and from all those having eligibles in the event.

(f) (1) At meetings of MORE THAN FIVE DAYS duration, overnight events may be postponed and carried over not to exceed two racing days.

(2) At meetings of a duration of FIVE DAYS OR LESS, overnight events and late closing races shall be cancelled and starting fees returned in the event of postponement, unless the track member is willing to add the postponed races to the advertised program for subsequent days of the meeting.

At the option of management any postponed races may be contested in single mile dashes. Where races are postponed under this rule, management shall have the privilege of selecting the order in which the events will be raced in any combined program.

Rule 16.—Starting.

Section 1. With Starting Gate.—

(a) **Starter's Control.**—The Starter shall have control of the horses from the formation of the parade until he gives the word "go".

(b) **Scoring.**—After one or two preliminary warming up scores, the Starter shall notify the drivers to come to the starting gate. During or before the parade the drivers must be informed as to the number of scores permitted.

(c) The horses shall be brought to the starting gate as near one-quarter of a mile before the start as the track will permit.

(d) **Speed of Gate.**—Allowing sufficient time so that the speed of the gate can be increased gradually, the following minimum speeds will be maintained:

(1) For the first ⅛ mile, not less than 11 miles per hour.

(2) For the next 1/16 of a mile not less than 18 miles per hour.

(3) From that point to the starting point, the speed will be gradually increased to maximum speed.

(e) On mile tracks horses will be brought to the starting gate at the head of the stretch and the relative speeds mentioned in sub-section (d) above will be maintained.

(f) **Starting Point.**—The starting point will be a point marked on the inside rail a distance of not less than 200 feet from the first turn. The Starter shall give the word "go" at the starting point.

(g) WHEN A SPEED HAS BEEN REACHED IN THE COURSE OF A START THERE SHALL BE NO DECREASE EXCEPT IN THE CASE OF A RECALL.

(h) **Recall Notice.**—In case of a recall, a light plainly visible to the driver shall be flashed and a recall sounded, but the starting gate shall proceed out of the path of the horses.

(i) There shall be no recall after the word "go" has been given and any horse, regardless of his position or an accident, shall be deemed a starter from the time he entered into the Starter's control unless dismissed by the Starter.

(j) **Breaking Horse.**—The Starter shall endeavor to get all horses away in position and on gait but no recall shall be had for a breaking horse except as provided in (k) (5).

(k) **Recall—Reasons For.**—The Starter may sound a recall only for the following reasons:

(1) A horse scores ahead of the gate.

(2) There is interference.

(3) A horse has broken equipment.

(4) A horse falls before the word "go" is given.

(5) Where a horse refuses to come to the gate before the gate reaches the pole ⅛ **of a mile before the start,** the field may be turned.

(l) **Penalties.**—A fine not to exceed $100, or suspension from driving not to exceed 15 days, or both, may be applied to any driver, by the Starter for:

(1) Delaying the start.

(2) Failure to obey the Starter's instructions.

(3) Rushing ahead of the inside or outside wing of the gate.

(4) Coming to the starting gate out of position.

(5) Crossing over before reaching the starting point.

(6) Interference with another driver during the start.

(7) Failure to come up into position.

A hearing must be granted before any penalty is imposed.

(m) **Riding in Gate.**—No persons shall be allowed to ride in the starting gate except the Starter and his driver or operator, and a Patrol Judge, unless permission has been granted by this Association.

(n) **Loudspeaker.**—Use of a mechanical loudspeaker for any purpose other than to give instructions to drivers is prohibited. The volume shall be no higher than necessary to carry the voice of the Starter to the drivers.

The penalty for violation of this section shall be a fine of not to exceed $500.00 or suspension not to exceed thirty days after a hearing by the President or Executive Vice-President.

§ 2. **Holding Horses Before Start.**—Horses may be held on the backstretch not to exceed two minutes awaiting post time, except when delayed by an emergency.

§ 3. **Two Tiers.**—In the event there are two tiers of horses, the withdrawing of a horse that has drawn or earned a position in the front tier shall not affect the position of the horses that have drawn or earned positions in the second tier.

Whenever a horse is drawn from any tier, horses on the outside move in to fill up the vacancy.

§ 4. **Starting Without Gate.**—When horses are started without a gate the Starter shall have control of the horses from the formation of the parade until he gives the word "go". He shall be located at the wire or other point of start of the race at which point as nearly as possible the word "go" shall be given. No driver shall cause unnecessary delay after the horses are called. After two preliminary warming up scores, the Starter shall notify the drivers to form in parade.

§ 5. The driver of any horse refusing or failing to follow the instructions of the Starter as to the parade or scoring ahead of the pole horse may be set down for the heat in which the offense occurs, or for such other period as the Starter shall determine, and may be fined from $10 to $100. Whenever a driver is taken down the substitute shall be permitted to score the horse once. A horse delaying the race may be started regardless of his position or gait and there shall not be a recall on account of a bad actor. If the word is not given, all the horses in the race shall immediately turn at the tap of the bell or other signal, and jog back to their parade positions for a fresh start. There shall be no recall after the starting word has been given.

§ 6. **Starters.**—The horses shall be deemed to have started when the word "go" is given by the Starter and all the horses must go the course except in case of an accident in which it is the opinion of the Judges that it is impossible to go the course.

§ 7. **Overhead Barrier.**—A member may use an overhead barrier or counting start in starting races and any driver who fails to obey the orders of the Starter or Assistant Starter operating same may be fined or ruled out of the race.

§ 8. **Unmanageable Horse.**—If in the opinion of the Judges or the Starter a horse is unmanageable or liable to cause accidents or injury to any other horse or to any driver it may be sent to the barn, but the entry and declaration fees on the horse shall then be refunded. When this action is taken the Starter will notify the Judges who will in turn notify the public.

§ 9. **Bad Acting Horse.**—At meetings where there is no wagering, the Starter may place a bad acting horse on the outside at his discretion. At pari-mutuel meetings such action may be taken only where there is time for the Starter to notify the Judges who will in turn notify the public prior to the sale of tickets on such **race.** If tickets have been sold, the bad acting horse must be scratched under the provision of Section 8 herein.

§ 10. **Snap Barrier.**—All handicaps shall be started with a snap barrier, unless a starting gate or walk-up start is used, and sprung simultaneously with the announcement of the word "go". Any driver allowing his horse to go into the barrier before the word "go" shall be fined $10 to $100.

§ 11. **Post Positions—Heat Racing.**—The horse winning a heat shall take the pole (or inside position) the succeeding heat, unless otherwise specified in the published conditions, and all others shall take their positions in the order they were placed the last heat. When two or more horses shall have made a dead heat, their positions shall be settled by lot.

§ 12. **Shield.**—The arms of all starting gates shall be provided with a screen or a shield in front of the position for each horse, and such arms shall be perpendicular to the rail.

Rule 17.—Drivers, Trainers and Agents.

Section 1. **Licensing of Drivers.**—No person shall drive a horse in any race on a track in membership with this Association without having first obtained from this Association an Active Membership including a driver's license. The proper license shall be presented to the Clerk of the Course before driving.

Any person violating this rule shall be automatically fined $10.00 for each offense and no license shall be issued thereafter until such fines shall have been paid. In addition, thereto, the track member shall automatically be fined the sum of $5.00 for permitting a driver to start without a license. In the event of a driver's license being lost or destroyed, a replacement may be obtained upon payment of a fee in the sum of $1.00.

The Executive Vice-President shall require the applicant to:

(a) Submit evidence of good moral character.

(b) Submit evidence of his ability to drive in a race and, if he is a new applicant, this must include the equivalent of a year's training experience.

(c) Be at least 14 years of age for an (MA) or (M) license and 16 years of age for an (F) license.

(d) Be at least 18 years of age for a (P) license.

(e) Furnish completed application form.

(f) When requested submit evidence of physical and mental ability and/or to submit to a physical examination.

(g) Applicants, other than for an M or an MA license shall submit to a written examination at a designated time and place to determine his qualification to drive or train and his knowledge of racing and the rules. In addition any driver who presently holds a license and wishes to obtain a license in a higher category who has not previously submitted to such written tests shall be required to take a written test before becoming eligible to obtain a license in a higher category.

A license will be issued in the following categories:

(A) A full license valid for all meetings.

No full license will be granted until the applicant has had, (1) at least one year's driving experience while holding a (P) Provisional license, and (2) 25 satisfactory starts at an extended pari-mutuel or Grand Circuit meeting.

(P) A Provisional license valid for fairs and for extended pari-mutuel meetings subject to satisfactory performance.

(Q) A license valid for fairs and a license for qualifying and non-wagering races at extended pari-mutuel meetings with the approval of the Presiding Judge. The Presiding Judge shall make a report to this Association relating to the performance of such a driver in a qualifying race. The Horsemen's Committee may appoint an Advisory Committee of three drivers at any meeting to observe the qualifications, demeanor and general conduct of all drivers and report in regard thereto to the Presiding Judge, copy of any such report to be in writing and forwarded to the Association.

(F) A license valid for fairs and all meetings with the exception of extended pari-mutuel meetings.

Drivers holding a license valid for fairs only who have driven at fairs must demonstrate an ability to drive satisfactorily before they will be granted a (Q) license valid for qualifying races.

(MA) A license valid for matinee meetings and amateur racing at othermeetings providing he is an amateur at the time of the race.

(M) A license valid for matinee meetings only.

(V) A probationary license indicating that the driver has been guilty of rule violations and has been warned against repetition of such violations. When a driver with a probationary license commits more than one rule violation, or one major violation, proceedings may be started and he will be given a hearing either before the Executive Vice-President or the District Board of Review in the District where the last penalty was imposed, to determine if his license should be revoked.

(T) Trainer.

No Provisional license will be granted to women drivers for extended pari-mutuel meetings, and no full license will be granted to women drivers who have not previously held such a license for extended pari-mutuel driving.

Repeated rule violations shall be considered grounds for refusal to grant or grounds for revocation of any driver's license. A provisional, qualifying, or fair license may be revoked for one or more rule violations, or other indications of lack of qualifications, and the qualifications of drivers in these categories may be reviewed at any time, with written examinations if necessary, to determine if a driver is competent.

All penalties imposed on any driver will be recorded on the reverse side of his driver's license by the Presiding Judge.

§ 2. Any licensed driver who shall participate in a meeting or drive a horse at a meeting not in membership with this Association or the Canadian Trotting Association shall be fined not to exceed $100 for each such offense: PROVIDED HOWEVER, that nothing herein contained shall prevent any person from driving at a contract track or from participating in a meeting conducted at such a track.

(a) No driver's license other than a matinee will be granted for the first time to any person 60 years of age, or over, until such application and the supporting papers have been submitted to the Driver's Committee of the Board of Directors and favorable recommendation made thereon.

(b) **Physical Examination.**—An applicant for a driver's license 65 years of age or over may be required to submit annually, with his application for a driver's license, a report of a physical examination on forms supplied by the Association. If the Association so desires, it may designate the physician to perform such examination. However, in such event, the cost thereof shall be paid by the Association.

(c) In the event any person is involved in an accident on the track, the Association may order such person to submit to a physical examination and such examination must be completed within 30 days from such request or the license may be suspended until compliance therewith.

§ 3. The license of any driver **or** trainer may be revoked or suspended at any time after a hearing by the President or Executive Vice-President for violation of the rules, failure to obey the instructions of any official, or for any misconduct or act detrimental to the sport. **The President or Executive Vice-President may designate a proper person as a hearing officer who will conduct a hearing and furnish a transcript to the President or Executive Vice-President.** The license may be reinstated by the President or Executive Vice-President in his discretion upon application made to him and upon such terms as he may prescribe. Any suspension or revocation of license made hereunder may be reviewed by the Board of Appeals as provided in Article IX of the By-Laws.

§ 4. The following shall constitute disorderly conduct and be reason for a fine, suspension, or revocation of a driver's or trainer's license:

(a) Failure to obey the Judges' orders **that are expressly authorized by the rules of this Association.**

(b) Failure to drive when programmed unless excused by the Judges.

(c) Drinking intoxicating beverages within four hours of the first post time of the program on which he is carded to drive.

81

(d) Appearing in the paddock in an unfit condition to drive.

(e) Fighting.

(f) Assaults.

(g) Offensive and profane language.

(h) Smoking on the track in silks during actual racing hours.

(i) Warming up a horse prior to racing without silks.

(j) Disturbing the peace.

(k) Refusal to take a breath analyzer test when directed by the Presiding Judge.

§ 5.   Drivers shall, when directed by the Presiding Judge, submit to a breath analyzer test and if the results thereof show a reading of more than .05 per cent of alcohol in the blood, such person shall not be permitted to drive, and an investigation will be started to determine if there has been a violation of Section 4 (c) of this rule.

§ 6.   Drivers must wear distinguishing colors, and shall not be allowed to start in a race or other public performance unless in the opinion of the Judges they are properly dressed.

No one shall drive during the time when colors are required on a race track unless he is wearing a type of protective helmet, constructed with a hard shell, and containing adequate padding and a chin strap in place.

§ 7.   Any driver wearing colors who shall appear at a betting window or at a bar or in a restaurant dispensing alcoholic beverages shall be fined not to exceed $100 for each such offense.

§ 8.   No driver can, without good and sufficient reasons, decline to be substituted by Judges. Any driver who refuses to be so substituted may be fined or suspended, or both, by order of the Judges.

§ 9.   An amateur driver is one who has never accepted any valuable consideration by way of or in lieu of compensation for his services as a trainer or driver during the past ten years.

§ 10.   Drivers holding a full license, or registered stables participating at an extended pari-mutuel meeting, shall register their racing colors with this Association. Colors so registered shall not be taken by any other person. The fee for such registration is $10.00 for lifetime registration. All disputes on rights to particular colors shall be settled by this Association.

§ 11.   Any person racing a horse at a meeting where registered colors are required by Section 10 hereof, using colors registered by any person or persons except himself or his employer, without special permission from the Presiding Judge, shall be fined $10.00.

§ 12.   **Trainer.** An applicant for a license as trainer must satisfy the Executive Vice-President that he possesses the necessary qualifications, both mental and physical, to perform the duties required. Elements to be considered, among others, shall be character, reputation, temperament, experience, knowledge of the rules of racing, and duties of a trainer in the preparation, training, entering and managing horses for racing.

Rule 18.—Racing and Track Rules.

Section 1.   Although a leading horse is entitled to any part of the track except after selecting his position in the home stretch, neither the driver of the first horse or any other driver in the race shall do any of the following things, which shall be considered violation of driving rules:

(a) Change either to the right or left during any part of the race when another

82

horse is so near him that in altering his position he compels the horse behind him to shorten his stride, or causes the driver of such other horse to pull him out of his stride.

(b) Jostle, strike, hook wheels, or interfere with another horse or driver.

(c) Cross sharply in front of a horse or cross over in front of a field of horses in a reckless manner, endangering other drivers.

(d) Swerve in and out or pull up quickly.

(e) Crowd a horse or driver by "putting a wheel under him."

(f) "Carry a horse out" or "sit down in front of him," take up abruptly in front of other horses so as to cause confusion or interference among the trailing horses, or do any other act which constitutes what is popularly known as helping.

(g) Let a horse pass inside needlessly.

(h) Laying off a normal pace and leaving a hole when it is well within the horse's capacity to keep the hole closed.

(i) Commit any act which shall impede the progress of another horse or cause him to "break."

(j) Change course after selecting a position in the home stretch and swerve in or out, or bear in or out, in such manner as to interfere with another horse or cause him to change course or take back.

(k) To drive in a careless or reckless manner.

(l) Whipping under the arch of the sulky, the penalty for which shall be no less than 10 days suspension.

§ 2. All complaints by drivers of any foul driving or other misconduct during the heat must be made at the termination of the heat, unless the driver is prevented from doing so by an accident or injury. Any driver desiring to enter a claim of foul or other complaint of violation of the rules, must before dismounting indicate to the judges or Barrier Judge his desire to enter such claim or complaint and forthwith upon dismounting shall proceed to the telephone or Judges' stand where and when such claim, objection, or complaint shall be immediately entered. The Judges shall not cause the official sign to be displayed until such claim, objection, or complaint shall have been entered and considered.

§ 3. If any of the above violations is committed by a person driving a horse coupled as an entry in the betting, the Judges shall set both horses back, if, in their opinion, the violation may have affected the finish of the race. Otherwise, penalties may be applied individually to the drivers of any entry.

§ 4. In case of interference, collision, or violation of any of the above restrictions, the offending horse may be placed **back one or more positions** in that heat or dash, and in the event such collision or interference prevents any horse from finishing the heat or dash, the offending horse may be disqualified from receiving any winnings; and the driver may be fined not to exceed the amount of the purse or stake contended for, or may be suspended or expelled. **In the event a horse is set back, under the provisions hereof, he must be placed behind the horse with whom he interfered.**

§ 5. (a) Every heat in a race must be contested by every horse in the race and every horse must be driven to the finish. If the Judges believe that a horse is being driven, or has been driven, with design to prevent his winning a heat or dash which he was evidently able to win, or is being raced in an inconsistent manner, or to perpetrate or to aid a fraud, they shall consider it a violation and the driver, and anyone in concert with him, to so affect the outcome of the race or races, may be fined, suspended, or expelled. The Judges may substitute a competent and reliable driver at any time. The substituted driver shall be paid at the discretion of the Judges and the fee retained from the purse money due the horse, if any.

(b) In the event a drive is unsatisfactory due to lack of effort or carelessness, and the Judges believe that there is no fraud, gross carelessness, or a deliberate inconsistent drive they may impose a penalty under this sub-section not to exceed ten days suspension, or a $100.00 fine.

§ 6. If in the opinion of the Judges a driver is for any reason unfit or incompetent to drive or refuses to comply with the directions of the Judges, or is reckless in his conduct and endangers the safety of horses or other drivers in the race, he may be removed and another driver substituted at any time after the positions have been assigned in a race, and the offending driver shall be fined, suspended or expelled. The substitute driver shall be properly compensated.

§ 7. If for any cause other than being interfered with or broken equipment, a horse fails to finish after starting in a heat, that horse shall be ruled out.

§ 8. Loud shouting or other improper conduct is forbidden in a race.

Whipping a horse underneath the arch of the sulky shall be considered improper conduct and is forbidden.

After the word "go" is given, both feet must be kept in the stirrups until after the finish of the race.

§ 9. Drivers will be allowed whips not to exceed 4 feet, 8 inches, plus a snapper not longer than eight inches.

§ 10. The use of any goading device, chain, or mechanical devices or appliances, other than the ordinary whip or spur upon any horse in any race shall constitute a violation of this rule. In the discretion of the Judges, brutal use of a whip or spur or indiscriminate use of a whip or spur may be considered a violation punishable by a fine of not to exceed $100 or suspension.

§ 11. No horse shall wear hopples in a race unless he starts in the same in the first heat, and having so started, he shall continue to wear them to the finish of the race, and any person found guilty of removing or altering a horse's hopples during a race, or between races, for the purpose of fraud, shall be suspended or expelled. Any horse habitually wearing hopples shall not be permitted to start in a race without them except by the permission of the Judges. Any horse habitually racing free legged shall not be permitted to wear hopples in a race except with the permission of the Judges. No horse shall be permitted to wear a head pole protruding more than 10 inches beyond its nose.

§ 12. **Breaking.**

(a) When any horse or horses break from their gait in trotting or pacing, their drivers shall at once, where clearance exists, take such horse to the outside and pull it to its gait.

(b) The following shall be considered violations of Section 12 (a):

(1) Failure to properly attempt to pull the horse to its gait.

(2) Failure to take to the outside where clearance exists.

(3) Failure to lose ground by the break.

(c) If there has been no failure on the part of the driver in complying with 12 (b), (1), (2), and (3), the horse shall not be set back unless a contending horse on his gait is lapped on the hind quarter of the breaking horse at the finish.

(d) The Judges may set any horse back one or more places if in their judgment any of the above violations have been committed.

§ 13. If in the opinion of the Judges, a driver allows his horse to break for the purpose of fraudulently losing a heat, he shall be liable to the penalties elsewhere provided for fraud and fouls.

§ 14. To assist in determining the matters contained in Sections 12 and 13, it shall be the duty of one of the Judges to call out every break made, and the clerk shall at once note the break and character of it in writing.

§ 15. The time between heats for any distance up to and including a mile shall be not less than twenty-five minutes; for any distance between one and two miles, thirty minutes. No heat shall be called after sunset where the track is not lighted for night racing.

§ 16. Horses called for a race shall have the exclusive right of the course, and all other horses shall vacate the track at once, unless permitted to remain by the Judges.

§ 17. In the case of accidents, only so much time shall be allowed as the Judges may deem necessary and proper.

§ 18. A driver must be mounted in his sulky at the finish of the race or the horse must be placed as not finishing.

§ 19. Any violation of any sections of Rule 18 above, unless otherwise provided, may be punished by a fine or suspension, or both, or by expulsion.

Rule 19.—Placing And Money Distribution.

Section 1. Unless otherwise provided in the conditions, all purses shall be distributed on the dash basis with the money awarded according to a horse's position in each separate dash or heat of the race.

Purse money distribution in overnight events shall be limited to five moneys.

§ 2. Dashes.—Unless otherwise specified in the conditions, the money distribution in dashes shall be 45%, 25%, 15%, 10%, and 5%. In Early Closing Races, Late Closing Races or Added Money Events, if there are less than five (5) starters, the remaining premium shall go to the race winner unless the conditions call for a different distribution. In overnight events if there are less than five (5) starters the premium for the positions for which there are no starters may be retained by the track.

If there be any premium or premiums for which horses have started but were unable to finish, due to an accident, all unoffending horses who did not finish will share equally in such premium or premiums.

If there be any premium or premiums for which horses have started but were unable to finish and the situation is not covered by the preceding paragraph, such premium shall be paid to the winner.

§ 3. Every Heat a Race.—The purse shall be distributed as in dash races with nothing set aside for the race winner.

§ 4. Placing System.—If the placing system is specified in the conditions, the purse shall be distributed according to the standing of the horses in the summary. In order to share in the purse distribution, each horse must complete the race and compete in each heat to which he is eligible. A horse must win two heats to be declared the race winner and such horse shall stand first in the summary. In deciding the rank of the horses other than the race winner, a horse that has been placed first in one heat shall be ranked better than any other horse making a dead heat for first or any other horse that has been placed second any number of heats; a horse that has been placed second in one heat shall be ranked better than any other horse that has been placed third any number of heats, etc.; e.g., a horse finishing 3-6 would be ranked ahead of another horse finishing 4-4. A horse finishing in a dead heat would be ranked below another horse finishing in the same positon and not in a dead heat. If

85

there be any premium for which no horse has maintained a position, it shall go to the race winner, but the number of premiums awarded need not exceed the number of horses that started in the race. Unless otherwise specified in the conditions, the money shall be divided 50%, 25%, 15% and 10%.

§ 5. **Two In Three.**—In a two in three race, a horse must win two heats to win the race, and there shall be 10% set aside for the race winner. The purse shall be divided and awarded according to the finish in each of the first two or three heats, as the case may be. If the race is unfinished at the end of the third heat, all but the heat winners or horses making a dead heat for first shall be ruled out. The fourth heat, when required, shall be raced for the 10% set aside for the winner. If there be any third or fourth premiums, etc., for which no horse has maintained a specific place, the premium therefor shall go to the winner of that heat, but the number of premiums distributed need not exceed the number of horses starting in the race. In a two-year-old race, if there are two heat winners and they have made a dead heat in the third heat, the race shall be declared finished and the colt standing best in the summary shall be awarded the 10%; if the two heat winners make a dead heat and stand the same in the summary, the 10% shall be divided equally between them.

Rule 20.—Conduct of Racing.

Section 1. No owner, trainer, driver, attendant of a horse, or any other person shall use improper language to an official, officer of this Association, or an officer of an Association in membership, or be guilty of any improper conduct toward such officers or judges, or persons serving under their orders, such improper language or conduct having reference to the administration of the course, or of any race thereon.

§ 2. No owner, trainer, driver, or attendant of a horse, or any other person, at any time or place shall commit an assault, or an assault and battery, upon any driver who shall drive in a race, or shall threaten to do bodily injury to any such driver or shall address to such driver language outrageously insulting.

§ 3. If any owner, trainer, or driver of a horse shall threaten or join with others in threatening not to race, or not to declare in, because of the entry of a certain horse or horses, or a particular stable, thereby compelling or trying to compel the Race Secretary or Superintendent of Speed to reject certain eligible entries it shall be immediately reported to the Executive Vice-President and the offending parties may be suspended pending a hearing before the District Board of Review.

§ 4. No owner, agent or driver who has entered a horse shall thereafter demand of the member a bonus of money or other special award or consideration as a condition for starting the horse.

§ 5. No owner, trainer, driver, agent, employee, or attendant shall bet or cause any other person to bet on his behalf on any other horse in any race in which a horse owned, trained, or driven or in which he in anywise represents or handles as a starter.

§ 6. **Failure to report fraudulent proposal.** If any person shall be approached with any offer or promise of a bribe, or a wager or with a request or suggestion for a bribe, or for any improper, corrupt or fraudulent act in relation to racing, or that any race shall be conducted otherwise than fairly and honestly, it shall be the duty of such person to report the details thereof immediately to the Presiding Judge.

§ 7. Any misconduct on the part of a member of this Association fraudulent in its nature or injurious to the character of the turf, although not specified in these rules, is forbidden. Any person or persons who, individually or in concert with one another, shall fraudulently and corruptly, by any means, affect the outcome of any race or affect a false registration, or commit any other act injurious to the sport, shall be guilty of a violation.

§ 8. If two or more persons shall combine and confederate together, in any manner, regardless of where the said persons may be located, for the purpose of violating any of the rules of this Association, and shall commit some act in furtherance of the said purpose and plan, it shall constitute a conspiracy and a violation.

§ 9. In any case where an oath is administered by the Judges, Board of Review, or Officer of this Association under the rules, or a Notary Public, or any other person legally authorized to administer oaths, if the party knowingly swears falsely or withholds information pertinent to the investigation, he shall be fined, suspended, or both, or expelled.

§ 10. **Financial Responsibility.**—Any participant who shall accumulate unpaid obligations, or default in obligations, or issue drafts or checks that are dishonored, or payment refused, or otherwise display financial irresponsibility reflecting on the sport, may be denied membership in this Association or may be suspended on order by the Executive Vice-President.

§ 11. Any violation of any of the provisions of this rule shall be punishable by a fine, suspension, or both, or by expulsion.

Rule 21.—Stimulants Drugs.

Section 1. At every meeting **except as stated herein** where pari-mutuel wagering is permitted, the winning horse in every heat and/or race shall be subjected to a saliva test for the purpose of determining thereby the presence of any drug, stimulant, sedative, depressant, or medicine. **At any meeting where there is a pre-race blood test of all horses and where the Commission requires a post-race urine test of the winner, a saliva test will not be required.** In addition, the Judges at any meeting may order any other horse in any heat or race to be subjected to the saliva test or any other test for the purpose of determining thereby the presence of any drug, stimulant, sedative, depressant, or medicine. Also, the Judges may order any horse in a race to be subjected to a urine test. At all extended pari-mutuel meetings and at Grand Circuit meetings at least 25% of the horses subjected to a salvia test shall be given a urine test. Such horses to be selected by the Presiding Judge by lot. Such tests shall be made only by qualified veterinarians and by laboratories approved by the Executive Vice-President. In addition to the above, the winning horse in every heat or dash of a race at any track with a total purse in excess of $5,000.00 shall be subjected to both a saliva and a urine test. However, such urine test shall be counted in determining the 25% required above.

§ 2. The Executive Vice-President may, in his discretion, or at the request of a member, authorize or direct a saliva, urine or other test of any horse racing at any meeting, whether or not tests are being conducted at such meeting, provided that adequate preliminary arrangements can be made to obtain proper equipment, and the services of a competent and qualified veterinarian and an approved laboratory.

87

During the taking of the saliva and/or urine sample by the veterinarian, the owner, trainer or authorized agent may be present at all times. Unless the rules of the State Racing Commission or other governmental agency provide otherwise, samples so taken shall be placed in two containers and shall immediately be sealed and the evidence of such sealing indicated thereon by the signature of the representative of the owner or trainer. One part of the sample is to be placed in a depository under the supervision of the Presiding Judge and/or any other agency the State Racing Commission may designate to be safeguarded until such time as the report on the chemical analysis of the other portion of the split sample is received.

Should a positive report be received, an owner or trainer shall have the right to have the other portion of the split sample inserted in with a subsequent group being sent for testing or may demand that it be sent to another chemist for analysis, the cost of which will be paid by the party requesting the test.

§ 3. Whenever there is a positive test finding the presence of any drug, stimulant, sedative or depressant present, **in the post-race test,** the laboratory shall immediately notify the Presiding Judge who shall immediately report such findings to the Executive Vice-President of this Association.

When such positive report is received from the State Chemist by the Presiding Judge, the persons held responsible shall be notified and a thorough investigation shall be conducted by or on behalf of the Judges. Then a time shall be set by the Judges for a hearing to dispose of the matter. The time set for the hearing shall not exceed four racing days after the responsible persons were notified. The hearing may be continued, if in the opinion of the Judges, circumstances justify such action. At County Fairs and non-pari-mutuel meetings, in the event the Judges are unable to perform this action, the Executive Vice-President shall forthwith set a date for a prompt hearing to be conducted by him or some person deputized by him for the purpose of determining all matters concerning the administration of such drug, stimulant, sedative or depressant and the care and the custody of the horse from which the positive sample was obtained.

The decision of the Executive Vice-President or the person deputized by him shall be reduced to writing and shall be final unless the person or persons aggrieved thereby shall within 30 days appeal in writing to the Board of Appeals as provided in Article IX of the By-Laws.

Should the chemical analysis of saliva, urine or other sample **of the post-race test** taken from a horse indicate the presence of a forbidden narcotic, stimulant, depressant, or local anesthetic, it shall be considered prima facie evidence that such has been administered to the horse. The trainer and any other person or persons who may have had the care of, or been in attendance of the horse, or are suspected of causing such condition, shall be immediately stopped from participating in racing by the Judge and shall remain inactive in racing pending the outcome of a hearing. The horse alleged to have been stimulated shall not run during the investigation and hearing, however, other horses registered under the care of the inactive trainer may, with the consent of the Judge of the meeting, be released to the care of another licensed trainer, and may race.

§ 4. Any person or persons who shall administer or influence or conspire with any other person or persons to administer to any horse any drug, medicant, stimulant, depressant, narcotic or hypnotic to such horse within forty-eight hours of his race, shall be subject to penalties provided in Section 9 of this rule.

§ 5. Whenever the **post-race** test or tests prescribed in Section 1 hereof disclose the presence in any horse of any drug, stimulant, depressant or sedative, in any amount whatsoever, it shall be presumed that the same was administered by the person or persons having the control and/or care and/or custody of such horse with the intent therby to affect the speed or condition of such horse and the result of the race in which it participated.

§ 6. A trainer shall be responsible at all times for the condition of all horses trained by him. No trainer shall start a horse or permit a horse in his custody to be started if he knows, or if by the exercise of reasonable care he might have known or have cause to believe, that the horse has received any drug, stimulant, sedative, depressant, medicine, or other substance that could result in a positive test. Every trainer must guard or cause to be guarded each horse trained by him in such manner and for such period of time prior to racing the horse so as to prevent any person not employed by or connected with the owner or trainer from administering any drug, stimulant, sedative, depressant, or other substance resulting in a **post-race** positive test.

§ 7. Any owner, trainer, driver or agent of the owner, having the care, custody and/or control of any horse who shall refuse to submit such horse to a salvia test or other tests as herein provided or ordered by the Judges shall be guilty of the violation of this rule. **Any horse that refuses to submit to a pre-race blood test shall be required to submit to a post-race saliva and urine test regardless of its finish.**

§ 8. All winnings of such horse in a race in which an offense was detected under any section of this rule shall be forfeited and paid over to this Association for redistribution among the remaining horses in the race entitled to same unless it is clearly shown that the horse was not stimulated. No such forfeiture and redistribution of winnings shall affect the distribution of the pari-mutuel pools at tracks where pari-mutuel wagering is conducted, when such distribution of pools is made upon the official placing at the conclusion of the heat or dash.

§ 9. **Pre-Race Blood Test.—Where there is a pre-race blood test which shows that there is an element present in the blood indicative of a stimulant, depressant or any unapproved medicant, the horse shall immediately be scratched from the race and an investigation conducted by the officials to determine if there was a violation of Section 4 of this rule.**

§ 10. The penalty for violation of any sections of this rule, unless otherwise provided, shall be a fine of not to exceed $5,000, suspension for a fixed or indeterminate time, or both, or expulsion.

§ 11. All Veterinarians practicing on the grounds of an extended pari-mutuel meeting shall keep a log of their activities including:

(a) Name of horse.
(b) Nature of ailment.
(c) Type of treatment.
(d) Date and hour of treatment.

It shall be the responsibility of the Veterinarian to report to the Presiding Judge any internal medication given by him by injection or orally to any horse after he has been declared to start in any race.

§ 12. Any veterinarian practicing veterinary medicine on a race track where a race meeting is in progress or any other person using a needle or syringe shall use only one-time disposable type needles and a disposable needle shall not be re-used.

Rule 22.—Fines, Suspensions, and Expulsion.

Section 1. **Fines—Suspension Until Paid.**—All persons who shall have been fined under these rules shall be suspended until said fine shall have been paid in full.

Fines which have been upaid for a period of five years may be dropped from the records of the Treasurer of the Association, however, such action will not affect the suspension.

§ 2. **Recording and Posting Penalties.**—Written or printed notice thereof shall be delivered to the person penalized, notice shall be posted immediately at the office of the member, and notice shall be forwarded immediately to the Executive Vice-President by the Presiding Judge or Clerk of the Course. The Executive Vice-President shall transmit notice of suspension to the other members; and thereupon the offender thus punished shall suffer the same penalty and disqualification with each and every member.

§ 3. **Effect of Minor Penalty on Future Engagements.**—Where the penalty is for a driving violation and does not exceed in time a period of 5 days, the driver may complete the engagement of all horses declared in before the penalty becomes effective. Such driver may drive in Stake, Futurity, Early Closing and Feature races, during a suspension of 5 days or less but the suspension will be extended one day for each date he drives in such a race.

§ 4. **Disposition of Fines.**—All fines which are collected shall be reported and paid upon the day collected to the Executive Vice-President.

§ 5. **Effect of Suspension Penalty.**—Whenever the penalty of suspension is prescribed in these rules it shall be construed to mean an unconditional exclusion and disqualification from the time of receipt of written notice of suspension from the Member or the President, or Executive Vice-President, from any participation, either directly or indirectly, in the privileges and uses of the course and grounds of a member during the progress of a race meeting, unless otherwise specifically limited when such suspension is imposed, such as a suspension from driving. A suspension or explusion or denial of membership of either a husband or wife may apply in each instance to both the husband and wife. The suspension becomes effective when notice is given unless otherwise specified.

§ 6. **Effect of Penalty on Horse.**—No horse shall have the right to compete while owned or controlled wholly or in part by a suspended, expelled, disqualified or excluded person. An entry made by or for a person or of a horse suspended, expelled or disqualified, shall be held liable for the entrance fee thus contracted without the right to compete unless the penalty is removed. A suspended, disqualified or excluded person who shall drive, or a suspended or disqualified horse which shall perform in a race shall be fined not less than $50, nor more than $100, for each offense.

§ 7. **Fraudulent Transfer.**—The fraudulent transfer of a horse by any person or persons under suspension in order to circumvent said suspension, shall constitute a violation.

§ 8. **Indefinite Suspension.**—If no limit is fixed in an order of suspension and none is defined in the rule applicable to the case, the penalty shall be considered as limited to the season in which the order was issued.

§ 9. **Suspended Person.**—Any member wilfully allowing a suspended, disqualified or excluded person to drive in a race, or a suspended or disqualified horse to start in a race after notice from the President or Executive Vice-

President, shall be together with its officers, subject to a fine not exceeding $100 for each offense, or suspension or explusion.

§ 10. **Expelled Person.**—Any member wilfully allowing the use of its track or ground by an expelled or unconditionally suspended man or horse, after notice from the President or Executive Vice-President, shall be, together with its officers, subject to a fine not exceeding $500 for each offense, or suspension or expulsion.

§ 11. Whenever a person is excluded from a pari-mutuel track by the track member, this Association shall be notified.

§ 12. An expelled, suspended, disqualified or excluded person cannot act as an officer of a track member. A track member shall not, after receiving notice of such penalty, employ or retain in its employ an expelled, suspended, disqualified or excluded person at or on the track during the progress of a race meeting. Any member found violating this rule shall be fined not to exceed $500.

§ 13. **Dishonored Check, Etc.**—Any person being a member of this Association who pays an entry, a fine or other claim to this Association or an entry or fine to another member of this Association by a draft, check, order or other paper, which upon presentation is protested, payment refused or otherwise dishonored shall be by order of the Executive Vice-President, subject to a fine not exceeding the amount of said draft, check or order, and the winnings of the horse or horses declared illegal and said persons and horses suspended until the dishonored amount and fine are paid and the illegal winnings returned.

§ 14. **Penalty of Racing Commissions.**—All penalties imposed by the Racing Commissions of the various states shall be recognized and enforced by this Association upon notice from the Commission to the Executive Vice-President, except as provided in Section 15 of this Rule 22.

§ 15. **Reciprocity of Penalties.**—All persons and horses under suspension or expulsion by any State Racing Commission or by a reputable Trotting Association of a foreign country shall upon notice from such commission or association to the Executive Vice-President, be suspended or expelled by this Association. Provided, however, that, for good cause shown, the Board of Appeals may, upon consideration of the record of the proceedings had before such State Commission or foreign Association modify or so mould the penalty imposed to define the applicability thereof beyond the jurisdiction of the State Commission or foreign Association. Provided further that, whether or not a penalty has been imposed by a State Racing Commission, the District Board may make original inquiry and take original jurisdiction in any case as provided in Sections 2 and 15 of Article IV of the By-Laws.

§ 16. **Modification of Penalty.**—Any suspension imposed by Judges can be removed or modified by the Executive Vice-President upon the recommendation of the Judges and Member on whose grounds the penalty was imposed.

§ 17. An application for removal of expulsion imposed for starting a horse out of its class or under change of name, or both, shall not be docketed for a hearing by the District Board until all the unlawful winnings are returned for redistribution and a fine of $250 is paid.

Rule 23.—Protests And Appeals.

Section 1. **Protests.**—Protests may be made only by an owner, manager, trainer or driver of one of the contending horses, at any time before the winnings are paid over, and shall be reduced to writing, and sworn to, and shall contain at least one specific charge, which, if true, would prevent the horse from winning or competing in the race.

§ 2. The Judges shall in every case of protest demand that the driver, and the owner or owners, if present, shall immediately testify under oath; and in case of their refusal to do so, the horse shall not be allowed to start or continue in the race, but shall be ruled out, with a forfeit of entrance money.

§ 3. Unless the Judges find satisfactory evidence to warrant excluding the horse, they shall allow him to start or continue in the race under protest, and the premium, if any is won by that horse, shall be forthwith transmitted to the Executive Vice-President to allow the parties interested an opportunity to sustain the allegations of the protest, or to furnish information which will warrant an investigation of the matter by the District Board of Review. Where no action is taken to sustain the protest within thirty days, payment may be made as if such protest had not been filed.

§ 4. Any person found guilty of protesting a horse falsely and without cause, or merely with intent to embarrass a race, shall be punished by a fine not to exceed $100 or by suspension or expulsion.

§ 5. When a protest has been duly made or any information lodged with the Judges alleging an improper entry or any act prohibited or punishable under these rules, the same shall not be withdrawn or surrendered before the expiration of thirty days, without the approbation of the Executive Vice-President. If any member shall permit such a withdrawal of protest or information with a corrupt motive to favor any party, the executive officers so permitting it may be expelled by the District Board of Review.

§ 6. **Appeals.**—All decisions and rulings of the Judges of any race, and of the officers of Member Tracks may be appealed to the District Board of Review within ten (10) days after the notice of such decision or ruling. The appeal may be taken upon any question in the conduct of a race, interpretation of the rules, decisions relative to the outcome of a race, application of penalties, or other action affecting owners, drivers, or horses, but it must be based on a specific charge which, if true, would warrant modification or reversal of the decision. In order to take an appeal under Rule 18, a driver must have first made a complaint, claim, or objection as required on Rule 18. The District Board of Review may vacate, modify, or increase any penalty imposed by the Judges and appealed to the Board. In the event an appellant fails to appear at the hearing of his appeal without good cause the District Board may impose a fine not to exceed $100.00 or a suspension not to exceed thirty days to be effective at the first meeting at which he has horses entered for racing.

§ 7. Nothing herein contained shall affect the distribution of the pari-mutuel pools at tracks where pari-mutuel wagering is conducted, when such distribution is made upon the official placing at the conclusion of the heat or dash.

§ 8. All appeals shall be in writing and sworn to before a Notary or one of the Judges of the Meeting. At the time the appeal is filed, a deposit of $100, or an agreement to forfeit the sum of $100 in the event the Board determines the appeal is not justified, must accompany the appeal. In the event the District Board of Review feels that the appeal was justified, it will refund the money to the appellant. This procedure does not apply to protests.

§ 9. In case of appeal or protest to The United States Trotting Association, the purse money affected by the appeal or protest must be deposited with the

Executive Vice-President pending the decision of the District Board of Review. Any purse or portion thereof withheld for any reason shall be forthwith sent to the Executive Vice-President together with a full statement showing the reason for such withholding.

§ 10.   Any track member that fails to send the Executive Vice-President, within one week of the date on which it was filed, any protest or appeal filed with the member or its Judges, may be fined or suspended.

§ 11.   The license of any Presiding Judge may be revoked for refusal to accept a protest or appeal, or for refusing to act as witness for a person seeking to swear to a protest or appeal.

Rule 24.—Time and Records.

Section 1. Timing Races.—In every race, the time of each heat shall be accurately taken by three Timers or an approved electric timing device, in which case there shall be one Timer, and placed in the record in minutes, seconds and fifths of seconds, and upon the decision of each heat, the time thereof shall be publicly announced or posted.   No unofficial timing shall be announced or admitted to the record, and when the Timers fail to act no time shall be announced or recorded for that heat.

§ 2.   **Error in Reported Time.**—In any case of alleged error in the record, announcement or publication of the time made by a horse, the time so questioned shall not be changed to favor said horse or owner, except upon the sworn statement of the Judges and Timers who officiated in the race, and then only by order of the District Board of Review, or the Executive Vice-President.

§ 3.   **Track Measurement Certificate.**—In order that the performances thereon may be recognized and/or published as official every track member not having done so heretofore and since January 1st, 1939, shall forthwith cause to be filed with the Executive Vice-President the certificate of a duly licensed civil engineer or land surveyor that he has subsequently to January 1st, 1939, measured the said track from wire to wire three feet out from the pole or inside hub rail thereof and certifying in linear feet the result of such measurement. Each track shall be measured and recertified in the event of any changes or relocation of the hub rail.

§ 4.   **Time for Lapped on Break.**—The leading horse shall be timed and his time only shall be announced.   No horse shall obtain a win race record by reason of the disqualification of another horse unless a horse is declared a winner by reason of the disqualification of a breaking horse on which he was lapped.

§ 5.   **Time for Dead Heat.**—In case of a dead heat, the time shall constitute a record for the horses making the dead heat and both shall be considered winners.

§ 6.   **Timing Procedure.**—The time shall be taken from the first horse leaving the point from which the distance of the race is measured until the winner reaches the wire.

§ 7.   **Misrepresentation of Time—Penalty.**—(a) A fine not to exceed $500 shall be imposed upon any member of this Association on whose grounds there shall be allowed any misrepresentation of time, and time shall be deemed to have been misrepresented in any race, wherein a record of the same is not kept in writing. A fine imposed under this rule shall include the officers of the member.

(b)   Any person who shall be guilty of fraudulent misrepresentation of time or the alteration of the record thereof in any public race shall be fined, suspended or expelled, and the time declared not a record.

§ 8. **Time Performances.**—Time performances are permitted subject to the following:

(a)   Urine and saliva tests are required for all horses starting for a time performance.

(b)   An approved electric timer is required for all time performances. In the event of a failure of a timer during the progress of a time performance, no time trial performance record will be obtained.

(c)   Time trial performances are permitted only during the course of a regular meeting with the regular officials in the Judges' stand.

(d)   Time trial performances are limited for two-year-olds who go to equal or to beat 2:10, three-year-olds who go to equal or to beat 2:05 and aged horses that go to equal or to beat 2 minutes.

(e)   In any race or performance against time excessive use of the whip shall be considered a violation.

(f)   Any consignor, agent or sales organization or other person may be fined or suspended for selling or advertising a horse with a time trial record without designating it as a time trial or who sells or advertises a horse without showing the gait of its parents or grandparents.

(g)   Time trial performance records shall not be included in a race program.

(h)   Time trial performances shall be designated by preceding the time with two capital Ts.

Rule 25.—Export Certificates.

Section 1.   The Executive Vice-President may appoint export agents at various ports of shipping, who shall upon examination and identification of the horse to be exported, indorse the application for export certificate. Every application for an export certificate must be accompanied by a certificate of registration in the current ownership and a fee in the sum of $35.00. The export certificate shall be issued and signed by the Executive Vice-President of the Association and the corporate seal affixed thereto. No such certificate will be issued for the export of any horse under expulsion nor for any horse currently under suspension by this Association. The fee for a duplicate certificate shall be $10.00.

§ 2.   Any party or parties giving false information to procure an export certificate shall be deemed guilty of fraud and upon conviction thereof shall be fined or expelled and the horse in question may be expelled.

§ 3.   If any horse registered with this Association is exported from the United States of Canada to any other country without making application for an export certificate, then the said horse will be stricken from the records of The United States Trotting Association.

Rule 26.—Registration Of Horses.

Section 1.   In order to register a horse the owner thereof must be a member of this Association.

§ 2.   **Standard Bred.**—Horses may be registered as Standard bred with any of the following qualifications:

(a)   The progeny of a registered Standard horse and a registered Standard mare.

(b) A stallion sired by a registered Standard horse, provided his dam and granddam were sired by registered Standard horses and he himself has a Standard record and is the sire of three performers with Standard records from different mares.

(c) A mare whose sire is a registered Standard horse, and whose dam and granddam were sired by a registered Standard horse, provided she herself has a Standard record.

(d) A mare sired by a registered Standard horse, provided she is the dam of two performers with Standard records.

(e) A mare or horse sired by a registered Standard horse, provided its first, second and third dams are each sired by a registered Standard horse.

(f) No horse over seven years of age is eligible for registration.

(g) The Standing Committee on Registration may register as Standard any horse which does not qualify under the above six rules, if in their opinion he or she should be registered Standard.

§ 3. **Non-Standard Bred.**—Any horse may be registered as Non-Standard upon filing application showing satisfactory identification of the horse for racing purposes. This identification may be accomplished by furnishing the name, age, sex, sire, dam, color and markings and history of the previous owners. A mating certificate must accompany this application, showing the sire to be some type of a registered horse.

§ 4. The breeder of a horse, for the purposes of registration, is the owner or lessee of the dam at the time of breeding, and when held under lease, bred on shares or in partnership, only such lease or partnership will be recognized for such purposes which is filed in the offices of The United States Trotting Association.

§ 5. **Mating Certificates.**—Mating certificates shall be signed by the owner or if the horse is under lease a letter must be filed with this Association signed by the owner of the horse stating to whom and for what period of time the horse is under lease. In addition to the letter signed by the owner a letter signed by the lessee stating that he will accept responsibility for the accuracy of the mating certificate during the period of time covered by the lease must be filed. In such event the lessee must sign the mating certificate. A mating certificate must be on file in the office of the Association before a certificate of registration will be issued.

§ 6. **Artificial Insemination.**—A colt conceived by semen transported off the premises where it is produced is not eligible for registration.

§ 7. **Breeding Records.**—Stallion owners shall keep a stallion record showing the mare's name, sire and dam, color, markings, owner, breeding dates, and color, sex and foaling date of any foals born on the stallion owner's premises. The records shall be available for inspection by officers or authorized representatives of The United States Trotting Association, and shall be kept at least ten years or filed with The United States Trotting Association.

All persons standing a stallion at either public or private service shall file with this Association a list of all mares bred to each stallion, together with the dates of service. This list must be filed by **August 1st** of the year of breeding. **In addition to the service report, a list of standardbred foals dropped on the farm with foaling dates and markings must be filed by August 1st.** Failure to comply with this provision may subject the owner or lessee of the stallion to a fine of not less than $10.00 nor more than $50.00. Application for registration may be refused from any person not complying with this rule.

§ 8. Names.—

(a) Names for proposed registration shall be limited to sixteen letters and three words.

(b) Horses may not be registered under a name of an animal previously registered and active.

(c) Names of outstanding horses may not be used again, nor may they be used as a prefix or suffix unless the name is a part of the name of the sire or dam. A prefix or a suffix such as Junior, etc., is not acceptable.

(d) Use of a farm name in registration of horses is reserved for the farm that has registered that name.

(e) Names of living persons will not be used unless the written permission to use their name is filed with the application for registration.

(f) No horse shall be registered under names if spelling or pronunciation is similar to names already in use.

(g) Names of famous or notorious persons, trade names, or names claimed for advertising purposes, except names, or parts of a name, of a registered breeding farm, will not be used.

(h) The United States Trotting Association reserves the right to refuse any name indicating a family or strain which may be misleading, or any name which may be misleading as to the origin or relationship of an animal.

(i) Horses may be named by January 1st, subsequent to their foaling, without penalty.

§ 9. Fees for Registration.—Complete application submitted for foals prior to October 1st—$10.00. Complete applications submitted subsequent to October 1st and prior to the date on which the foal becomes two years of age—$15.00. Complete applications submitted thereafter—$25.00. Canadian owned horses registered with the Canadian Standard Bred Horse Society Records may be registered with The United States Trotting Association upon presentation of the Canadian certificate in the applicant's name and a $5.00 fee.

§ 10. Fees for Transfer.—For each change in ownership, if application is received within one month after date of sale $2.00; one to three months $5.00; three to six months $10.00; and (effective on sales after January 1, 1962) six months to one year $25.00; one to two years $50.00; over two years $100.00.

§ 11. Fee for Duplicate Registration Certificate.—A duplicate registration certificate shall be issued for $5.00 upon receipt of a satisfactory written statement from the owner stating why duplicate papers are needed.

§ 12. Fees for Tattooing.—The fee for tattooing horses foaled on or after January 1, 1960 will be $5.00.

§ 13. Fees for Re-registration to Change the Name.—Fee for re-registration of a yearling prior to January 1st when it shall become two years old, which re-registration is solely for the purpose of a change of name, shall be $1.00. After a horse becomes a two-year-old the fee for change of name shall be $15.00. **No change of name will be permitted once a horse has raced nor will any change of name be permitted for stallions or mares that have been retired for breeding purposes.**

§ 14. Notice of Sale.—Any party selling a registered horse shall immediately notify The United States Trotting Association, giving the full name and address of the new owner and the date of sale. No horse shall be transferred unless a registration certificate, together with a transfer signed by the registered owner, is filed with this Association.

§ 15. Skipping Transfers.—Any person who is a party whether acting as agent or otherwise, to skipping or omitting transfers in the chain of ownership of any horse, may be subjected to the penalties and procedures set forth in Section 16 hereof.

§ 16. **Penalty for Executing False Application for Registration or Transfer.**—The President, Executive Vice-President, Registration Committee or District Board of Review may summon persons who have executed applications for registration or transfer that have become subject to questions, as well as any other person who may have knowledge thereof. Failure to respond to such summons may be punished by a fine, suspension or expulsion. If the investigation reveals that an application for registration or transfer contains false or misleading information, the person **or persons** responsible may be fined, suspended or expelled, and in addition may be barred from further registration or transfer of horses in the Association **and such animal may be barred from registration.** The decision of the President, Executive Vice-President, Registration Committee or District Board of Review, as the case may be, shall be reduced to writing and shall be final unless the person or persons aggrieved thereby shall, within ten (10) days appeal in writing to the Board of Appeals as provided in Article IX of the By-Laws.

§ 17. **Fine for Careless Reporting of Markings.**—Any person filing an application for registration with incorrect information **shall** be fined $10.00 for each such incorrect application.

§ 18. **Cancellation of Incorrect Registration.**—If, upon any proceeding under the provisions of Section 16 of this Rule 26, it shall be determined that any outstanding registration is incorrect, the Executive Vice-President shall order immediate cancellation of such outstanding incorrect registration and shall forthwith forward notice of such cancellation to the owner of the horse which is incorrectly registered.

§ 19. Failure by a member to submit requested information relative to the breeding and/or transfer of a horse to this Association may subject the member to suspension by the Executive Vice-President.

Beginning Of A "Fix"

An entire book could be written on the effects of breeding on the results of a race or racing in general. Horses are bred for speed. They can not get it any other way. A great many things may be done to bring out the inbred speed, but if it is not inherent within the horse, absolutely nothing is going to prompt a good performance. Some of the inherited factors that contribute to speed are all closely related to the various anatomical systems that makes up all mammals. These systems are: 1. Skeletal, 2. Muscle, 3. Gastro-intestinal, 4. Circullatory, 5. Nervous, 6. Endocrine, 7. Urinary and sexual.

A real top performing race horse inherits the best combination of all of these. He may inherit the best or worst system of either sire or dam so the odds are aginst getting a top animal every time with any particular mating. In other words breeding a good mare to a plowhorse is not likely to produce a good race horse. If both parents are top performers, prior to breeding, chances are considerably better for coming up with an offspring that will do as well or better than either parent. The colt may, however, inherit the worst of both parents and not be half as good as either one. If neither parent has any system weakness or have dominant systems to overcome weaknesses on the part of the other parent then a good cross results. Some mares are producers regardless of what they are bred to and some stallions have a tendency to reproduce winners on a variety of bloodlines whereas other stallions seem to produce worthwhile offspring from very few dam bloodlines. These stallions just do not have dominant factors to overcome weaknesses in the mares they are mated with. Once a good cross is found it should be pursued. It is a well known fact that some families or bloodlines produce the best offspring when mated with other known families.

Let's pursue the systems in more detail—Beginning with the skeletal or bone structure of the horse. There are 283 bones making up the framework of a horse. To be a good race horse all of these must be well developed and properly placed. The legs are the most important. The legs are the main support of a lot of weight and are subjected to a great many severe stresses in races. They must be strong, straight, and set squarely under the animal. The most frequent problem encountered with legs is interference—that is a foot striking one of the other legs. Regardless of the gait (trot, pace or gallop) there is very little clearance or room for error when a horse is in full stride. If they are toed-in, toed-out, cow-hocked or have any other deformity that takes the feet out of a perfectly straight line the chances of interference are greatly increased. If a horse strikes his knee or foot going at full speed an injury can result that will not only eliminate him from that race but quite possibly from ever racing again.

Straight legs are an inherited characteristic and utmost care should be exercised in selecting a racehorse with particular attention paid to the legs. Plenty of things can happen to legs even if they seem perfect to start with. It might, also, be well at this point to mention some of the things that can be done to correct inferior gaits—keeping in mind the best remedy in proper selection of the individual from families that have good legs and feet.

Again, it would be impossible to point out all of the corrective measures in the space allotted here so we will just hit the high points and suggest you read a more detailed literature related to the specific problem at hand. A good horseshoer will be the best ally of any horseman regardless of whether his horses have perfect or impossible legs. A good horse can be soon made servicably sound racers by skillful horseshoers. The length of toe determines (they grow like fingernails), how far the horse will reach and how quick they will 'break over' to take another step. The angle of the hoof has to be very exact for the same reasons. If a horse has no bone, muscle, or tendon impairments, the sole must be dressed to set perfectly level. If they toe out or in, this may be corrected by leaving the inside or outside hoof wall a little longer. The amount will vary with the severity of the condition and in most cases will be corrected gradually over a long period of time. Any drastic change in the foot usually causes the horse to go lame because some tendons are tightened by the change and others are left slack thus not carrying their full load. Severe damage can result from sudden changes in the foot. If it is necessary to make a change in the length or angle, approach it with all due caution making the change a little at a time. The shoe may have to be reset several times with an interval of time between each setting to permit the horse to adapt to the changes. Horseshoes are not just put on for luck. They serve a very important purpose of keeping the trimmed foot from wearing unevenly.

The shoes that are put on after the foot is properly trimmed are discussed in another part of this book. They must be the right type, the right weight, and put on right. Right in this case means what the horse has been used to wearing. Any slight change may change his gait enough to lose a race. By the same token, if he has been racing on the regular track and is put in a turf race, some shoe changes may be in order to compensate for the change. A wet or sloppy track may require a shoe change for some horses. Some need heels raised while others need pads. Horsehoeing can be classified as a scientific art when properly done.

Lets get back to the inherited framework of the horse. Unsoundness may not be inherited as much as they are acquired, but many of the predisposing or underlying causes are inherited. I certainly would favor breeding to a sound horse that had a history of having been sound throughout his racing career. The one possible exception to this rule would be a real contender that became incapacitated for racing by some accident. A little study of the offspring of any given sire or dam can be quite revealing. Allowances can be made for feeding and handling, but if the greater percentage do not remain sound and in racing condition structural weaknesses probably are at the root of the problem. Such weaknesses can be bred out of racing stock and every attempt should be made to select the best frame for a future race horse. The following will illustrate what this frame should be.

Conformation
of Feet and Legs

A perpendicular line drawn downward from the point of shoulder should fall upon the center of the knee, cannon, pastern, and foot No. 1 represents the correct conformation. Nos. 2 to 7 inclusive, represent common defects. No. 2, slightly bow-legged. No. 3, close at knees and toes out. No. 4, toes in. No. 5, knock-kneed. No. 6, base narrow. No. 7, base wide.

A perpendicular line drawn downward from the center of the elbow joint should fall upon the center of the knee and pastern, and back of the foot, and a perpendicular line drawn downward from the middle of the arm should fall upon the center of the foot. No. 8 represents the righ conformation. No. 9, leg too far forward. No. 10, knee sprung. No. 11, calf kneed. No. 12, foot and leg placed too far back.

A perpendicular line drawn downward from the hip point should fall upon the center of the foot and divide the gaskin in the middle; and a perpendicular line drawn from the point of the buttock should just touch the upper rear point of the back and fall barely behind the rear line of the cannon and fetlock. Correct position of the leg from this view is most important in a horse.

No. 13 represents the correct conformation. No. 14, leg too far forward and hock crooked. No. 15, entire leg too far under and weak below hock. No. 16, entire leg placed too far backward.

A perpendicular line drawn downward from the point of the buttocks should fall in line with the center of the hock, cannon, pastern and foot.

No. 17 represents the correct conformation. No. 18, bow-legged. No. 19, base narrow. No. 20, base wide. No. 21, cow-hocked and toes out. Very serious fault.

Conformation of Feet and Legs

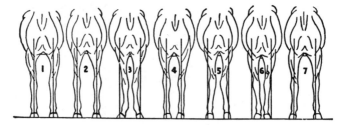

Front view of fore limbs.

A perpendicular line drawn downward from the point of shoulder should fall upon the center of the knee, cannon, pastern, and foot.

No. 1 represents the correct conformation. Nos. 2 to 7, inclusive, represent common defects. No. 2, slightly bow-legged. No. 3, close at knees and toes out. No. 4, toes in. No. 5, knock-kneed. No. 6, base narrow. No. 7, base wide.

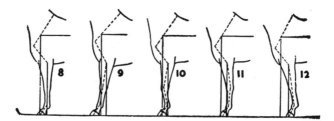

Side view of fore limbs.

A perpendicular line drawn downward from the center of the elbow joint should fall upon the center of the knee and pastern, and back of the foot, and a perpendicular line drawn downward from the middle of the arm should fall upon the center of the foot.

No. 8 represents the right conformation. No. 9, leg too far forward. No. 10, knee sprung. No. 11, calf kneed. No. 12, foot and leg placed too far back.

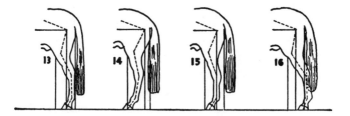

Side view of hind limbs.

A perpendicular line drawn downward form the hip point should fall upon the center of the foot and divide the gaskin in the middle; and a perpendicular line drawn from the point of the buttock should just touch the upper rear point of the back and fall barely behind the rear line of the cannon and fetlock. Correct position of the leg from this view is most important in a horse.

No. 13 represents the correct conformation. No. 14, leg too far forward and hock crooked. No. 15, entire leg too far under and weak below hock. No. 16, entire leg placed too far backward.

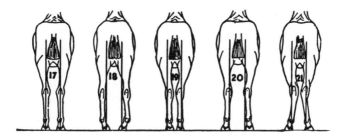

Rear view of hind limbs.

A perpendicular line drawn downward from the point of the buttocks should fall in line with the center of the hock, cannon, pastern and foot.

No. 17 represents the correct conformation. No. 18, bow-legged. No. 19, base narrow. No. 20, base wide. No. 21, cow-hocked and toes out Very serious fault.

Fixing By Training, Running And Riding

If the training, running, and riding of race horses is not to be considered as a science, I think it may fairly be admitted, that it is a very special species of knowledge that can best be acquired by early experience. Boys growing up with horses getting good practical training under a good groom or trainer for several years are likely to determine future races by thier superior acquired ability. Early impressions made on the minds of attentive boys, while they are going progressively on throughout the whole practical gradations, both in and out of the stables, of a well managed racing establishment will fit together and become a lasting image to guide them later.

To determine the tremendous effect training personnel and horses has on fixing future races a sort of groundwork or introduction to preparatory essential matter will be injected in this chapter. Many readers have had little previous knowledge on the subject of training race horses that is necessary to understand just how they are conditioned for racing and the adverse effects that enter the picture if they are not properly trained and handled. I will endeavor to lay down the rules for training race horses with as much perspicuity as possible within the realm of my experience. Most of this experience has been gleaned from critical study of many of the nation's big name trainers methods and related results.

In training and running of horses, the changing circumstances must occasionally alter things, which of course will be the cause of exceptions to some of the rules. Training not being an exact science permits a wide range of confusion and many heated arguments about various methods of handling different situations. Matters of judgment requiring horse sense (stable thinking) or common sense which we repeat is not too common. I could readily point out a wide variety of examples, but such quotations would be of little use, beyond that of enlarging this book—a sort of thing I wish to avoid as much as possible. A better approach seems to be to lay down generally the whole of the practical principles as well as all the minute details and point out a few variations as we go. Many of the general principles will be repeated frequently. I believe this is necessary because those who know what little trifling circumstances of neglect or mismanagement will cause a horse in training to change considerably for the worse, can well understand the necessity of my being thus particularly minute and repetitious. My point is to be very clear on all matters relative to the management of race horses while they are being trained so the reader can appreciate this may be the place or time of the biggest fix in any given race.

Like any other specialized occupation, racing has its own language (if it may be so termed). Many of these terms will be used in this presentation, not to confuse anyone who has not had this association, but because it should give readers engaged in racing in any capacity a conversational plane with race horse people. This language, used by trainers, jockeys, stable boys, and owners when they are conversing with each other on business, is very expressive, that is to say, they understand each other in a very few words; and with apologies to you pros, where I have thought the terms used not generally intelligible, I have explained them, i.e., if you are a bug on grammer, it may be a shock to your system to hear a well-bred owner tell you about his horse by saying, "He win", when it happened yesterday or last year. If you are a new owner and your trainer comes over to tell you your six year old gelding broke his maiden, you may want to wait until the children are in bed to discuss this unless you know a maiden, in horse racing, is any horse, male or female, that has never won a race. Indeed, that my meaning may not be misconstrued, I will endeavor, as I proceed with the management of the condition of thoroughbred horses to point out as clearly as possible the manner of feeding, clothing, watering, exercising, or working of all of them, agreeably to their ages and constitutions.

I am convinced the public is comparatively unacquainted with the manner in which the noble horse is brought into the admirable condition in which he is exhibited at the post. The secrecy and halo that surrounds many trainers has sent many owners away talking to themselves. They just can not understand why this business can not be operated on sound business principles, nor can I.

There are a few owner-trainers, but most horses are owned

105

by people in other lines of endeavor and sent to privately hired trainers or to public stables that may own a few horses, but work for a number of owners, usually on a per day basis (present scale is from $10 to $20 per horse per day plus shoes, veterinary bills, etc.). The flat fee is for feed, care, training, and racing. It is for this type of owner and for the potential owner, this chapter is undertaken. It might be well to point out there is an extremely wide range in the abilities and operation of public trainers, from the best to the impossible like the "Fix the Owner" (FTO) trainer found in another chapter.

I would suggest very close scrutiny when selecting a trainer for any owner that wants to do more than see his horse run occasionally. In any race of importance, when the powers of the horses may be deemed nearly equal, or when they have been brought to that point by being handicapped with weights, the better trainer's horse will naturally win. Thus the race is fixed by good training (or the lack of it). Most owners are not too concerned about expense so when an inexperienced observer (or owner) walks down the shed-row and sees an ample supply of the best, food, clothing and plenty of water he may conclude the horses are getting the best care. Nothing could be further from the truth. Many trainers and grooms lack basic knowledge of the principles of training, lack confidence (they make up for this by doing a lot of talking) and will put horses on the track absolutely unfit to run. A lot of these break down and is considered a normal course of events—a pathetic and unnecessary loss in most cases. I have known cases where horses were kept muzzled forty eight hours without food or water before a race. This is shear folly as a horse starts to weaken about four hours after he has eaten if not fed again and to deprive a horse of water for forty eight hours is downright cruel.

There are thousands of owners from all walks of life that own race horses, it is a huge business of deep speculation.

Where there are such enormous sums of money depending on the results of many great stakes we ought to bear in mind that no pains which promise any chance of success should be spared, nor any accommodations that might in any way be advantageous to horses in training should be lost sight of.

106

Many tracks have lost sight of this matter of stables. Many others are building excellent stables or replacing the old ones with commendable structures, fireproof, comfortable and utilitarian.

Stables should be built on a dry level surface, as close to the track as is practical avoiding as much automobile traffic as possible. Ideally all stables should face the South. Horses enjoy sunshine as much as people and are more responsive when they get it.

Everyone associated with race horses should be aware how delicate and highbred a creature we have to deal with, in the training of a race-horse, and how much the circumstances of air, temperature, methods of feeding, clothing, watering, exercising, working, etc. may affect his powers for the race. They appreciate and respond to the simplest things and fail to respond when the routine of near perfection is broken or tampered with.

Grooms and stable help are also sensitive human beings and proper quarters should be provided for them. After all they do most of the work that is routine, at best, and at times very boring. Any cheer should be helpful in the form of better accommodations. From observation, psychologically most must feel they are playing second fiddle to the horses and with good reason. At least the horse gets his stall cleaned and freshly bedded everyday while the grooms do the best they can. No establishment can be said to be complete in which any person or thing, necessary to execute any work in the best manner, is wanting; nor even if these be all present, can it be said to be well conducted, unless every person about it is suitably accommodated, and everything so well adapted to its proper use, and set in its proper place, that it may always be ready at the shortest notice, to do its work in the most perfect manner. It is necessary to point this out because many races are lost, indeed predetermined, because some item was not available that should have been. A trainer that has had experience as a groom can appreciate how much labor can be saved by having the right equipment in the proper place. Their duties can be performed with greater facility with the best prospect for success. Everything necessary to do the best job should be available without superflous items in the way.

A stable door should be five feet wide and at least nine feet high. A very good added precaution would be rounded edges on the door or even rollers so the flighty horse could not injure himself going in and out. The floor of the stall should be well drained and kept level.

The best hay for race-horses is first cutting alfalfa. I would prefer straight alfalfa if I could get it, but a mixture with timothy or clover is very good provided it is early cut and put up without any rain damage or heating. In the event of the last two the hay will be musty. This can be detected by breaking open a bale and smelling at close range. Good hay will have a nice clean ordor and be a bright green color. If it is cut at too late a stage of maturity it will be stemmy. If it has been rained on after it is cut it will be dark or a brownish color indicating the loss of much of its vitamin A as well as other valuable nutrients. Hay one year old is best for horses. New hay should not be fed to horses as it will loosen them or as they say in jolly old England, they become relaxed in their bowels, and they will sweat profusely with very little exertion. Hay that was put up before it cured sufficiently will heat. This type of hay causes the horse to drink more water which is a sufficient reason for its not being given to horses in training.

Oats is the universal grain for feeding horses. They constitute the principle food for horses for a number of reasons to be outlined under foods. For those horses in training, the very best oats attainable are not any too good. They should be heavy, recleaned or clipped with no chaf or tailings. Western oats are usually a heavier oat. The later oats are planted in the Spring, the lighter and less useful they are apt to be. As one sage farmer put it after an extended rainy season that kept him from seeding his oats, "they will be so light I will have to put rocks on them to hold them down in the bin."

Some corn can be fed to horses, but it produces a great deal of heat and race horses should be fed very small amounts (not over ¼ of the grain allowance).

Some race horses are very difficult to keep in proper flesh as they are quite delicate and irritable. They may eat and drink as much as they like under most circumstances. If a

108

little extra flesh can be put on, the trainer may be :
them a little harder (now and then steal an extr
go a little longer distance, thus build up stamina f
er distance with more ease to the horse. Horses
will usually eat from ten to twelve quarts of oats pe
may, also, be given a little corn, some sweet feed an(
ciate a bran mash once a week or so. It must be remembered
a horse can founder on too much grain so it should always be
kept in a safe place if there is any danger of them getting loose.
Bran mashes help keep the animal in good shape as they are a
bit laxative as is linseed oil meal.

Most of the feeding will be covered under the chapter on
nutrition, but one more point will be discussed here related
to freshening up the stale horse. Horses that have been in
training for long periods of time or racing hard to become stale
and sooner or later renders them unfit for their best performance.
Some trainers turn them out from ten days to a month on good
pasture. There is nothing like Dr. Green to refresh a horse.
They will lose little of their condition in two or three weeks
and will return to their best form very rapidly. In the winter
when green grass is not to be had, carrots are an excellent sub-
sititute. They are cool, nutritious, and easily digested. When
washed and sliced they may be given daily in moderate quantities in each feed or once a day.

Nice bright wheat straw is the best bedding material, oat
straw may be used, in some areas sawdust is used, but different
kind of fungus diseases may develop on horses allergic to sawdust. Peat moss is satisfactory as is ground corn cobs and sugar
cane pith.

Water is a very important factor to race horses. For stake
winners that trained a lot, it may be a good investment to buy
bottled water from one source and keep them on it. Rain water
would be standard, also, and very good. If horses race at one
track they will adjust to local water. Water should never be
given immediately before or after food unless they have had
it in front of them all the time. Nor should water be given
immediately before or after work. They should be thoroughly
cooled out before given free access to water. A few swallows
now and again during the cooling out may be beneficial in

ng them—too much cold water could founder them. Soft
ater is best. If not available, a small quantity of salt could
be put in the pail, but this must not be overdone. The chill
could be taken off very cold water by adding some warm water
or letting it stand in a warm room. Race-horses should have
a pail of fresh water in their stall at all times except perhaps
immediately before a race.

Breaking Colts Fixes Races

To begin with a colt, your odds of ever seeing him race are
about seventeen to one. Your chances of seeing him run in the
Kentucky Derby are about twenty to thirty-six thousand and
of course his chances to win are one to thirty-six thousand.
The odds of getting them to the races could be greatly improved
upon, and racing in general could be greatly improved if two-
year olds were not raced at all. These are babies with bones
so soft they have not knitted at the ends. We would net think
of having a kindergarten football team, but we offer great
prizes in the way of stakes for two year old colts and fillies.
This is very wrong, and everyone in the business knows it is
wrong. There is no sensible reason for ruining, for life, over
fifty per cent of the two-year olds bred in this country. As
the situation now exists, breeders are forced to send these
babies to the sales where big money is paid for them. With
the big investment and an impatient urge to find out whether
they made a good investment or not, these are put on the track
—many just slightly over 1½ years old when they first go to
the post. This means they had to begin training when they
were about one year old. More than half will be broken down
before they get to the post, and many more shortly thereafter.
A shameful disgrace, and the betting public should refuse to
support the two-year old races. Except for the odd outstanding
colt or filly, they are not very consistent anyway. This is not
a crusade, but all racing could be benefitted and the public
better served if they are at least three. They are not mature
at three or even at four, for that matter.

Assuming this great sacrifice of young stock is going to continue, and attempt will be made here to point up some of the training procedures that will reduce the hazards as much as possible.

Most farms that breed with a view of either running or selling the young stock generally keep an experienced caretaker to manage the offspring. His method and manner of handling the young ones from the time they are sucklings a few days old should be such or to get them quite and gentle and acquainted with their surroundings. This is certainly an advantage whether they are sold as yearlings or kept and broke at a year and a half. Even if they are to be sold, to break and try them early to ascertain the power and speed each colt or filly possesses according to the results of the trials can give the breeder an idea about his asking price for each one.

Young ones are generally taken from their paddocks in July or August (the later, the better for the baby) and after five weeks they should be behaving well enough under saddle to follow each ride with a short gallop with a very light boy up. After this training period they should be sufficiently broke to be tried at three furlongs after which they should be returned to the paddocks to await the sale. If they are being kept to race, a better plan is to wait until late Fall to start training them as those few extra months mean a lot in their development and there is not going to be any stopping after they are put into training. Again, I would prefer this to start when they are two years old instead of as yearlings, but prohibition did not stop people from drinking. If they have been properly treated prior to bringing them to the stables they will not be alarmed at the people, new surroundings and things about them.

In public stables the trainer usually likes to supervise the breaking and training of the colts. Sometimes this is good, but many times it is not. He may be too busy racing to give them the extra care they need or he may just not have the patience and personality for a good 'colt man'. But whether they are broke at home or sent to some trainer is not as important as the methods used. The main object is to give them plenty of time until they are perfectly broke and established a routine the colt or filly understands. Everything should be done the same way at the same time. Do not try to introduce more than one new idea a day and it is best to repeat this not more than two or three times the same day. After one lesson is learned go the the next.

Even where facilities and trained personnel are not available a great start can be made in the training program. It is not necessary to have a rider to give the young horse some of his best training. To start, it will be sufficient to put first the bridle then the saddle on them and have them led out for a week or ten days. Lead them as many places as possible to acquaint them with new surroundings and if possible never let them get excited or get a fixed fear of anything. They can be muscled some by putting them on a long rope and lounging them now and again. This sort of treatment will steady them and teach them to respect those in charge. This is a very important point worthy of a lot of attention. Their entire future behavior will depend on how they are broke and handled early. There are two things to remember. 1. A horse will not punish himself and 2. Once a colt gets the better of someone he is going to be difficult to manage. Horses have great memories for both good and bad. The best way to break any horse, regardless of age, from a bad habit is to figure a way to make his bad habit inflict some pain to him. Once he has decided he is hurting himself, he will never do that again. They are a pretty stupid animal, though, and do not learn very fast (otherwise their great strength would never submit to man's handling). Patience and good judgment can get a horse to do nearly anything that does not cause him immediate pain.

Colts

When the young stock is first brought in there is a routine that can save much grief. First of all, the colts and fillies are separated. Having them thus arranged their education begins by teaching them to stand tied up in the stalls. This will prove no great problem if they have been used to wearing a halter and have been handled a great deal, as should have been the case. In any event, the halters and tie ropes should be very strong for this purpose. Care should be taken that the halters are adjusted so they can not slip out of them—remembering that once a horse does something they seldom forget. Some of them may be a little unruly at first and hang back a few times, but if they find they cannot get loose after repeated attempts, they become reconciled.

They should now have their feet cleaned out, trimmed and properly shod. Much care should be exercised on every movement and new procedure. They will gradually become accustomed to being brushed, combing out of the mane and tail, and picking out and washing their feet if they are handled with care without frightening them. They should be gradually taught the habit of being groomed every day. After a few days they can be taught to wear the bridle and saddle. Some colt men like to have them wear a roller with a girth around the chest when in the stable. This will prevent the roller from slipping back and getting into the flanks and make them less shy of a breast cloth when it is first put on. Some of them may be restless on being brought into the stable for the first time and be inclined to paw and tumble the bedding around. Those which indicate a disposition of this sort should have a boot or a strap with a short length of chain attached buckled on around the pastern joints. They should continue to wear these until they learn to stand perfectly still.

Breaking colts in is not something that should be hurried to find out what their potential is as quite often is the case. However promising in appearance or however well bred a colt may be, whatever properties he may possess, indeed the racer he will become greatly depends on the breaking. With bad management he may be totally ruined so we not only have fixed the outcome of some races; we have fixed his whole career. Little habits they pick up while being broke will cause them to misbehave while racing all of their life and that one race they should have won can be lost because of poor handling their first few weeks of training.

Again, horses have very retentive memories and seldom can be made to completely forget the unruly tricks or habits they acquire from being improperly handled on breaking. They can not think or reason very well so they are not capable of selecting a time or the most advantageous time to commit these so they usually catch the person in attendance completely off guard. In other words they do not think the way people do so sometimes they are hard to understand. They are, however, creatures of habit, a product of all they have learned at any time and quite predictable by anyone that tries to understand them. The man entrusted to break colts should be a man of experience who thoroughly understands what he is doing. Besides being a good horseman, he should be a man of excellent temper, never allowing his passion to get the better of his descretion when persevering with a colt. They actually are like working with retarded children. They can learn, but it takes tons of patience to bring them up right and have them throughly understand that what you are teaching them is good for them. Men raised around horses generally know better how to procede as colt breakers, but anyone with patience and good judgment can do an excellent job and be proud of his efforts. Horses, like dogs, respond to kindness when they understand and will reward the teacher with devoted effort. There are many ways of breaking colts, but for racing purposes it is a specialty and shoud not be left to cowboys that can subdue most any horse one way or another.

I will now outline some rather detailed procedures for breaking colts. A lot of it will seem ridiulous to many trainers, but there is a reason for every procedure and somewhere some colts have been ruined by neglecting some of the little things to be covered. they were, thusly, rendered useless or less useful by carelessness or lack of knowledge—the end results are the same.

The first step is putting on the cavesons, but before colts are led out of the stable they should have on long boots or have their legs wrapped well padded with cotton. This is assuming they are not used to being led. The reason for the leg protection is that when they first go out, they pull and hang back and then will plunge now and then. In doing so they strike their legs with their hoofs thereby inflicting bruises that become inflamed and can cause permanent damage to tendons and joints. Certainly no Standardbred should ever be hitched without proper bell boots and leg protection. It is sickening for me to recall the number of promising colts I have seen ruined by such carelessness. There may be even goers which may not appear to require boots, but it is a rather dangerous and foolhardy

114

experiment to attempt working colts without first putting on boots. When the colts come in from exercise or work the boots should be carefully observed for marks from blows. This can give a clue as to necessary changes in the shoeing. If corrected early they will stride better and have a much better gait. If allowed to settle into a bad way of going they may be nearly impossible to correct.

To start with there should be two people with each colt. On their first trip out one should walk in the rear in case the colt should hang back to urge him quietly on by gently shaking a whip behind him, but do not strike him. Colts with their cavesons and boots on and thus attended may be led out to the track or into a large paddock and be taught to lead quietly. As soon as they become tractable in this way they may be taught to work on a lounging line by first walking them in a small circle to the right or left. When they know how to go round at this pace, they may be quietly urged on into a trot, gradually increasing the size of the circle by giving them more length of rein. In three or four days or when they go boldly and freely at full length of the rein each way in the lounge for fifteen or twenty minutes with the pace gradually stepped up, then they are ready for mouthing bits, rollers and cruppers.

It might be well here to give a short description of the roller and crupper for those that have not used them. The roller may have a hook in the center of the pad, but must have a ring attached to the lower part of each side of the pad for the purpose of buckling on the side reins. In front of the bottom part of the pad straps should be attached. Straps should be attached to the crupper just over the loins and hang down to the hock joints level. It is best to put a buckle on the near side of the crupper to facilitate putting it on. When colts are out at exercise in this type of tackle these straps, from their action together with the wind blowing about are almost invariably striking against their legs and lapping under their bellies. They will be a little annoyed by the straps when first put on, but soon become accustomed to feel the straps which is what they are there for. By these means they are taught not to be alarmed when the wind blows a riders coat against them; or the wind blows their blanket against them as will happen when they are being walked to cool out; or if a strap comes lose in a race they would pay no attention to it, or even a muzzle improperly put on could hang down too low causing great alarm if he was not used to things hanging about him. A horse so alarmed may break loose and inflict all sorts of damage upon himself and others.

They should be handled in this manner until completely at ease. It is best for the same person dressed the same way to handle the colts for the first lessons. Now they are ready for the bits. For the first two or three days of their having the mouthing bits put on them, the bits should be allowed to play loosely in their mouths and in cruppering them, they should be handled boldly and without fear. The crupper should not be drawn too tight at first. The roller should be tightened very gradually because if colts are suddenly girthed up tight, most of them will set up their backs and plunge. If they get in the habit of this they will become very hard to saddle.

A horse which may have acquired this habit from being badly managed in his breaking requires great care and attention in saddling whenever he is going to run or he most likely will throw his jockey and fix a race for someone. Such a horse should best be saddled much earlier than the others. When the saddle is put on, the girth should be tightened up just enough to keep it in place. The horse may then be walked about for a short time with the girth tightened at intervals with a few more steps to let him forget. The surcingle can then be put on and the boy put up with more walking the horse until he is quiet. This will prevent an accident and assure a good start. Most horses get very excited when saddled knowing they are going to race. The greatest care observed on first girthing colts can pay big dividends later on.

When colts have had this tackle on two or three days and have been lounged and walked on the track a few hours each day, the next step is gradually to bear them up. This is done by attaching the side reins to the bits and rollers. This should be done gently at first. They should be shortened each day a hole at a time. From this treatment their mouths will become sensible to the pressure of the bit and they will bring their heads in naturally.

As some colts may take a little less time in breaking than

116

others, the colt breaker should now and then stop any of them he may see that are getting their mouths moist or frothy. Standing directly in front of these colts and taking hold of each side of the bit, he may, by a gentle pressure feel the state of the colt's mouth. If he finds it fairly sensitive to the pressure of the bit, he may by applying pressure to it at short intervals get the colt to rein back a little. Let the colt stand and pet him. Many repeated efforts will give him the idea of stopping or reining back by pressure applied to the bit when he is rode. It must be done in a very gentle way and he should be allowed to walk forward again. As each colt progressively improves, he should be handled in this manner.

Having gotten them this far along where they can be handled and pay no attention to the straps hanging down it is well to spend some time taking them to strange places merely with a view to accustom them to the different object they are likely to meet. They could even be taught to load at this point if proper facilities are available. Walking them over some boards would be a good start for this lesson. It would be best to have a truck or trailer they could walk into on the level with another horse already in it before trying to teach them to go up a ramp.

They can be taught proper respect for the whip now by instructing the person who is walking by the colts side to put their arms gently over the roller and lightly keep tapping his colt on his fore and hind quarters. This can be increased to give the colt the idea of moving on when tapped.

When they have learned this and had some practice they may be taught to wear the saddle. For the first few times of putting on the saddle, a little caution is necessary. The colt breaker should take the colt's head and at the same time pet him. There should be someone on either side. The one on the off side should hand the girths to the one on the near side who will not pull them too tight at first. The stirrups may be allowed to hang down and when the girth is drawn up sufficiently tight, the surcingle may be put on.

For a few days, the colts go on at their usual exercise of lounging and walking about the track for three or four hours a day or more time as may be necessary to steady those that may be rather flighty and unruly. The time will also have to

117

be regulated by their physical condition. These youngsters lose flesh rather rapidly sometimes when under the stress of breaking. It may be thought they are not doing a great deal but it is very trying for them and particular attention should be given their physical condition.

About this time of his breaking, the colt should be accustomed to be led by the colt breaker on his pony. This is very necessary before the colt is mounted or backed, as it accustoms him to see the man above him. He should be handled and fondled by everyone around in every possible way previous to his having someone placed on his back. The day on which he is to be mounted he should be kept working a little longer in the lounge or he may be led an hour or two longer than usual. A small paddock where he has been accustomed to being exercised will be the best place for his first ride. It should be a calm, still day with nothing to alarm him until he has become quite familiar with his rider.

For the first few times of mounting a colt or until he stands quietly there should be three men present. The colt breaker should place himself in front of the colt taking hold of each side of the bit and a man on the off side should have hold of the stirrup leather. While the man on the near side (who, of course, should be a good rider) is making attempts to mount, the one on the off side should give the necessary weight or strength in bearing down on the stirrup leather and yield his weight or strength, as occasion may require, to keep the saddle from moving out of its place; thereby annoying the colt at the time the man on the near side is making attempts to mount and dismount. He should start by first putting his foot into the stirrup and then taking it out again taking great care that his foot does not touch the colt's side. Lengthening the stirrup leathers a few holes may make this easier. He may repeat this once or twice if he finds the colt does not draw himself in or shy away. Having gotten his foot in the stirrup (taking care that his toe does not come in contact with the colt's side) he may raise himself gradually up from the ground until he is perfectly upright and bear, for a few moments, his whole weight on the stirrup. The colt breaker should, just at this period, try by kindness to engage the colt's attention while the man who is mounting may put his leg gently over and quietly seat himself in the saddle and while there he should pet and talk to the colt. He should then take up the reins, but at first he should handle them cautiously. The colt breaker should now lead the colt with the man on his back sitting perfectly still and unless he has to for safety sake, he should not immediately press his knees or calves of his legs too strongly against the colts sides. If he feels the colt getting ready to buck, the rider must sit firm and well down in the saddle making every effort to keep the colts head up. The colt breaker should check the caveson-rein and help in keeping up the colt's head. They should both keep working quietly at his head until he ceases to act up. He should then be led a few times each way around the paddock. If he appears fairly quiet he may be pulled up and made much of and led to the track with the man on him. The colt breaker should be riding by his side on his pony.

As soon as the colt is perfectly reconciled to his rider, he may be ridden back to the stable. The rider should pet and make a fuss over the colt before and after dismounting before putting him in the stable. This is all to impress the colt that this is a pleasant experience.

Some colts will be found to require more time and perserverence than others. Before mounting such colts, it may be as well to work them a little longer than the others, and at the time of mounting have someone give the colt a little corn or oats in a shallow dish to distract his attention. Once mounted, the rider should remain upon such a colt until he leads about perfectly quiet. The rider should occasionally pull him up and caress him letting him have a mouthful of corn now and then.

This sort of colt should be mounted and dismounted with the greatest care so as not to alarm him. He should be mounted and led every day until completely at ease with the rider up. It is best to have him in a group of other horses the first time he is turned loose. If the colt breaker thinks his colt will buck it is better to mount him on hard ground or a paved street where he can not get good footing and will be afraid to plunge. Excitable horses seldom try to throw a rider where they can not get good footing.

Giving time and taking pains with colts in this way, according to their different tempers, will give them confidence and they soon stand quietly to be mounted and dismounted with the rider being able to guide them any way they choose. Their cavesons may now be left off and in place of them use a plain head-stall martingale or running reins as required to enable their riders to get their heads in place.

The same person or as few persons as possible should continue to ride them under the direction of the colt breaker. There is much to teach them about riding well and to have good mouths. To accomplish this requires a light hand in application of the pressure with the bit on the colt's mouth. It should be done by the rider's giving and taking by gentle pulls and thereby keeping the colt's mouth alive to the pressure of the bit. The rider should occasionally gently press the calves of his legs and heels to the colt's sides to urge him on. Then pulling him up and letting him stand for a few moments and then reining him back a little and moving him forward teaching him to turn and go in any direction that may be required of him always treating him with kindness.

Some colts may become more sensitive on one side than the other. It is important to correct this which can be done by working or turning him more often to the insensitive side taking care not to neglect the other. This requires much patience and care.

All race horses will pull some, but this is of little consequence provided they pull evenly otherwise they will be very difficult to guide and control. How many times have you seen a race result fixed by a horse running wide on a turn or unable to be tucked into a pack of horses (putting them in a hole).

The horses are now ready to be exposed to noise and more alarming things to get used to the crowds. This should be done with a pony. Care should be exercised in exposing them to frightening situations. The main point is to get them to understand nothing will harm them. They soon acquire confidence in the rider in all sorts of situations. They will never make top race horses without this training. Never force a horse up to anything that has alarmed him. To punish him and force him at this point will only alarm him further. It is cruelty to force them when they are startled and indicates bad judgment. They become alarmed for two reasons. 1. The object they see excites them and 2. The correction they dread from the rider causes further concern. When they are frightened, no matter where or at what object, they should be treated kindly and petted to assure them. They should be kept wide in passing whatever they may have become frightened about. This sort of treatment with good riding and horsemanship gives the confidence to overcome their fears and they soon will pass boldly on without noticing anything they meet.

Saddle horses, ponies, and cow horses likely need to be taught to go right up to anything, but this is not true of racehorses. They are usually led where there is any chance of alarming situations and to not get excited when being led.

The colts should be taught to wear their bandages and blankets without any fuss both while in exercise and in the stall.

Colts sometimes may have a few hereditary vices or acquire tricks that are not in their best interest. These must be corrected. This takes a good and patient, yet, at the same time, a determined horseman. When he sets about to correct a fault of this sort he must not give up the contest. He must throughly defeat the colt (without severe punishment although some may be in order). A great deal can be accomplished by patience and tiring the colt out. When the rider has won his point and his horse is submissive he should pet him.

By this time the mouth should be accustomed to several bits and can be trained to keep their heads in place. They should be worked separately and in groups. They should be taught to pull away at the riders request.

In pacing a horse it is best to let them measure their own stride. To hold them back pulling with a give and take motion will keep them alive and alert.

It does not matter at first whether they lead with the left or right leg. They will learn this on the turns. They should be schooled in the starting gate with the same patience. Now with more training and galloping they are ready for the big one. If everything has gone as planned this will be one race lack of education did not adversely fix. There are so may little points along the way that can, when neglected, ruin an otherwise great race horse's future.

121

Training For The Race

Nothing fixes or predetermines a race with horses of equal ability more than the training or conditioning they have had prior to the race. Training is not a lot of hocus pocus or mysterious mastery of superior knowledge as a lot of trainers would let the owners believe. To dispell this commonly accepted facet of the horse racing business I am going to cover training from start to finish in utter simplified form. It must be remembered this is only a guide in principles. We are dealing in broad principles and every reader must remember that horses differ in character and constitution. These differences must be studied and taken into account for the overall training program to be the most successful and the ability to recognize the differences sets the good trainer apart from the ordinary. In short if the trainer's principles are sound, he will be able to deal with those individual cases that will require special treatment.

There are three stages of training: (a) Conditioning body health, (b) muscling and (c) winding with many points in each stage. It is well, at the beginning, to emphasize that three-quarters of the training is done in the horse's stall; he must be happy, contented, right inside, and eating well to properly be trained to race.

It may generally be stated that a horse is either improving or deteriorating. When he has reached his peak the trainer must be careful to ease him before he becomes stale and loses his form. A lot of races are left on the track with the morning workouts. Good trainers know they do not get purse money for crossing the wire first in the morning workouts. The proof of the pudding is the eating and the success gage of a trainer is how many races he wins (when they count).

If this chapter should succeed in creating more racing enthusiasts, or in aiding them on the road of dearly bought experience, it will have achieved its purpose.

Perhaps we should start by defining the term of training. The term "training" means the whole of the process to which the horse is subjected in order that he may perform his ultimate task, i.e., run his races with the maximum of speed, strength and endurance combined with the minimum of fatigue. As previously mentioned the training period may be definitely divided into three stages: (a) the conditioning of body health (b) muscling, and (c) winding or respiration period.

The first stage of conditioning body health has one main objective, that of getting the horse into the best possible conition. In other words, it is necessary, by all and any means, to get the horse to carry flesh. Many trainers complain about colts, bought through the sales, being too fat. They are too lazy or too impatient to take the time to reduce this fat to muscle or they just do not understand this forms a reserve which will later go to build up the horse's muscle and enable him to stand the hard preparation before him. No hard and fast rules can be laid down as to the length of time this first period will take, especially if the horse is in poor condition. The first considerations are: (a) check for worms, (b) bloodtest (c) check teeth, (d) get feet in shape and properly shod, and (e) most important get the horse happily adjusted and eating on a fixed schedule.

Successful training is a combination of the right feeding with the right work. During this period the horse should be given only such work as well enable him to digest his food to the best advantage and avoiding over-heating or over-tiring.

The feed should consist of the very best quality obtainable. As much may be given as the horse will eat. Green legumes or grass mixed with the hay will benefit the digestion. However, green food should not be given to excess or in the place of all hay as this will cause purging or diarrhea and thus defeat one's object, which is to fatten the horse.

Water is absolutely necessary for good digestion. A bucket or pail of clean water should be left in the stable and kept filled.

Ten to twelve pounds of crushed oats a day will be sufficient at this stage. Crushed oats or rolled oats are more easily and completely digested than the whole oats.

Hay and oats form the basis of the ration, but there are many tempting changes or additions that may be helpful, especially for the shy feeder. They generally benefit more by a variety of nutrition.

A double handful of bran in each feed will aid digestion, as it prevents a greedy horse from bolting down his food. If he

123

chews more he will lose less of the nutriment in the oats. A bran mash twice a week will refresh and benefit the digestive system.

Horses are fond of carrots which are high in Vitamin A and beneficial. A few slices in each feed will tempt a shy feeder to eat better. It is best to cut carrots lengthwise in order not to block the windpipe if they swallow them wrong—this seldom happens.

Sugar may be given, but the quantity should not exceed two pounds per day. Linseed or flaxseed is an excellent feed in small quantities. The oil cake or linseed oil meal may be used in place of the seed. The seed should be covered with boiling water to crack the seeds for more value. The best plan then is to mix this with bran, the resulting mash being given twice a week in place of the plain bran mash. I prefer just putting in a handful of linseed oil meal two or three times a week. Too much will have a laxative effect. The right amount will make the haircoat shine.

A little corn can be fed to advantage. It is very fattening and produces a lot of heat so should be limited.

Molasses are a good conditioner and horses are very fond of them once they have acquired the taste. Wet, dry, or sweet feed with molasses may be used. Cane molasses are better and sweeter than beet molasses. The best dried molasses are those dried on soybean hulls.

There are a number of supplements on the market. Most are harmless and some are really good. They are usually expensive and results should be the main consideration. Two of the best are Hemo-Blend and a pure diet put out by Theracon laboratories.

Poor feeders require special attention. Ascertain whether the horse's teeth require rasping. Sharp, rough teeth will prevent a horse from masticating his food as he should and will generally make him bear in or out when racing. For the bad feeder, vary the ration with the various extras mentioned. Feed in small quantities and more often. There are a number of digestive stimulants that can be resorted to in these cases. Good veterinary advice should be solicited in problem cases. Bad teeth will cause some horses to bolt their food. Bran in the feed will largely prevent this after giving the teeth the required attention. Two or three fist-size stones in the feed tub will answer the same purpose or some trainers put the salt block in the feed tub so the horse will have to nose around it.

There are a number of signs indicating the state of the horse's health. A horse badly out of sorts will indicate this by the condition of his hair coat, which loses its glossy sheen and becomes dry and dull. The skin loses its pliability and the eyes lack lustre. The droppings should be observed closely. Hard dry droppings indicate fever or over-heating. Loose, frequent droppings mean enteritis. Horses that eat their droppings require salt and a block should always be available in the manger for the horse to lick.

Enteritis is an inflammation of the intestine or bowel. This diarrhea is evidenced by frequent, very soft, and foul—smelling droppings. There are many good remedies available from the local veterinarian. Whole oats in the droppings indicate poor digestion due to a lack of mastication. Rolling, crimping, or crushing the oats will help.

The next few paragraphs will deal with stable management. Feed at least four times a day for best results. Three times a day is an absolute minimum. A light feed first thing in the morning, a feed at 10 or 10:30 a.m., at 4 p.m., and the last and largest feed at 8:30 or 9 p.m. is the best program. Many trainers give the large feeding around 4 p.m. which is the last feeding in a three times a day schedule. Most horses eat better at night. The stable should be airy, but not drafty; in cold weather use more blankets—do not reduce the ventilation or use artificial heat.

The bedding should be removed every day, the foul straw being separated from the clean and thrown away. The floor of the stable should be allowed to air for as long a time as possible before the bedding is replaced. This is done by cleaning the stall as soon as the horse goes out to work or exercise and spreading the straw just before he is returned to the stall after being cooled out.

A good disinfection program consists of a monthly washing of the stalls with creosol or other disinfectant and limeing the floor once or twice a month.

The feed tub should be thoroughly cleaned before every feed with no trace of the previous meal being allowed to remain in it. Grain and forage should be kept free of dirt and dust and should be protected from cats, dogs and mice. The smell of these disgusts most horses to a point they may refuse to eat.

The absolute necessity of a thorough grooming every day cannot be exaggerated. In the winter it is best to clip the horse. This facilitates grooming and prevents sweating at work, chills and colds.

All horses need exercise. The horse may be ridden, at a walk, every other day for an hour or an hour and a half and led beside a quiet horse on the intermediate days at a walk or trot. The periods of trotting may be gradually increased up to ten minutes at a time, but the horse's sweating should be taken as the first indication of the work to be given. The horse at this stage should do the minimum work which will keep him healthy.

Horses are largely creatures of habit and it is during this first period that we must encourage good habits and discourage the bad ones. The horse should be allowed to develop the habit of eating at regular intervals and looking forward to his food; of becoming in fact a good "doer" by habit. Moreover, it is well known that fat, placid—tempered horses suffer less from nerves than thin, fidgety ones. A hearty appetite and comparative immunity from nervous distraction are invaluable assets in a racehorse.

Next comes the muscling period now that we have the horse in a good health state so he will be able to stand a lot of work without falling apart. He is fat, round and soft. This fat and flesh must be turned into muscle by methodical and progressive work. At first a slight increase of exercise and a prolongation of the period of trotting will be all that is necessary. After a week or two the horse may be given short canters of two to three minutes duration. If we divide the whole period into three parts, each lasting one month, the following program of work may be taken as a rough guide with the amount of trotting and cantering being gradually increased throughout the peroid. Monday—walking exercise, a little trotting. Tuesday—walking exercise, a canter. Wednesday—Walking and trotting exercise. Thursday—Walking and a little trotting. Friday—

Walking and trotting exercise. Saturday—Walking exercise and a canter. Sunday—Rest.

The first exercise is critical. On no account should the horse be allowed to approach his full extension during these canters. He should be made to develop an effortless, swinging stride and learn how to handle and use himself. Towards the end of the third month he will require half—speed gallops on good going, the length and frequency being gradually increased. The object of the muscling period is to prepare the legs to withstand the really severe strain of the fast work in the third and last period. Undue hurry may well cause a breakdown and loss of time, if not worse. At all times during exercise the horse's attention must be kept on his work and not allowed to wander. Horses, like humans, must concentrate in order to derive benefit from physical exercise. He should be made to walk out at a good four miles per hour, to trot briskly collected well into the bridle, and to canter with his head out and down with his center of balance well forward. In his canters he should be taught to lead with either leg. All work should be done out of doors.

Horses that have not been in training before may have to be taught to gallop properly. For this a standing martingale may be found to be very useful. If used, it should be so adjusted that the horse cannot raise his nose higher than his withers, this being the only fault that will necessitate its use.

Horses work better with company. Whenever possible two or more horses should be galloped together, the pace being fixed by one of them. The others are forbidden to exceed it on any pretext.

A horse that pulls too hard to be galloped in company must be worked alone at this stage. It is very bad for a young horse to find himself left behind during an exercise gallop. Horses should therefore gallop level and close together.

All work must be regulated by the state of the horse's health, appetite, and legs, which should remain unaffected or the amount of work regulated to prevent further complications. The horse's legs require constant attention. No work should be attempted unless you are satisfied that there is no sign of tenderness or puffiness in the legs. Tender or swollen legs may be treated

127

as follows: A flannel bandage soaked in as hot water as one can stand should be wrapped *loosely* around the affected part. A piece of oiled silk or plastic should be then wrapped over the flannel bandage to retain the heat. This can all be kept in place by a second over all bandage. Clay plastered on a swollen limb and left to dry for 24 hours is an excellent reducer of inflammation. By applying clay to two legs the presence of heat in one or the other, otherwise undetectable, can be established, the clay on the affected leg drying sooner than that on the sound leg. Bumps and swellings of small importance may be painted with iodine or mild blister. The hair should be cut off or clipped off before the application is made. This iodine treatment may be continued for a week or so or as long as is necessary to get results. Bandages in this case should be left off as they cause the iodine to set up too much irritation. Shoes are discussed elsewhere, but they are better too heavy than too light and must be equal to the wear and tear required of them. Ordinarily service shoes are too heavy and racing plates are too light. Something in between is ideal.

The ration during the muscling period should be more substantial than during the first or "health" stage. The green food and mashes should be reduced and the oats increased gradually from 12 pounds to 16 pounds per day. Sugar, or such additional food as is productive of heat and energy, may be continued, but care should be taken that this is not overdone. Loss of appetite will generally mean that the horse is doing more work than is momentarily good for him. The remedy is obviously, to slack off a bit. A linseed and bran mash once a week, on the evening preceding the day on which the horse rests, will help to keep the system in good order and his digestive processes functioning better.

It is very important for the trainer to have a clear idea of the recognized exercising paces. These are called the canter, the half-speed gallop and the fast gallop.

First of all the canter is actually a gallop at a pace greatly inferior or less than the racing pace. It is a very slow even swinging gallop.

Secondly, the half-speed gallop needs to be well understood and practiced with utmost care. The horse is well extended but kept down to a pace considerably below his fastest. Such a gallop keeps him from getting over nerved up, heated up, and hard to cool out.

Third is the fast gallop. This allows a horse, *over a short distance*, to gallop at his best pace or maximum effort. A sluggish horse may even have to be pushed in his fast gallops, though this is rarely the case, especially when horses work in company. Fast gallops should not be given during the muscling period and half-speed gallops only with discretion, alternating with canters of gradually increasing length. Pushing the horse to faster speeds during the muscling period will help nothing and likely will be of considerable damage.

Now we will get to the respiratory or last stage of fixing the horse to run. The horse's wind can only be developed by means of fast gallops or work such as swimming, trotting up long steep hills, etc., which exercise the lungs in the same way. A swimming pool for lame horses is a great way to keep them in shape without aggravating the injury in most cases. Such alternatives could be employed, also, when the ground is frozen or too muddy for regular work. Fast gallops entail very great muscular effort. They should be given as often as possible with caution regarding the state of the horses health. They form in themselves an ample days exercise, especially if the horse is walked two or three miles before the gallop. They are by far the most severe part of the preparation of a horse for racing and only careful and progressive work in the earlier stages of training will enable the horse to undergo them without grave risk of injury. Two fast gallops a week, for a period of two months are about all a horse should be given. Begin with 400 to 500 yards and increase the distance little by little to 1500 yards or a mile. The distance should depend entirely on what the horse can do each time. Never try to do a certain distance in a certain time while training. This is what a lot of well meaning trainers do every morning and get their horses stale before they get to the races. The general rule should be to ease up on the horse as soon as he stops pulling. When two or more horses are galloped together, take care that the distance is within the powers of the least fit one. Let them all be eased up together lest the weaker one becomes a quitter. Having due regard to individual

129

peculiarities and to the length of the race for which you propose to enter the following is a suggested weekly program during the last period of training: Monday and Thursday—fast gallop, 400 to 1500 yards. Tuesday and Friday—walking exercise or ponying. Wednesday—Two 1000 yard canters. Saturday—Half-speed gallop 1½ to 2 miles. Sunday—Rest. This is, of course, a rough guide only. Nervous horses are inclined to run up light or lose weight with fast work, but these are usually better in their wind and would require less work to get in shape.

Regularity of the routine is a very important point in the training of racehorses. Arrange every other part of the work so that the horse leaves and returns to his stable at approximately the same hours each day. Two hours out of doors on the move will be enough and a great deal more than most horses get which is one of the reasons there are so many lame horses. Many races are fixed every day with too much or too little exercise.

The amount of weight carried at exercise is an important factor. The horse should invariably be ridden in his fast gallops by a light weight. This not only reduces the risk of injury to his legs but also gives a better idea of the horse's progress. A horse that will gallop a mile with a light jockey and pull all the way is probably fit to run and just because he would not do this with a lot more weight does not make him less fit. On his slower work, the question of weight is less important but of course, real heavy weights should be avoided. I would say 150 pounds at the outside is as much as the average horse can carry, even at slow exercise, without great risk of injury.

The working distances are not as critical as might be supposed.

It is not necessary to work the horse over long distances. One trained over a short distance properly may well win races over a longer distance. A horse can stand training to stay up to three and a half miles, but this will not necessarily help him to win shorter races.

Since every aspect of the training period has a bearing on the outcome of every race it may be well here to include some comments on the training saddlery. As a general rule use a thick racing snaffle bit with arms or large rings. A light-mouthed horse will go better in a rubber snaffle. Avoid double snaffles except for fast work and even then whenever possible. The horse will play with the steel in his mouth and may develop a faulty head-carriage. Reins should be solid, preferably of plaited leather or rubber covered. Use a nose band adjusted to prevent the horse opening his mouth wide and yawning. A standing martingale will help to fix the position of a young horse's head and prevent him pulling to one side or the other. Be sure his teeth are not bothering him if he seems to want to pull either way. Except for galloping, use a large, comfortable hunting saddle. For galloping, a smaller steeplechase saddle weighing five to six pounds is best. Always use two girths and take care that the girth buckles lie flat on the saddle and are not next to the horses skin. Use a light pad or saddle-cloth and if necessary use a wool pad over the withers.

Training boots are better than bandages as the bandages take time and great care to put on and when badly adjusted may easily cause lameness owing to the uneven pressure. Actually, the force of impact on the horse's forelegs at a gallop is so enormous (several tons) that any form of boot or bandage is practically useless except against knocks, blows, etc. from the hind feet. Trotters and pacers in most instances should be well booted to prevent injuries. The rule, therefore, should be: Nothing on the horse's legs, except for galloping in heavy going or jumping then boots rather than bandages.

Now for a few remarks about the walk and the trot. Do not ride walking or trotting exercise with your stirrups adjusted as though for a flat race. It is useless, unsightly, and uncomfortable; moreover, it throws much dead-weight on to the horse's back—a thing to be avoided at all times. Keep the horse up to his work. Keep a straight line and continuous contact with his mouth, but hold the reins long rather than short, consistent with the contact. To keep the young horse up to his bridle at a walk entails more riding (leg and hand) than one would think. When trotting the upper part of the body should be forward, the hands low. Encourage the horse to carry his head low and to use his shoulders. Avoid posting in a saddle or descending with a bump into the saddle at every other stride; ride fairly long from the thigh.

Now for the canter and the gallop. In the gallop, and to a

131

lesser degree, in the canter, the horse's weight is thrown forward; he pursues, in effect, his center of gravity. The weight on the forelegs at the gallop is very great making it very necessary to adopt a position which will relieve the horse of the riders weight as much as possible. This weight should be over the horse's center of gravity. At slow paces the center of gravity is roughly above the girths or a trifle behind them. At fast paces it is, vertically above the withers. This is due to the advanced and lowered head carriage of the horse when extended. The actual length of the stirrup will vary in each individual case of man and horse and no rule can be laid down. Just remember that is why they were made adjustable to get them right. The stirrup should be shorter for a fast exercise gallop on the flat than for a race involving obstacles. Time speed is the sole object of the fast gallop.

Position in the saddle must also be right to accomplish our goal. Do not stand up in the stirrups in the generally accepted sense of the term. The knee should be below and slightly behind the withers. The lower part of the leg should incline backwards from the knee, the grip being maintained from the knee to the calf. The seat should be as far back as possible without touching the saddle, the head and shoulders correspondingly forward and down. The whole body should pivot from the knees, which must remain fixed and the lower leg should be wedged between the stirrup and the knee to prevent the latter moving from its pivoting point. I should throw in the proper positions for the bettor while watching and after a race as I have seen a great many contorted figures after every race, but this action on the part of the fans really has no bearing on the outcome of the races so we will omit proper posture for them.

The reins are a lot of your communication with the horse. As a general rule hold the reins as long as possible consistent with being able to hold your horse. In a race, you may at any time have to give the horse all the rein you can to enable him to recover from a blunder. Also, within reason, the longer your reins are, the less your horse will pull.

Horses work best in company. Horses at exercise should gallop in company, except very hard pullers or excitable horses which will have to be worked alone. The horses must remain knee to

132

knee throughout the gallop. This is absolutely essential, since it is very bad for a racehorse, especially a young one, to be left behind during a gallop. He will get in the habit of staying there and think it is where he belongs.

Now you fans know how some of your horses were trained that should have won to save the grocery money. Every exercise gallop should be preceded by a canter of a few hundred yards, to warm up the horse and set him on his legs; the gallop should not start from a standstill, but the horse should walk, trot, and finally gallop off level. Never allow an exercise gallop to develop into a trail. After the gallop the horses should pull up gradually—any undue strain on tired tendons may cause a breakdown.

Now, provided everthing has gone well, we are ready to race. If it is a young horse he has been schooled in the starting gate. Always plan a race with a full knowledge of the horse's and jockey's capabilities. Practice alone can give the correct tactics to be employed in ever-varying conditions. Sometimes the track is deep on the inside and it is best to stay out etc., if your horse has a burst of speed for the finish you can afford to let someone else set the pace for three quarters of the way, but do not let any horse get so far ahead that you will not be able to catch him. This sounds simple, but you must know what your horse and everyone in the race can do. If, on the other hand, your horse is a "one-pace" horse, you must keep him at that pace throughout the race, regardless of your position at any time. A waiting race can be ridden just as well in front of the field as among or behind it, but a complete knowledge of the fastest pace your horse can maintain over the whole distance is essential. Take the shortest way without interfering with other horses. In rounding a bend, begin your turn before the corner actually begins. Notice the other horses. If a certain horse is lugging in or out be on the other side. Avoid being level with and on the outside of a hard puller going round a bend. He may run out and take you with him. At best you will prevent him from running out, which he might otherwise do giving you an advantage. If you are riding level with a tired horse force the pace. This will disturb him using up his energy at a faster pace. Do not fight it out with a hard pulling horse. Let him go his own pace for a bit, then ease him up to the pace you desire, it will be easier on both of you and in any case a bit of early lead is a good thing to have gained. If your horse blunders and loses ground do not hustle him to make up for this loss all at once. This will unsettle him and you will never finish as you should. Let him make up his distance gradually when he has recovered from the incident. Always try to get a good start out of the gate; it is so much ground gained which others must make up and in no way alters your waiting tactics should you have decided to use them. Getting a horse settled after coming out of the starting gate is just as important as being in front. Once he is set he is gaining on all of those that are not. Any protests or objections should be calmly presented. It is scarcely necessary to stress the necessity of avoiding any apparent lack of good manners, courtesy or discipline. If you can not be in the money you might as well be last, so do not force your weary horse (I am saying this for the owners benefit) into a position that means nothing. He will be all the better for being allowed to finish quietly in such a case. Weigh out.

If you can avoid using your whip do so. A single sharp cut is usually better than constant use. To be of any use a whip must be properly used. To begin with, to use a whip and keep still at the same time is extremely difficult; those that can do it require no advice on the subject of riding races. This comes from long practice. The point is—shifting weight may do more harm than the whip does good. The beginner will generally do better to ride his horse home with his hands.

Before the race the horse should be given his regular morning feed and groomed then given a half hour's walk. Five hours before the race starts he should be tied up or muzzled to prevent him from eating or drinking. The exception to this is a high quality low residue diet. This can be fed with an extra boost of energy about four hours prior to the race. If boots or bandages are to be used they should be put on with the utmost care just before the horse leaves to go to the paddock.

After the race let the horse have a few swallows of water. Give him a bath rather hurriedly. Remove the excess water with a scraper and put a blanket over him from head to tail. Walk him until dry. He can then be given a rub down with alcohol or liniment and bandaged. Give him a mash, bed him down and level the stall. The legs should be massaged briskly after having been subjected to the strain of exercise gallops or a race.

Keeping the horse in condition will be a problem. Once he is fit to run holding racing condition is a challenge especially if he is a stakes horse with time lapes between engagements. The racing calendar will have to be studied and decide on a plan of campaign, keeping in mind certain races which you think your horse can win. Once a program is decided upon it should only be modified in cases of necessity caused by illness, etc. In your programming you should include (a) races, specially selected to suit your horse and which you definitely hope to win and (b) races which take place a week or so before each of your selected events and which will serve as training gallops. Here we are back behind the scenes fixing races—a necessary evil to giving a top performance and all the more reason fans should understand the whole business of racing. It will be more enjoyable and more profitable that way. Your horse will, of course, always run to win, but the racecourse is, within reason, the best final training ground and you may justify, for this reason, entering a horse in a race in which he stands a poor chance. The cardinal rule is as to distances should be borne in mind. Do not, for instance, run your horse over a long race October 1 if you hope to see him win an important event October 8 over the same distance. Few horses can take this rigorous a schedule. Most can race once a week, but not an all out effort every week. As a general rule, a horse, once in racing condition, will require comparatively little work provided his engagements are not too far apart. Two fast gallops a week during which he is to run, with one canter and walking exercise on the other days will be ample for most horses.

A few words on punishment and reward might be appropriate at this juncture. It is unhappily a fact that consciously or otherwise, the majority of people responsible for the education of young horses are a good deal more free with punishment than rewards. The following points should be borne in mind:

1. Punishment for refusing something he likely did not understand or was not in the habit of doing is not constructive. A

reward for doing it right will give the horse a definite liking for his work.

2. Make sure that the horse deserves punishment before you inflict it. A young uneducated horse never needs severe punishment. He will be ruined by any such treatment. Slovenly work or ill-temper on the part of a horse known to be sweet-tempered and a capable performer is almost invariably due to ill-health, to pain caused by ill-fitting saddlery, tight bandages, sharp teeth or some such reason and the cause, not the effect, requires treatment and understanding or vice-versa.

3. Never lose your temper on any provocation. You are dealing with a dumb animal. Do not reduce yourself below him by getting angry with him—besides he is much stronger and a fit of anger can be very dangerous. He could fix you before you get a chance to fix the next race. Good luck.

Ability To Stay Fixes Races

The ambition of every man that breeds racehorses is to produce a good stayer or distance horse. Proof positive that this is no small task is made evident by the large number of horses entered in the Kentucky Derby and the few that run. Roughly sixteen thousand were eligible last year when they were born with only a dozen starters. Further proof of this is the number of short races (seven furlongs or less) at any given meet.

It is only natural then to ask the question: Why cannot all horses run a distance? The answer to this question is that all horses can run a distance; it's the time they take that makes the important difference. There are three important factors to contend with relating to "staying". We must take into consideration: 1, Distance; 2, Time, and 3, Weight. We must try and find out the difference between horses that can sprint six furlongs in 1.12 and the horses that can go two miles in 3.24 and ask how they differ from horses that can go 80 miles from sunrise to sunset.

If a number of racing trainers, breeders, and owners were shown a group of racehorses not knowing the horses or their pedigrees, I seriously doubt that they could distinguish the sprinters from the distance horses just by observation. Two horses can be built almost exactly alike with one being a sprinter while the other will go the long mile. I have made close inspections of most of the Champion Thoroughbred and Standardbreds of the last decade. Very few have features so outstanding as to place them far above others in appearance alone.

If it were possible to tell a horse's total ability by their conformation then yearling sales would go out of business. The best horsemen of the generation go to sales and bid for what they think is best—not from just conformation. They have the pedigrees, performances of close relatives and a wealth of other information at hand. With all of this they still get fooled. Some pretty cheap yearlings have won the Kentucky Derby as well as all other stakes and conversely some pretty expensive horses never make it to the post or if they do they never get to the winners circle even in a cheap race.

What, let us ask, is the secret of a good horse and more specifically "staying power".

We may preconclude that all horses expected to race will have the required bone and muscle structure with proper development of these components. However, this development must be of a particular pattern. This, of course, is obvious; a Clydesdale has far more muscle and bone than any racehorse, but the type of muscle is of no use for speed, though suitable for endurance and we shall see later on that this kind of endurance is very different from the staying power we are discussing. Mere size is not the secret. Many excellent stayers are relatively small horses while some of the finest looking horses are non-stayers. But it is because size so largely influences one's mind that high prices are paid for well-grown colts in the hope that they will prove to be Derby winners. If we study the history of the evolution of the racehorse we shall find some justification for this idea, for the present day racehorse is a bigger animal than he formerly was and they perform better. While the average horse nowadays, among the better horses, would be over 16 hands, we find, if we go back to 1745 that 15.2 (the height of Sampson) was considered very large. Captain Hayes thought that English horses had increased an average of an inch in height between 1867 and 1897 and that

137

the average horse was six inches taller than he was 200 years ago. The smaller horses seldom win the Derby so size is somewhat of a factor.

Native Dancer proves the size of the horse is not the essential point; with size there must go a particular type of heart, if a horse is going to stay. While large size is the rule among stayers, many small horses may be good stayers and have the required pace.

We may admit that some sprinters are different in conformation from stayers yet the real difference lies hidden from the sight of everyone for the difference is in the particular kind of heart that the animal has inherited. It may be concluded then, that staying sires produce staying stock which has long been observed. We are only pointing out that the "staying heart" is the reason. Of course there are exceptions, but these only go to prove the rules.

It must be recognized, as a fact, that just as a man may transmit his nose, his eyes, or his ears to his sons and daughters, just so may a horse transmit his bone, his muscle, his color and his *heart* to his sons and daughters. So we have solved the secret: It matters not whether a horse is black or brown or Chestnut—the essential thing the animal has to possess in order that he may stay is a staying heart (an inherited characteristic). While we are discussing the sire, it must be remembered the mother or dam has just as much influence so her pedigree must be carefully considered also.

Some horses begin their careers in brilliant fashion and look from their first performances as if they would stay. They go off at peak performance and never return. These horses likely had poor hearts to start with and were used too much when they were two year olds or even as three year olds they may be asked to do more than their hearts can stand. The results are a dilated heart that makes them a failure later on. They likely put out an honest effort but their strained hearts just cannot respond. These horses can be useful for shorter distances if used with care.

Let me make my meaning about the dilated heart quite clear. First of all, one must understand that the heart is a pump; that its walls are composed of muscle—though not of the same kind of muscle that the flesh of the body and legs is made of. The valves of this wonderful pump are made of very strong tissue like a thick plastic sheet. Considering the amount of work that the heart is called upon to do, getting no entire rest either day or night, the wonder is that it can keep on for sixty or seventy years in man and twenty or more years in the horse, in such a very efficient manner.

Now, if a man who has been working in an office gets "run down" from overwork, and decides to take a vacation and part of that vacation is devoted to climbing mountains he will often come back to his office in worse condition than when he started. What has happened? He has tried to make his heart muscle do work which it was not prepared to do. He has strained his heart (and perhaps could have had a heart attack). In other words, this wonderful pump has done its best to cope with the extra work that it was called upon to do and while it may have succeeded, the effort has effected it and the results of the extra work performed is that the heart has become dilated. For the time being, it is not able to do the ordinary work that it is called upon to perform. This heart may come back, providing it is rested and properly nursed, but if the subject in question tries to drive it further and does not rest it to allow complete recuperation then this heart will fail to do ordinary work and will most certainly fail if asked to perform extra work.

What happens to the untrained office man happens over and over again on the racecourses to horses that are asked to win races when they are not "ready"—that is they are only half trained; and while they may succeed they often dilate their unprepared hearts in their honest efforts to succeed. They may never be able to turn in a top performance again even though they show no lameness or other outward symptoms of distress.

To simplify, when a horse is "ready" and his muscles are fit and he is quite able to run a mile and carry a decent weight, he is asked to run a mile and a half; he makes a mighty effort and from that day on he never does himself justice in a race, for his effort has strained his heart and not being allowed to rest, his heart remains dilated till the end of his days at the track. Many of these horses could be saved for useful careers if due consideration was given before asking them to do something they were not prepared for or even giving them proper care after discovering some damage had been done. Thus the heart fixes a lot of races, even unbeknowns to the owners and trainers.

Let me say that a heart that is dilated may recover if the animal is properly rested and many came back to redeem themselves after some very poor efforts.

It may be properly concluded that you can't make a stayer out of a horse that has not inherited a staying heart regardless of the training. The idea that if you want a mile and a half horse then train him over that distance is absurd. You must, of course, get the animal's muscles in a fit condition and this can be done by slow, long work, and by running him at a fast pace from time to time over shorter distances. However, you can't make his heart carry him two miles at the requisite pace if he does not inherit the proper kind of heart, no matter how you train him! It is also true that a horse, in most cases, stays better the older he gets, because his heart improves (he has had more training).

After all, in staying, it is the pace that tells. In other words, a great stayer must have the power to run at a great pace all the way and to have something out of the ordinary to finish with and unless the horse has inherited a staying heart it is quite impossible for him to finish well.

It has often been observed that great stayers are inclined to hang behind in the early stages of a long distance race. This is quite characteristic of the stayer. If you hurry him too much in the eary stages of a long race you will defeat him. The reason is that his heart must not be asked to do too much too quickly. You must let him gradually get his heart beating in a slow, methodical way, and then he adjusts well. When the time comes everything is coordinated and functioning in rhythm. His lungs being unimpeded in their work cooperate with the heart and supply the necessary oxygen for staying power. If, however, you hurry the stayer too much in the first part of the race the circulation becomes upset—that is, the circulation in the lungs causes an engorgement that interferes with the breathing of the horse and impairs the smooth working of his heart.

140

Some stayers have a particular kind of heart which enables them to sprint and at the same time it allows them to begin quickly in a distance race, to get a good position early and to keep their places. These horses can sprint like pure sprinters and be perfect stayers because they can take up any position they like in a field regardless of distance. They can go the distance or sprint with the best of them—a great combination to have as they can get in nearly any race and do well.

There are some horses who can run in front of the field in a distance race and keep up the pace. They run a waiting race in front. These horses, however, are often not true stayers and can be beaten by one that is a stayer.

I must throw in a few words on endurance which is not the same thing as staying. The difference between the two is a matter of pace. For instance, quarter horses can outrun most any Thoroughbred for 440 yards, but cannot go fast for any distance yet they are capable of going all day long with many short bursts of speed which make them excellent for working cattle. There is a different type of heart than one that enables a horse to go two miles at a very rapid pace. The quarterhorse has to have lots of heart and must be a good type of heart, but it is a different type to the staying heart. The endurance heart is also well illustrated when we come to deal with jumping horses. We all know of horses that could only get a mile on the flat track yet when these horses become steeplechase horses or hurdlers they win in brilliant fashion. The simple explanation is that it is only a matter of pace. A hurdler can run two miles, but the time he takes would leave him a furlong or two behind in a weight-for-age race. Therefore, when we say a horse can stay, we imply the possession of a heart that can stand the enormous strain of running two miles in, say, 3.26 carrying a good weight.

If we walk and carry a weight we can go a certain distance and not feel fatigued, but if we attempt to run with the same weight we soon find out the difference. In walking we always have one foot on the ground; in running we are entirely off the ground part of the time. In walking we put little strain on the heart, for the foot that is always on the ground helps us. While in running we have to lift the whole weight of the

141

body from the ground so we call on the heart to do much more work. If then, we have to carry a weight and run, we have not only to lift the body from the ground but also the weight. Naturally, the heart is called upon to do more work and becomes exhausted in proportion to the amount of weight carried, the distance it is carried, and the time consumed. The heart muscle, as matter of fact, in great exertion has to work at eight times its normal rate and so becomes tired and the effect of fatigue is simply to reduce the output of the heart. This is the reason it is fairly easy to accurately handicap horses with a few extra pounds of weight.

Weight acts on the heart in the same way that distance does— that is weight tires the heart after a certain amount of energy has been expended and distance exhausts the heart in galloping on account of the amount of work required from the heart. A horse may trot fifty miles that cannot gallop two. The reason being that in the trot his body is not entirely off the ground whereas in the gallop it is. It is the pace that tells. This is the reason a chapter covering locomotion is included to explain why the very actions of the horse fix races. Top trainers keenly observe how the horse leaves the ground on the gallop as well as how he lands. The time lapse and the distance he reaches each time greatly affect pace and the amount of energy expended.

There are many horses capable of carrying a huge weight at a fast pace for a short distance and yet they cannot carry a light weight for a long distance. Therefore, to fix a race in ones favor the trainer must know what kind of heart his horse has, i.e., just what the particular animal is capable of doing.

With electrocardiographs a great deal can be determined about a horses ability. This can be detected at a very young age and should be used more as a basis for selecting racing stock. Properly trained personnel is the main bottleneck, but as more experience is gained in interpreting the electrocardiograms more of the risk will be removed from buying horses that do not have the heart to do the job and hopefully fewer will be ruined at an early age when this whole situation is better understood by everyone interested in horses.

The bettors and racing fans will do well to study past performances and consider whether the horse has been subjected to any great stress in his last race or two. This explains why many favorites get beaten every day around the world. Many factors fix the outcome of any given race. The type and conition of the horse's heart has the most influence on the outcome and gets the least consideration. A careful study of past performances as well as the horses pedigree will reveal more than a stethoscope. Horses inherit the ability to run. If pushed beyond their ability there is trouble ahead. Heart muscle heals very slowly under ideal conditions and never with less favorable treatment.

Fixing Races With Sex

Even sex gets into the act of fixing horse races and it is more deeply seated than romantic involvement notwithstanding Tesio's Contention that this is definitely a factor. Many concede Tesio is one of the foremost authorities on breeding race horses. One of his most accomplished race horses resulted from an unplanned mating where romance intervened. As this romantic Italian tells the story, the mare was being walked to a selected stallion for service. She would have nothing to do with this well planned mate. Finally in disgust, she was being led back to her stable by a different route which took them by another stallion. It was definitely love at first whinny and both the mare and stallion carried on until Tesio decided to breed her then and there even though this stallion was not regarded as being worthy of this mare. A real champion resulted from this mating. Could be the chemistry was affected by whatever attraction there was between these two equine lovers. It is hard to argue with results and Tesio went on to breed many more very successful campaigners for the turf.

Delving into the statistics of Kentucky Derby winners gives us further evidence sex is a factor in racing results. While there are many nominated for this Classic and usually one or more female starters, only one has ever won the Derby. A handful of geldings have won the roses, but by and large it is a contest for the real he-man horses with all of their being. The same is true of the second leg of the triple crown with only a few

143

more of the distaff side making it to the Winners Circle. Among the Standardbreds there have been some pretty fair records set by fillies and mares, but the four greatest namely, Greyhound, Billy Direct, Adios Butler and the great Bret Hanover all prove the males get there first and are the fastest.

When it is a choice between evenly rated stallion, geldings or mares in the same race, the educated bettor will chose them in that order.

Hormones, especially testosterone for geldings is used quite extensively as an equalizer. A combination of male and female hormones under the proper conditions and in proper balance are more effective as this more nearly approximates the natural production of these same hormones. Indiscriminate use of any hormones will likely do more harm than good which rules out the use of these very potent drugs as stimulants. There can be no question that well regulated sexual drive has a great bearing on race results.

Sex can have a very adverse affect on racing results. A mare in heat will not only upset the field, but is not likely to perform very well. Since few mares are spayed or unsexed their careers as racing animals are somewhat limited. There are hormone implants that can be placed under the skin to help keep them under control. With the advent of birth control pills for humans the time will likely soon be here to control estrus in racing mares.

Not all of the unpleasant aspects of sex are confined to the female. Many males become uncontrollable as studs and must be castrated to become more manageable. There is little doubt in my mind that this is too often resorted to by trainers that have ran out of ideas or patience. Of course many colts are castrated on the farm so they can be run with the females. While we are being philosophical about this matter, racing could be greatly benefited if many more were castrated. This would include many standing at stud. All sincere advocates of improving the breed will agree there are too many counterfeits producing inferior racing stock. This is true of neariy everything bred for performance, but Thoroughbreds and Standardbreds lead the parade. With the stakes getting higher and the competition keener every year more and more mediocre stallions will have

144

to be retired from service as better breeding is available to take their place.

There is a lot of irony associated with sex and racing. One of the greatest of all race horses in the Thoroughbred world is Kelso, a gelding. Nor is he alone, as many are castrated before they get a chance to prove their ability.

After a stallion has proved he is a great racehorse and is retired to stud he must prove he can reproduce his greatness. Some never get a proper chance to accomplish this since the best mares are mated to already proven sires. Thus a new stallion must prove his ability on mares that even the proven stallions might flunk out on. Once a stallion produces a stakes winner he gradually gets more select mares and families that helps his chances of becoming a great producer of racing stock.

At best the stallion is only 50% of the success of any breeding program. If he is mated with families that he does not 'nick' with he will be a great deal less than 50% effective. Mating by known families is a better plan than just mating two outstanding individuals.

Another observation over the years indicates most stallions that race hard take a few years to settle down to being good breeders. Few have produced outstanding individuals in their first or second crop of foals even if they were lucky enough to be mated to good producing dams. Apparently the body chemistry gets calmed down after a year or two and if the stallion has not been written off or relegated to breeding inferior mares his true ability comes to light. By the same token horses that made good records and were retired early, usually because of an injury, have produced better first foal crops than those that had several years of hard racing.

This might be a good place to put in a few comments to defend the, all too prevelant, practice of castrating horses without proper reasons.

Now, I will be the first to admit there are too many second rate studs in the racing business and recognize the fact that the whole industry could be upgraded by castrating well over half of those standing for service. However, the other side of the coin must be dealt with. A fair number of potentially great stallions have been reduced to geldings simply because the trainers couldn't think of any other excuse for their non productive training efforts at the time.

Most "horses" race better than their gelding counterparts, just as most horses have a slight edge over mares. It would seem, then, that the horse's potential is being reduced by a couple of quick slashes with the scapel and a few seconds with the emasculators. This may be necessary to change the habits of some very "studdish" "bull-headed" horses and may be desirable where males and females have to run together. Although it has not been scientifically documented, there is some belief that stallions tend to get heavy on the neck and forequarters that has a tendency to break them down. If this theory could be proven it would be a valid reason for very early castration of colts that do not have the very best bloodlines.

I can recall many instances of recomendations by veterinarians, that horses be castrated that I felt were unjustified. In many instances I felt their only reasons had to be: 1. They couldn't find anything else wrong or 2. They thought the surgical fee would come in handy or 3. Maybe they did it at the trainers request simply because he had temporarily ran out of ideas.

True, castration, is a simple operation that is not very hazardous, but it is so permanent more consideration should be given to this elective surgery. Not only is some of the horse's ability being sacrificed, a great deal of his value goes down the drain when his procreative ability is removed. A stallion that proves himself and goes lame can be used for breeding and have as much or more value for that purpose than for racing. The same is true for a mare. When she can't run any more she can be valuable as a broodmare, but when a gelding can no longer make it at the races he is generally sold by the pound—not a very glamorous ending for an aristocrat, with a long line of ancestors that made the grade then had a chance to carry on and except the someone's sudden whim this noble stud might have done the same, but Cest la vie; into the can or glue pot.

The point is that a lot of races are fixed by the emasculator. Many horses could have raced better and some great geldings might have joined the ranks of our better sires if that simple little operation had been postponed for a while. There are many that will argue the other way. They will hold steadfastly that

146

the horse in question would never have made it to the races without the operation. I will concede this is likely true in a very few cases, but a little more patience with those might have been rewarded.

The whole point is, that too many promising horses are gelded without sufficient reasons and too many not so promising ones are kept for breeding. Performance and pedigree should be the criteria for selecting breeding stock. When gelded, a lot of horses lose some of their performance ability. Every particle of ability is needed to win races and have good racing. Let's at least take a second look before performing that simple operation that will fix that horses racing ability for the rest of his life.

Pain Fixes Races

A book on races being fixed may not appear at first sight, to be the place to discuss pain. However, horses are subject to many painful conditions that do affect their performance. A probe in depth of the whole subject of pain and factors that lower the threshold of pain are quite revealing. Richard Behan published a book on pain in 1915 quoting over fifty pages of the names and writings of scientists that had attempted to define pain. This list included physiologists, anatomists and philosophers. Since pain is obviously an extremely complicated fact of life it will serve our purpose here to accept it as a reality and aspire only to enumerate the occurrences and the detrimental effects on race horses.

The phenomenon of pain has evolved for a definite purpose. It is so common a thing among all higher forms of animal life that we must conclude it is probably for the good of the individual and not punishment or for the harm, as pain is sometimes considered. Briefly, it is an important device employed by nature to protect the individual from injury or from the result of injury. Certainly any measures taken to relieve pain should be accompanied with consideration of why the pain exists and what damage will be done to body structures if the pain is "blocked" or "killed". Indescriminate use of pain killing drugs can ruin a horse permanently. In other words the cause

147

of the pain should be diagnosed and eliminated instead of just trying to eliminate the pain.

A single definition of pain is "a mental interpretation of injurious stimulus." The whole reason for pain interpretation is for protection. A horse that is sore on one leg automatically shifts as much weight as possible to the opposite. This extra burden generally results in damage or unsoundness to the side opposite the original trouble if excessive demands are made while the horse has a sore spot. This is the reason most unsound conditions require a rest period before racing or training is resumed. It is proper to assume there is no pain associated with physiological or normal body processes, therefore, one has to assume something is wrong when pain shows up. "There is no physiological function in the body which gives rise to pain in the normal course of health."

There are two main types of pain that fix races. The first known as cutaneous pain which seems to exert an exhilarating action causing the animal to want to move on. When the whip is used for instance. This is useful in that it gets the horse away from any hostile environment which will first hit the skin. Secondly, we have deeper pain that has an altogether different effect. Sore tendons, joints or abdominal pains are not going to be benefited by any movement so they exert a depressing effect with less activity. He can not run away from a sore leg.

In addition to these two types of pain there are different qualities or recognizable differences of intensity. There, also, exists a pain threshold. The intensity of two pains existing separately at the same time is no greater than that of the more intense of the two. This is capitalized on by the trainer. He will warm the horse up to warm him out of a pain or he will pack his legs in ice to reduce the intensity. It is possible to block pain with a number of drugs, but most are illegal on the track. Another pain or ultra sonic waves can raise the threshold for preception of another pain. This is the reason we bite our lips or dig our fingernails into our flesh when in pain. Intensity of deep pain may be reduced by tactile pressure and heat applied to the skin. Hot water or ice packs help the deeper pains as do blisters to the skin.

Then there is 'referred' pain—a sore foot may make the whole

148

leg painful making it difficult to locate the seat of the trouble. In the management of painful conditions, it must always be a foremost consideration that the function of pain is an indicator of disease and if blocked or ignored great damage can be done— a sore horse should not be forced to run. The presence of any pain should alert the trainer to investigating the cause of this pain.

Horses that bear in or out may have a bad tooth or a sore leg. The pain should not be relieved until the cause is determined for effective treatment. Sore horses can not win races over sound ones so find and treat the causes. It is not normal to have pain. If it exists, it is a warning flag to be observed. Don't let pain fix your next race. The bettor can, by careful observation tell if a horse is in pain when they parade onto the track. The head will bob when they step on a sore front leg and go down when the sound leg hits the ground. They will drag the sore hind legs or the hips will be noticed going up and down unevenly.

There is one other very important consideration while discussing pain. Pain lowers the red blood cell count thus limiting the horses ability to race as effectively for some time (up to four weeks) after the pain has subsided. A blood count might be valuable information to get a horse back in shape after any painful condition. Then, of course, if there is inflammation present the white cell count will be up (over 9,000 is high). It must be remembered that corticosteroids are given for painful conditions. These will double or triple the white cell count and reduce the red cell count.

Slipshod Fixing

Horses do not wear horseshoes for luck. These good luck charms are on to protect the feet. They are, at best, a necessary evil and a poor shoeing job may not only fix a race. If bad enough it can ruin the horse for life or fix him permanently.

Generally, very little is done to the horse's feet prior to starting them in training. While roving about in a state of

149

nature they are generally sound and healthy. It is well to check the young stock and if any foot is showing uneven growth, they should be trimmed. However, when horses are stabled and put in training to be conditioned, a great many changes take place. First of all, he must get along on a ration of dry feed which affects his health. The average horse can adapt to this change quite well and is not a point of great concern. He will assist (if allowed to do so) the digestion of the dry food he eats, by the quantity of water he chooses to drink at different intervals during the day. But he has no power to meet or counteract the very great change which is, at the same time taking place with his feet. This must be left partly to the groom who looks after him and partly to the horseshoer with any aid the trainer can give. They should all give their best attention to this point immediately on the horse's coming into the stable, while his feet are in good shape. If they are neglected or become diseased, it is, difficult to get them sound under such adverse conditions.

Race horses get almost continuous exposure to all kinds of causes which injure their feet. They are training or racing nearly the year around. While most horses have intervals of time for their feet to recover from injuries, race horses must keep on going.

A race-horse, unless an accident happens to him, is kept up longer and therefore more constantly in an artificial state, than any other horse. The race-horse can not be so very conveniently laid up to rest, especially if the owner does not have a farm.

Two and three year old colts which are bred for racing are generally well staked and often in training as yearlings, in winter as well as summer. Most have to come to post early in the Spring and run until late Autumn or Fall. Their feet require much care as they are still growing and some may be training on frozen ground imparting tremendous shock to soft undeveloped tendons, muscles, and bones. When all factors are considered it is surprising as many as do ever get to be aged racehorses. A lot of races get "fixed" along the way.

It is almost unnecessary to observe here, that the bedding of a race-horse cannot well be dispensed with at any time, as horses in strong work require rest by day as well as by night and many of them do lay down during the day, stretching and resting their limbs and muscles. Thus for sixteen or eighteen hours out of every twenty-four they are standing or laying with their hoofs constantly covered up with the warm bedding. This keeps their feet very hot and dry and is one of the principal causes of contracted feet. The horse has no power within himself of remedying this change produced in his feet. It is an artificial state that he can not correct for without someone's help.

All trainers and grooms should acquaint themselves with the natural state of different horses feet. If they can recognize the normal they will be aware of any abnormal changes. Prevention is always better than trying to affect a cure and early treatment without complications holds far more promise than advanced stages of diseases. The trainers should see that the grooms are attentive in the normal care of their horse's feet —such as picking them out and washing them to preserve their horse's feet in as healthy a state as possible. They should also make themselves acquainted with some of the most advantageous remedies to apply to give relief when the horses feet do become diseased or out of order. Race-horses can not perform when their feet hurt any more than they can run with bad legs. Most grooms do a good job on the legs, but I have seen many instances of neglected feet with very disastrous results. Any time a new man shoes a horse it is well to be particularly attentive. Unless he is used to the horse he may unwittingly make a minor change that will affect the gait of the horse. There are good shoers and very bad ones at most race-tracks, unfortunately, so they must be watched. On all occasions the utmost attention should be given the feet.

The feet of most race horses are usually quite small and strong with a deep or high wall. Their heels are high and strong and the soles concave. Some likely could race without shoes, but this is not very practical for most race-horses. The feet will wear too much.

The feet of most horses are subject to contraction when kept in dry stalls. Their heels contract. Many horses with their feet in this state may go sound, but many more will become unserviceable. If the condition develops gradually nature sometimes accommodates to the slow progress of the disease

151

and with the foot growing in length the lameness is obviated. But when contraction is sudden, lameness is generally the results. If the horse receives proper attention in the stall he is not likely to get contracted feet. They are sound when they come into the stable because outside their feet are almost constantly moist. Even in the summer their feet are moistened by the dew of the grass. While in the paddocks they are almost always in action; their feet are exposed to air on a soft, cool surface. They are, also, heavier when out, which may assist in keeping the feet expanded.

It is evident race-horses feet have a great bearing on the race results. Before I proceed with remedies necessary to be applied to horses feet with a view of keeping them sound and healthy, I would like to give a description of the external horny covering of the horses foot and how it is divided. I will compress and be as brief and simplify the matter as much as I can. This is not a lesson in anatomy, but it may be advantageous to everyone with concern for the horse, or his ability to perform, to know how he is put together. We will start with a plain description of the external foot covering. The entire upper part of the crust or hoof wall is connected or joined with the skin at the lower part of the pastern and this juncture is termed the coronet or coronet band. The sides of the foot are called the quarters and the quarters terminate in the heels. The front and lower part of the hoof is the toe. The sole is arch shaped on the bottom of the foot and has limited motion when the foot is in action. The bars on the under side are a continuation of the hoof wall. They are convex and extend along the sides of the frog. The frog is composed of soft, elastic horn, is convex and wedge-shaped, situated in the middle of the sole. It is pointed towards the toe and spreads as it advances to the heel. In the center of the broad part is a fissure, which, when diseased is termed thrush. These horny parts composing the hoof are for the protection of the sensitive or internal parts of the foot.

There are various opinions with regard to the uses of the frog of the horse's foot. Whatever may be the functions that nature intended it should perform, it is a very important part of the foot and anyone working with horses or shoeing them should become well acquainted with this part of the foot. This is a cushion to absorb shock. Constant pressure from bar shoes is not good for frogs as they will deteriorate from artificial pressure applied for an extended period of time. Canker is caused from a lack of frog pressure. The best cure is lowering the horses heels to put as much pressure as possible on the frog. Natural pressure by allowing the frog to come into contact with the ground is the best way to preserve a healthy state. Regardless of disease of the foot or the cause, it most likely begins in the frog and if neglected spreads to the other parts of the foot so we could have entitled this chapter, "Letting the Frog Fix the Race."

Some horses hoof walls are too oblique, with low weak heels and convex soles. These ill-formed feet are likely inherited and should be avoided if possible. They are trouble with a Capital T. Proper shoeing will help these cases but it will likely take heavy shoes that will retard their speed rather than help it. Neither mares nor stallions should be kept for breeding stock with these difficulties or future generations will be "fixed". To correctly shoe this type of horse the hoof walls should be encouraged to grow below the sole and the toes kept short to give strength to the heels. A bar shoe may be necessary. A mild blister on the coronet band promotes growth of the hoof wall.

Most race horses have good feet, but it they do have convex soles special care must be given to keep them sound. First of all, these are weak feet and as little paring as possible should be done. Shoes should be as light and narrow as possible. The shoe must not come in contact with the sole of the foot. If this happens the horse will go lame sooner or later. The heels should be kept moderately low and the frog pared as little as possible in order to keep natural pressure. This type of horse should be shod often with the toes kept short to give strength to the heels. When the wall has grown ordinary shoes can be used. A good foot dressing two or three times a week will help.

Navicular disease deserves some special mention because it ruins many otherwise good horses. They act similar to foundered horses and usually stand pointing with one foot. That is, the affected foot is placed a foot or so in front of the other and this stance is maintained.

The locality of this disease is between the navicular bone and the flexar tendon which passes over the navicular bone as it passes downward to be inserted into the coffin bone. The surface of the navicular bone and the part of the tendon immediately over it becomes feverish and inflamed. The immediate cause is probably concussion, produced in the rapid pace of the horses striking hard surfaces. Frequent repetition of these inflammatory conditions may result in orsification of the parts which deprives them of their natural actions (or all action) causing the horse to go as much as they possibly can on their hind quarters.

Heavier horses are more susceptible to navicular disease, but any horse can get it. Overwork under heavy loads on hard training grounds cause more trouble than would normally be encountered.

Horses, in the early stages, have a tendency to "warm out" of this condition so all that may be noticed is that the horse goes a little stiff in his fore feet when first taken from the stable. The horse should be given rest at the first signs of trouble. When the inflammation subsides, he will appear to go sound to any, but the very accurate observer. The best remedy is to sell the horse, because when he is put back in hard training the condition will return. He walks cautiously and gallops stiffly and short in his stride. Prevention is the only answer to this problem.

Unless sufficient mosisture is properly applied to horses feet much of the natural expansion and elastic parts of their heels and quarters will be destroyed. Then these parts become hard, dry and brittle greater concussion takes place in the feet causing injuries that would not otherwise exist.

Horses that have convex feet, have the largest and most healthy frogs. It is only necessary to remove any detached or ragged parts before shoeing. I can not stress enough that as little trimming as practical is best for abnormal feet. The secret is to encourage them to grow by any means at your disposal, because as they grow they will become more normal in appearance and service to the animal. Keeping the feet moist, properly shod, and using a mild blister on the coronet band occasionally all help to stimulate growth of the feet. Nutrition, also, plays a very important role. Since all cells and especially the horny parts are protein basically, a good source of proteins that supplies all of the amino acids, is necessary to get proper foot growth. Gelatin, which is derived from hoof and bone, has been used quite widely. In my opinion there are many more useful and cheaper protein sources that do a better job. Plenty of good alfalfa hay, linseed oil meal and oats will provide the protein requirements. There are several excellent protein supplements on the market to fill the gap on problem cases. Good feed, good care, and proper shoeing will prevent most foot problems from getting a start.

Theoretical knowledge is useful in explaining the principles of the different arts and sciences, but can not always be applied to the letter. This is true with knowing which is truly an art. The best advice is to find a horseshoer that knows his business, tell him all you can about the way the horse is going and let him decide how best to shoe the horse. All imperfections that may cause unsoundness should be closely watched and attempts made to correct them. However, all of these are individual cases that could take up an entire book explaining. A horseshoer has long practical experience and possesses exclusive advantages with respect to his trade. Give him a trial walk and trot after each shoeing to be certain there are no nails picking. If a horse is lame (even in his head) pull the shoe off until the lameness is located. Long striding horses on short tracks with bad turns will do better with the hind shoe tips turned up slightly, especially if the shoes extend beyond the heels. The course to be run over must be considered.

Taking shoes off is an important operation and should be done with utmost care so as to not damage the wall. Some horseshoers use more strength than judgment. More care could preserve the foot and have more wall to nail to. In removing shoes from thin walled or bad feet the shoer should first turn up the clinches with one end of the buffer and with the other he should start the nails. Then he should draw them out with the pincers one by one until the shoe falls off. The groom or trainer knows when he has weak hoof walls and he should insist on the horse's shoes being taken off so that the horn may be preserved as much as possible.

Fixing A Race With Horseshoes

There is no question about horse shoes being lucky, especially if they are the right ones on the right horse. They can also be extremely unlucky. Horseshoes have likely caused as many horses to lose races they would otherwise have won as any other single factor. Just how horsehoes fix races are many and varied. The variations run from poor shoeing to losing a shoe in the race (which might also be classified as poor shoeing). One must always wonder when a horse loses a shoe and the race if it was not deliberate sabotage by the otherwise trusty "smithy". I think in all cases the answer is no. If a horses feet are not growing properly or the shoes have been changed several times within a short time, the hoof wall becomes weakened and will not hold nails as well as they should. A nail that is a bit too brittle can break under the tremendous stresses racing demands. Suffice to say horseshoes can be lucky and unlucky in a horse race.

A horse's feet need careful attention. They continue to grow throughout the horse's life. Neglected feet may grow long and uneven, so that the weight will be thrown on the foot unnaturally and may lead to tendon strain, unsoundness, or interference and even broken bones.

The most important thing is that the hoof wall be kept level and even so that the horse stands squarely upon it. If neglected there is a tendency for the toe of the front feet to grow long, causing the horse to stand forward, with the uneven pressure on the hoof wall inviting a quarter crack. The heels of the hind feet may grow too high, the horse then standing too straight behind. Either of these conditions will fix a horse to where they can not race at all, if neglected for very long.

From the front, the feet should rest true and square on the ground. The horse that stands pigeon-toed will need the inside of the wall trimmed down, while the horse that toes out will need the outside of the foot shortened. Keeping the foot level is especially important with colts and young horses. Some faults in conformation of feet and legs may be remedied or greatly improved by careful trimming and shaping when the colt is young and the bones are immature. The use of light shoes or half plates may be advisable in some cases where wear on one part of the foot is excessive. An occasional look at the foot can determine the points that need correcting. A rasp should not be used on the outer surface of the hoof wall.

Nearly all race horses are kept shod as a practical necessity. The primary object of the shoe is to prevent breakage and excess wear on the foot wall. Shoeing may also affect the straightness, balance, length of stride, height of action, etc. A skillful shoer can correct or improve certain faults such as winging, interfering, or going wide behind. The use of such extreme weight as to greatly increase the concussion as the feet strike the ground, or shoeing the foot with very long toe and shallow heel may, however, lead to undue strain. Good shoeing is truly an art, and this type of work should be done by a competent, experienced shoer who knows his job.

Shoes are usually reset every three to five weeks. If new shoes are not needed, the old ones may be used again after the foot has been trimmed where necessary. Many horses are reshod for each race depending on conditions of the race and the track. Pads are not usually used for cinder, gravel, or dirt surfaces. Calks, borium, and other grabs may be used when necessary.

Shoes vary greatly in design and weight. They all have a purpose and a bearing on racing. As little as ½ ounce of extra misplaced weight can affect the results of a race by throwing the horses performance completely off. This is nothing for the average bettor to be greatly concerned about because once a trainer determines what is the best shoes for his horse he will make very few changes. Trying to handicap a horse by tampering with his footwear can be very dangerous business. There are other ways that do not involve as much risk.

Nevertheless it is well to know a few of the things that can happen by default and by design involving the shoeing. A misplaced nail can and has put many potential winners out of the race or out of contention. A nail prick is similar to cutting into the quick when trimming ones finernails. It is painful and when such trauma involves a horses foot where the pain will be present every time he puts that foot down he can not possibly turn in a top performance.

If a horse is shod several days before a race and the angle

of the foot is changed the horse may be too sore to win or even run well if he does enter the race. Such things are usually an accident or cases of the shoer being given faulty information. Most shoers know their business and shoe the horse exactly like they are told to. It is the trainers responsibility to be very sure they are shod properly—the outcome of the race depends upon it.

Bugged And Fixed

When proper disease prevention, control and treatment are not given first priority horsemen are not only big economic losers; the fact is, such waste is more than loss to the individuals, it is an act of sabotage aginst the loyal supporters of the sport of horse racing. When a bettor puts his money on a horse (which is the only thing that makes racing possible) he has a right to expect the horse has been kept in the best possible condition so that horse will perform up to his inbread ability. Whether it is unconsciencious unintentional, lack of knowledge, or just pure neglect, there is an unmerciful amount of this kind of sabotage going on. It is unthinkable that fewer than two per cent of the horses racing wind up their careers without some unsoundness. The fact that very few retire in racing condition is a very poor testimonial to the care they get during their racing days. A great many diseases are unavoidable, but a far greater number could be prevented with close cooperation of track owners, horse owners, trainers, grooms and veterinarians. More concern to keeping the horses well and sound would pay the best dividends towards winning races as anything the racing business could do.

Poor stables, poor care, poor sanitation and poor treatment methods all must share some of the blame for a lot of races fixed by disease.

In very recent years some money and talent has been devoted to research of problems concerning the race horses. To date this is far too little and too slow. With more movement of horses back and forth across the country, with ever increasing numbers and concentrations of horses a real threat exists around the corner if proper safeguards are not instituted—and soon. There is never any excuse as good as a satisfactory performance. Some race meets have practically been closed by outbreaks of various controllable diseases. This could become serious enough to not only fix a race, but could fix racing.

More strict rules and enforcement of vaccination, sanitation and disease prevention are needed to protect the future of racing. At some tracks approximately half of the horses stabled there are on the disabled list. It is very good that management does not permit these animals to run and thus deceive the public by letting a horse race not up to his inbred ability. On the other hand it is a waste of stable room, time, money and potential jeopardy to all the other horses there. A great deal of this could be eliminated by management practices.

Some of the most productive changes could be made in the archaic drug regulations. The blame for any horse being drugged rests solely with the trainer unless it can be proven that it was given by someone else without his approval (a very difficult task). However, when there is a drug scandal the racing commission, generally an appointed group to regulate racing, comes under fire by the press and the public. Thus since they make the regulations, they attempt to ban anything in the drug line that could in any way affect a horses racing ability.

On the surface this would appear to be a good practice. It is not, in fact it condemns a lot of horses to unnecessary suffering. Since possession of any drug or medicine on the banned list is grounds for conviction and subsequent loss of license, the trainers liscense and his livelihood, the trainers can not even treat his sick and lame animals with the best drugs available—many are banned.

Before becoming too critical let's offer a solution. The main objective should be to see that drugged horses do not race. This can be accomplished by simply drawing a blood test on every animal before they go to the post. If they show a positive test simply scratch them from the race with no penalty. Such a procedure would be far more effective in detecting horses that have been drugged than the hit and miss procedure of testing just the winners as is present practice, with only a urine test.

159

The "test and scratch" method would permit trainers and veterinarians to use any drug of choice to best treat the animal. If he came to the post still carrying a residue that might affect the horse or the outcome of the race, he would be withdrawn before running. This would protect everyone and guarantee more honest racing. As it stands today most trainers and veterinarians hands are tied to do their best to keep horses in racing shape. This results in them taking chances and when caught creates great monstrous scandals—like witchcraft used to do. Many good veterinarians will not practice on the tracks for this reason. Why place their license in jeopardy to do what they know is right? Butozolidine is a good example. Few knowledgeable people will deny this is one of the most effective drugs for relieving pain and reduce inflammation in the race horse.

Butozolidine is banned in spite of its curative powers. Rather than provide for effective regulation the commissions just declare it illegal for use with no consideration for the trainer or the horse's welfare—not a very good way to treat the life-blood of the world's greatest sport. The betting public paying for the sports is also cheated to a degree as horses could be put in condition to race more nearly up to their potential. This is one of many many effective treatment drugs on the unacceptable list because too little consideration has been given this matter.

When men that have to work have a headache or pain, they take an aspirin and go on to work. The poor horse must suffer until he can recover (and in many cases is run while hurting) because effective drugs are barred from use. This in no way protects the public and it is inhuman in many cases.

Another possible solution is requiring veterianarians to report all drugs used and the date given. This would permit them to use any drug and still provide safeguards for the public. Some tracks pay little attention to the use of drugs other than out-and-out stimulants and depressants. These tracks have as good or better racing and they have a lot healthier horses without a lot of adverse publicity which certainly benefits no one. There needs to be effective controls, but these need to be tempered with good judgment and consideration for the welfare of the horse.

Trainers And Owners Do Their Share Of Fixing

After the condition book has been prepared for the conditioned races the owners and trainers must determine which of their stable fit the various conditions. They take into account which horses they know from other stables that would fit these same conditions that they feel they would have a chance to beat. Determining which conditioned races to enter requires a great deal of serious thought and a miscalculation can cost the owner a race where he might have won easily had he entered against another field of horses.

To better explain how this system works, we will use a simple set of conditions, but you must realize they are seldom this simple. In this case the Racing Secretary has made a race for two year olds that are non winners of three thousand dollars. First the trainer knows he has four two year olds in his stable. One is lame and will not be ready for this race. One has made six thousand dollars this year, so he is out. This narrows his entries down to two. One is a filly and he knows there are several colts on the grounds that fit these conditions so it would be better to keep the filly for another race more in her own class. This decision leaves this trainer with only one choice for this race. His colt has only won two races and has twenty-two hundred dollars to his credit whereas our trainer realizes there are at least four or five horses eligible for this race that have won more races and have more money on their card. He digs out the past performance records at this point to determine what kind of races they were in and how they ran. Obviously these other horses were running in cheap races to have won five or six races and still be under three thousand dollars in winnings. The one that gave our trainer the most concern was a little bay colt that had never won a race, but had twenty-nine hundred and seventy-five dollars in the bank. This horse had been in the money every race he had entered and had placed in the last four races. The trainers years of experience told him here was the horse to beat. He must study this one's performances exceptionally carefully to determine if he has any chance to beat him with his colt. The records showed the op-

161

positions colts did not leave the gate very well and the closest he had come to winning was when he had the inside post position. In that race a colt won that was a fast starter and had been beaten by our trainers colt in a later race. The bothersome thing was the way this slow starter could come home. A decision must be made whether to enter this colt in a race with a faster horse. There were some things in the trainers favor as final deliberations were being made. He had as good a chance as the other man of drawing the inside post position or pole. In any event his horse could leave faster than the other one and he could likely be out in front a few lengths to start with. Just plain racing luck might shuffle the other speedster back in the pack to where he would have to run pretty wide around the homestretch turn to get racing room. This was a short race and better still this track had a fairly short stretch (distance from the last turn to the wire). All of these factors were against a slow starter that would not have time to pick up speed and pass the front runner.

The trainer decided to give it a try. He called the owner to tell him when the race would be and his reasons for thinking he could possibly win this race if he got the breaks. There is always the possibility that another horse he had not considered would take it all. This is what makes racing the great sport it is. He could draw the outside post position and not be able to get out in front which would seriously hamper his chances of winning. If it rained this would be even more of a detriment. All of these probabilities were given careful consideration and with any co-operation from dame fortune or lady luck our trainer felt he could win this one so he goes to the secretary's office, fills out the proper form to officially enter the race, then waits to see how it will all come out. No one will know until they cross the wire at the finish. If this horse is not the favorite and wins at least one person in that crowd will say, or at least think, this race was fixed. Sure enough it was and a lot of thought, study, experience, and honest sincerity went into the fixing. The photo finish attested to the fair match. Had our disgruntled bettor known his horses, done his homework, and not listened to the tauts and watched the toteboard for the favorite, he just might have figured this one out with the same logic our trainer

162

used. He could have been at the cashiers window cashing that five to one ticket with looks of admiration, envy, questions, and suspicion from the crowd that had thrown their losing tickets away. Instead this bettor will mill around until a few minutes before the next race is to be off at which time he can determine which horse the toteboard predicts will win. In this mans aimless wonderings he will briefly join many others on the cashiers side with his share of suspicious glances at the winners. Besides some of his friends might recognize him near the window and congratulate him for having the brilliance to pick this one. He does not knowingly do this, but susconsciously being among the winners adds balm to the wounds and mental anguish of losing. A far better thing to do, since he likes to bet and likes to win, would be to spend this wasted time studying past performances of the horses in the next race. This would not guarantee him a winner every time, but it will greatly reduce the chances of losing when considered along with all of the other bits of information and conditions that exist. You know, betting on a horse race is pretty risky business. After all there is usually only one winner (unless it is a dead heat) and this leaves several losers in every race.

The trainer fixes the race by information and logic with a deep understanding that many things happen in the actual race that can not be predetermined. However, he enters the races where he has the best chance to win and trusts the luck to whoever is in charge of that department. His chances are always as good as anyones in the same race whether it is a good tract, bad track, good weather, bad weather or the draw for post position —anyway, you can't win them all.

In this same situation he may very well have decided the slow starter could have beaten him in spite of this handicap. He might have accidentally found out that there was a real outstanding horse being shipped in from another track that could probably beat him. His colt might not have been just as sharp as he would have liked on this mornings workout so it would be better to wait for a more opportune race that would not demand almost perfect performance, luck, etc. All of these could have been reasons to just decide not to enter the aforementioned race.

163

The big stake races provides a setting for high level conferences with guessing games mixed with good and bad decisions. For these elite affairs, horses are shipped up and down, back and forth across the country and even across the ocean with the same purpose that business people fly from coast to coast—go where the money is if you have any chance of picking up some of this green stuff. A hundred thousand dollar purse understandably makes owners and trainers eyes light up like pinball machines, especially if they have a contender for this event. Fifty thousand dollars to the winner will buy a lot of oats, besides the fun they will have knocking off this one. In many cases revenge is the motivating factor. A trainer just gets nipped at the wire by some goat that he knows he can beat with any kind of breaks (chances are that he can too).

There are usually several of these big stake races around the country on any given Saturday or Holiday so it gets to be a matter of which one to enter. The question may be, "Shall we ship out and beat them on the coast or take our chances here," or there is a sure thing at a neighboring track. True, the purse is only fifty thousand and there is no prestige involved, but maybe we should take it easier this week and be ready for them next week. The smaller track might even pay the shipping expense to have our horse race there. Everyone likes to beat the champion and this is about the only way they get a chance.

At any rate big decisions have to be made and they involve a great deal of money. When an owner gets a top horse he has to make the most of it. In any given year there are several top horse and they are all out ot make the most of it. This means every angle had best be considered before investing several thousand dollars in entrance fees to say nothing of the expense of shipping long distances, usually by air. Horseracing being the sport it is leads every owner and trainer to want to test his good horse against the best at least once, win, lose, or draw. This, of course, is what makes good racing. However, economics enters into the picture and once tested they may wisely decide they do not want to race against some individuals. This is where the guessing comes in. A determination must be made which big race this super-horse is most likely to choose. Sometimes they let you know and sometimes they don't. When there is no advance information you may be unfortunate enough to select the wrong place and wind up racing against the very horse you would have preferred to avoid like the plague. This may be just the time things break your way and you take everything. After all the longshots do occasionally come in and this time you got all the breaks.

Illegal Fixing Of Races

Horseracing is likely the best policed sport in existence today and with good reason. Billions of dollars are involved. Every conceivable way to fix a race has been tried at least once. Percentage wise very few of these attempts have been successful. However, this is true only because of continued vigilance on the part of those with control authority and for the most part, exceptional cooperation from all of those that make up this great business of racing. With extremely large amounts of money riding on every race the potential danger is ever present that someone or some group will risk severe penalties to bring in a winner, perferably one with big odds, at the expense of the rest of the field.

Because this possibility exists many illegal practices will be mentioned and discussed to create an awareness that they exist as possibilities for attempting to illegally fix horseraces. In some instances they were successful the first time, but likely could not be successfully repeated. Hopefully this academic approach will allay some thoughts in the minds of uninformed individuals that most races have predetermined winners. Also, we would hope and expect continued honest racing that continues to thrill millions the world over.

Jockey Fixing Methods

There are many approaches to fixing a horse race. With proper cooperation from all of the jockeys of any given race this would likely be the easiest method—just let them decide which horse to bring across the finish line first. The major drawback to this method is integrity on the part of most jockeys. They have likely gotten to their present position by playing the game fair and their entire future is tied to remaining honest. If one gets very far out of line the others are in a good position to put him back in line or out of business. I am not saying there are not good and bad jockeys, but I do know there are more honest ones than dishonest. Perhaps this is true only because they have to be to stay in business. I am not here to argue that point. The fact remains that if all jockeys in any given race decided who would win most likely the chosen horse would win every time. However, even if one did not agree to this arrangment he would either win himself or foul up the others plans. Therefore, I submit that jockeys fixing entire races seldom if ever happens. They may try, but more times than not, their efforts will not be very gratifying.

There have been, and I am sure will continue to be from time to time, efforts made by one or two jockeys conniving to cut out a potential winner or even help the second best horse home. With stewards, judges, film patrols, and well informed patrons looking on this is pretty difficult to accomplish. The slightest rule infraction will bring a protest from the abused jockey or one of the officials and the films will be re-run before the results are made official. If the complaint is found to be legitimate, the offending horse is "set down" (moved back a place or two or all the way to last). The betting public makes horseracing possible and their interest must be protected at all costs. Judges must be flint hard and unwavering. Fortunately they are not in contact with the public they serve so can not possibly be swayed by the crowds reaction. There is no reaction until the decision is made and posted as official —then it is too late for any change.

Weather Fixes Races

One consistant thing about horseracing is that they like the postman in good or bad weather, rain, sleet or snow—they go. It can rain pitchforks mixed with little toads or it can be so hot and dry the horses feet crack, and yet they race. I have seen the fog so bad that the announcer could not see the track.

His only call was "Here they come—I can hear them". This kind of peasoup will stop airplanes, boats, cars and most anything else, but not horseracing.

There is a little neon sign on the toteboard to let the fans in on information like whether it is a fast track, good or sloppy. It always seemed a bit facetious to bother with this last pronouncement when one does not have to be too observing to detect imperfect track conditions by watching the jockeys remove their mud bath following a race.

As indicated the show goes on regardless of the weather, but the weather has a great bearing on results and for reasons unfamiliar to many people closely associated with racing. It is reasonable and nearly everyone knows a horse with sore feet will put out a little better effort on a soft wet track than one that is hot and dry and hard. Horses hit very hard when running and if they are a little ouchy some extra cushion lets them try harder.

On the other hand most any horse that has ever slipped on a muddy track and hurt himself is likely to be slowed considerably by a muddy track. He will be overly cautious because horses have a remarkable capacity for remembering traumatic experiences. They may be dumb and slow to learn a lot of things, but they rarely forget a bad experience. Also, in this vein, a horse will under no circumstances volumtarily punish himself. This trait enables man to control such a powerhouse. Experienced trainers take advantage of this characteristic to break and train horses. They determine what they want to accomplish and figure out a way for the horse to teach himself. This method may be used to teach a horse new things or break bad habits. This will be dealt with in another chapter in depth. The point here is that having once been hurt on a muddy track a horse is going to rebel when urged to repeat a performance that caused him prior body harm.

Weather Fixes Races

One of the least exploited and perhaps one of the most potent environmental factors is sunshine. Sunshine, muddy water, and pretty scenery will not produce a top race horse, but the sunshine will do a great deal in that direction if the other necessary factors are present in proper amounts. The chemistry is rather simple. Sunshine provides Vitamin D. Vitamin D in turn stimulates the production of estrogen, a female sex hormone. The estrogen accellerates maturity, especially in the filly. Just how much sunshine (or other sources of Vitamin D) it takes to give any decisive advantage is not fully known. The advantages of extra growth and early maturity are obvious in that many of the richest stake races are for 2 year olds. Since all race horses have a birthday January 1st, those born any day after that have less time to mature and race as 2 year olds. Some being only a year and a half old on their second birthday. Horses are not fully grown and mature until they actually are around five years old. Positive evidence of this fact is their tooth development. This being the case, they are really babies at two, even if they are a full two years old.

Taking these factors into account may explain why horses raised in states with more days of sunshine race beyond their theoretical breeding potential. I think there is little question that Florida and California raised horses outdo their counterparts of equal breeding. The extra sunshine provides the Vitamin D that stimulates hormone produce to promote earlier maturity. Thus, we again have a weather factor fixing future races of horses. This will be especially true of two, three, and four year olds and possibly on through their fifth years. After five there should be little difference.

However, the fact of the matter is, there will always be a difference. A horse is raised only once. The best money an owner can spend is giving that colt or filly everything that in any way will be helpful for their development. The rest of their life and indeed the results of every race depend upon how they were raised! It may very well be from evidence at hand and an understanding of the chemistry and physiology evolved, we can now add, "every race depends upon where they were raised."

All of this is not to say a commendable job can not be accomplished anywhere. With an abundance of natural and synthetic vitamins, protein supplements and an ever increasing knowledge of the horses' requirements it is possible to duplicate nature's environment anywhere. In some places around the country this becomes a real challenge and even a bit hazardous. My only point here is that it can, and for the most part, is being done.

I do not want anyone to be mislead by making this foray into Mother Natures affairs seem a simple matter—it is not. We mentioned Vitamin D as being helpful. In the proper amounts it is most beneficial. However, in excess amounts Vitamin D can be very harmful. Recently scientific evidence indicates overdoses of Vitamin D in the very young prevents the normal development of one of the main arteries of the heart. It takes little imagination to envision what effect a limited blood flow is going to have on the racing career of any horse. Nature has a way of protecting against this hazard of too much Vitamin D by the stimulation of a layer of pigment in the skin to shut out unneeded Vitamin D. Where the vitamin is being fed precautions must be taken to feed the right amount every day. The right amount will be determined more exactly by its relationship to the total ration. To be more specific a good ration requires some forty three elements that not only must be present, but must all be in reasonably proper balance if best results are to be achieved. This will be covered more thoroughly under the chapter on Fixing the Race with Food.

While we are on the subject of sunshine it might be worth mentioning another factor it fixes. We all know a fast track means fast races, but did you ever stop to think that without sunshine to keep the track dry we might never have a fast track to race over. There is a lot of fixing in a horse race and old Sol does his share of the fixing so due consideration must be given when you lay that two dollars on the line. It may be sunshine or the lack of it that helped you to win or lose the big one.

Possibly, a much greater weather influence on the fixing of races is the barometric pressure. The form or program indicates certain horses are "mudders". There are three reasons for this with the last being the most important: (1) Some horses with sore feet or legs run better on the soft track, (2) Some are psychologically conditioned for muddy tracks and (3) Some horses blood count goes up when the barometer goes down as it always does prior to and during a rainstorm. In some horses this is a marked change while others show little response.

169

With an increased red cell count and the accompanying extra oxygen these horses can outperform their counterparts so they gain a reputation as mudders. These same horses could be kept at higher altitudes during training and brought down to sea-level to race with excellent results. In California this is easier to accomplish than in most states because the tracks are at sea level and there are some fairly high mountains close enough for trucking the horses back and forth to be practical. A horse freshened up at 3,000 to 5,000 feet for a few weeks will out perform those turned out at lower altitudes. At higher altitudes red blood cell numbers increase quite markedly providing the horse with more oxygen carring hemoglobin. The extra oxygen gives the horses more stamina or the ability to run at their full speed for a longer time than those not so conditioned.

This method of supercharging horses could easily be simulated by lowering the atmospheric pressure and oxygen content of an airtight stall. To be very effective, however, training would have to be done on a treadmill within the stall with the controlled atmosphere.

Conditioning a racehorse by such unorthodox methods and equipment would most certainly raise a few eyebrows. It would seem, however, this is a method utilizing physiological response to enviornment that does not do bodily harm nor get into the realm of stimulation. Therefore, it must be accepted for what value it would be to building endurance into race horses.

Some horses race best in hot weather while others favor cooler enviornments and, of course, any appreciable amount of wind is going to affect a race. It will affect the front runner more than the rest of the field and perhaps enough to be a determining factor in any given race.

The compensation horses make, when trained at high altitudes, is lost quite rapidly (within a few weeks) when they are raced at lower altitudes. Thus a lot of South American horses shipped over to this country race great for a while then tail off-permanently unless some drastic measures are taken to build them back up. The best method of doing this is to alter the electrolytic balance while providing the right balance of amino acids and blood building components.

There is another point concerning sunshine and its affects

on racing. Even on bright sunshine days tracks may not dry out after a soaking rain. Different tracks react differently with some taking several days to get back to normal. This is very important to the handicapper as he must know exactly the condition of the track to best determine how different horses will race. After the track does dry out it may be very fast due to the fact the water packed it some.

Fixing Horse Races With Food

When thinking in terms of only one race this matter of food brings up a large number of possible fixes. These will be dealt with first, but this by no means exhausts the subject. A great deal of the real fixing takes place before the foal is born and during his early years. Nutrition is playing a decisive role in the future performance of every horse long before they get to the track.

Lets dispose of the questionable practices first then come back to useful more worthy fixing of races with food. Logic and personal experience tells us getting right up from the table is the wrong time to go out and run the hundred yard dash in ten seconds flat, even if we were capable. The same is true with a horse. They can not have a belly full of hay, oats and water and put on their best performance around the oval. It follows, then, that food and most water should be withheld for several hours prior to the horse racing. Anything this elementary and simple to accomplish should not be overlooked, but it often is. Even if hay is left out of the stall, unless the horse is muzzled, he may eat the straw bedding to a harmful extent.

Our more immediate concern here are practices that do not arise from neglect, however. There are some instances of trainers not wanting their horse to do his best in a particular race so the betting odds will go up. This questionable practice is loosely referred to as handicapping. It can more appropriately be called cheating. Fortunately is is not a common or wide scale practice, but deserves mention because it does exist. One method of this type of 'handicapping' is to fill the horse up just prior to a race. There is no question that his performance will be off. The horse may develop a severe colic that could be fatal from such treatment. Even if most trainers were not honest they would not jeopardize their horses' health by such tactics. Another method of doing the same thing that is just as dishonest, but with few risks is giving the horse extra salt and allowing him access to water just prior to the race. The salt makes them extremely thirsty and they will drink several gallons of water. At roughly eight pounds per gallon, only a few extra gallons of water add a lot of weight. Even this practice is not without some danger and should be avoided for safety sake.

Many drugs that can be given orally could be discussed at length here, but saliva and urine tests can detect these and rarely do owners or trainers take a chance on feeding anything that could show up in these tests.

There have been attempts by commerical firms to put various stimulants in feed supplements deliberately or they got there by accident. These are usually detected before long and removed from the market. Since trainers are responsible for anything the horse gets they are usually very cautious about anthing new.

Here again, it must be admitted there is a very fine line between the legitimate and the wrong things to feed. The trainers job is to get the horses in condition to put on their best performance. Anything he can feed, inject, or rub on to help his cause is acceptable unless it comes under the broad heading of stimulants or depressants. There needs to be a lot more clarification on what should and should not be used. There, also, needs to be a reversal of the "heads-in-the-sand" attitude about the use of many products that could be helpful to racing without any more disadvantages than already exist.

To accomplish this goal, more is needed than these limited comments by a crusading veterinarian's limited literary ability. Some real thought and constructive planning by leaders from all levels of the racing industry is necessary to determine what should be acceptable, what is not, and a set of guidelines drawn up to make enforcement practical.

It would be totally unfair to take the industry to task for not having achieved perfection here, without mentioning that a great deal has been done in this department. However, much more needs to be done if we are going to continue to improve the sport and give the fans more consistant performances.

Specific rations will not be included here as it would take too much space to cover the great variety of conditions around the world that require different treatment in diets of race horses.

These general rules are very important and should be adhered to scrupulously for the best welfare of the horse. Horses are what they eat, in the truest sense of the word, from conception to retirement and there are few shortcuts in feeding that are not detrimental. Fixing races with food is one of the surest ways of making or breaking a stable.

It must be accepted that the most important part of animal husbandry is sound feeding of the animals. This is by no means, as might be supposed, a simple matter. In their natural wild state animals are free to roam wherever they please, that is they go to places where suitable food is abundant and remain there so long as it lasts. Under natural conditions animals are found in localities that supply their needs. Nature adapts animals to the place in which they live, but man does differently, hence while in nature animal nutrition is a simple matter, man has made it complicated. Further, from selected strains man breeds abnormal animals to perform abnormal feats and then, by sometimes failing to supply the right food to compensate for the abnormalities of his evolution, his horses fail in health and ceases to do what is expected of them. But by suitable and artificial feeding of his animals better results can be expected.

To feed horses so as to get the best results necessarily implies a knowledge of the basic principles of animal nutrition. Space will not permit a full treatment of this subject here. A brief attempt will be made to point out what the requirements are, and how these are to be supplied to help 'fix' better races. Knowledge concerning these fundamentals has been gathered from a life long association with horses including twenty years as a practicing veterinarian with the last half devoted to nutritional research and careful study of the vast amount of controlled experiments around the world.

Unfortunately there has not been enough research on the requirements of horse nutrition. Most owners and trainers feed

173

their horses according to their experience or the way grand-father did. While most of the present practices are sound, there are many mistaken notions handed down from generation to generation, and ultimately becomes accepted as veritable facts. Thus prejudices are established. Most notable among these is timothy versus alfalfa or clover hay. A horse is basically a hay burner and can handle all kinds. While timothy might have been the thing for Old Dobbin down on the farm, high-powered, high-strung racing stock need a better grade of fodder. They do best on high quality alfalfa. The most satisfactory feeding program is a combination of practical common sense and taking advantage of recent scientific knowledge. A definite advance has been made during recent years in the science and practice of horse nutrition, but there is still a great deal more to be learned about what might be considered the very rudiments of this important subject. On the other hand, while progress has been made by the scientific research worker, it cannot be said that the practical application of this knowledge has kept pace with information as it has become available. Far too often horsemen neglect to take advantage of valuable information that has been acquired for them and which, properly applied, would be the means of enabling them to get better results. Thus the horsemen are unwittingly fixing races with nutrition. They definitely could be doing better, for the most part, much per-formance is sacrificed through giving racehorses diets deficient in protein (thus the need for alfalfa hay which is rich in pro-tein). Few owners and trainers realize that hay, per nutritive unit, is one of the most expensive foods available. Recent re-search has kept horses for three years on a diet containing no long hay with superior results.

Were the hay rationed and high quality subsituted, at least in part, substantial savings could be made and the general welfare of the animal as well as performance be greatly im-proved upon. If the horseman were to keep an account of the quantity used and wasted (which can be greater than that actually consumed by average feeding conditions) he would probably be greatly astonished at the amount of money he could save in the course of a year.

Unfortunately many horsemen are very reluctant to discard

their prejudices and to adopt new methods that have been tested and found to be sound and practical. Particularly is this true of the older trainers and owners that can remember how grandpa did it. Nevertheless a new generation of well imformed dedicated men are doing some excellent work and are having good results. It is certain that as this progressive spirit extends more races are going to be fixed beyond the reach of those that do not keep up with scientific progress.

While taking advantage of scientific knowledge concerning horse nutrition the owner or trainer will realize the importance of attending to the practical details of animal husbandry. It takes breeding, feeding, and management (and a little luck) to win races. It is of little use constructing diets along scientific lines if the method of administration of the rations is faulty. Horses should be fed at least three times a day at as near the same hour as is practical and no excuse is as good as a satisfactory performance. A horses stomach is relatively small in comparison to his size and empties quite rapidly. After four or five hours he will start to weaken if working or is under stress of any kind.

An axiom to be remembered is that only the best quality food is worth buying. It costs a great deal to feed a horse, but it costs a lot more to not feed him properly and indeed give him the best money can buy. A race horse is an athlete, he cannot put out a winning performance on muddy water, course hay, dry oats, and tops of dry stable doors. Most trainers work on a flat daily rate and very often he may be tempted to purchase food because of its price per ton is less than that of good food. More often than not such food is found to be dear when an allowance is made for wastage, and frequently damaged and inferior grade food is responsible for animals going off their feed for some days, and losing condition that was obtained by hard work and consumption of expensive but good materials. Sometimes damaged foods causes colics, and serious losses from illness, and even deaths. A lack or oversight on the part of an owner or trainer that results in feeding moldy or decomposed feed can do extensive brain damage. Moldy corn is especially bad for horses. Proper storage can prevent these tragic events if good food is bought or put up in the first place. If large

175

quantities of hay or grain are stored, it should be periodically inspected. As a veterinarian, I came across many such cases that could have been easily prevented. Every horseman should know that musty feeds are definitely toxic to horses, and yet veterinarians time after time are called to stables to treat horses seriously affected by the careless use of musty or foxy oats. Unmarketable and weathered cereals are, of course, commonly used by farmers for their stock, and no harm results from such practices provided that the food is not musty or moldy to such a degree as to be dangerous. This is a questionable practice, at best, and certainly valuable race stock should not be subjected to such economy oriented practices. It has been my experience that in most cases doubtful foods are sold for much more than they are worth and a lot of potential trouble comes with the dubious bargain; they are often expensive to buy irrespective of the possible harm they may do.

It must always be remembered that a horse that is expected to perform must be kept in the top condition and that any unattractive or unpalatable food, which may be the cause of a setback in the well-being of the animal is scarcely worth consideration on the part of the horseman.

When about to buy foods for a horse it is necessary first of all to be quite clear as to the purpose for which the food is intended—for protein, for starchy matter, because it is rich in minerals, or for its bulk and so on. Relative costs can then be considered by knowing the various values of different feeds. consideration must also be given to palatability of the food— it is not a good diet if they will not eat it.

Unless a food is palatable and acceptable to an animal it is not likely to be eaten with relish, and may be declined altogether unless the animal is forced by hunger to eat it. Some horses will eat almost anything while others have more descriminating tastes. Most will resist sudden changes in their diet. If a change is to be made, it should be made gradually adding some of the new feed to their regular ration for a few feedings until they have grown accustomed to the new taste. If the mistake is made of attempting to use a new food in large quantities as a sub- stitute for the food to which the horse has become accustomed, very often, the food being strange, the horse declines to eat it right away and it is condemned forthwith. Common sense (which isn't too common) would indicate that the strange food should be offered only in small quantities to begin with, then it would be found with patience and perserverence the changed ration, provided it is good and sound, would become acceptable and probably be eaten readily. Many unpalatable foods may be improved by mixing them with some warm water, salt, molasses or other tasty substances, but this should be done only with good foods and not to foods so unpalatable through deterioration as to be really unfit for use otherwise.

All diets should be properly balanced, that is to say, there should be sufficient of each of the proximate principles of foods, and no more than is required for the purpose for which the diet is given. The proximate principles, protein, fat, carbohydrate and fiber must be in proper proportion the one to the other for the optimum results to be obtained. The diet must also contain sufficient mineral matter, vitamins and, of course, plenty of fresh water.

Regularity of feeding is essential and can not be over-emphasized if success is to be assured because there is nothing so detrimental to the health and well-being of horses as carelessness in regard to the time of feeding. Horses in stalls begin to fret and undergo serious stress if their routine is not adhered to closely. Definite times of feeding should be specified and the owner or trainer should see that his regulations in this respect are carried out. The hours of feeding should be so arranged that there is no long interval between meals. Horses being shipped long distances by van should be fed regularly, but small amounts. Failing to do so is a common cause of intestinal troubles.

Exercise is closely tied to feeding. It is not sufficient to open the door and let a horse look a mile, even if he is lame. Even limited exercise will help the digestive processes and help keep them healthy; this applies particularly to growing animals and breeding stock which are sometimes confined to strictly small spaces. Sunlight and fresh air have a wonderfully invigorating effect, and barns or stalls in which horses are confined should be constructed or altered if necessary, so as to admit as much direct sunlight as possible.

Grooming animals that are confined to houses, especially

if they are tied in stalls, has a very beneficial effect. All animals respond quickly to good treatment.

The Odds Are Fixed By The Bettors

The odds or expected payoff for those betting on a given horserace is the most important aspect of race fixing for racing fans and they do the fixing. Morning line odds are printed on race programs and published on the sport pages as approximately how the experts feel the race will turn out. These odds are based on past performances, are unofficial, in that they are meaningless except as a guide to start the betting. When one two dollar ticket is purchased the computers establish the odds and post them on the toteboard for the public to see and use as a further guide to make their decision as to which horse they want to play in this particular race. As more money is bet the odds change from time to time and every few minutes this is posted for the public so they can know where the money is being bet. In addition to the odds being posted, the toteboard shows the amount of money that has been wagered on the win, place and show pools and the amount that has been bet on each horse in each of these categories. Some fans have their programs marked ahead of time and pay no attention to the odds while others would not think of placing a bet until the last minute to see how the crowd feels about their choice. There are about as many ideas and systems of betting at any track as there are people present. Some only bet on the favorites. Others only bet the longshots (the ones with the biggest pay off odds). Many like to bet across the board. That is they place a six dollar bet which gives them two dollars on win, place, and show for the same horse. This system has merit for the cautious bettor because they get something if the horse comes in first, second or third. If the favorite does not win and their choice had fairly good odds they may make a little even if their horse finishes third. Most experienced race goers prefer to bet only to win. There is another group that never bets to win—feeling their chances are better with a place or show ticket. Regardless of where they put their money they are all helping determine the odds and the final payoff to those with the good tickets when the horses have crossed the wire and the judges have declared it official. Thus while a great many people have had a hand in fixing the race up to the time the betting starts, the betting public fixes the payoff.

While this all looks simple enough and on the surface seems fair without much chance for any hankie pankie lets look into some of the more sneaky aspects of this business of betting on horseraces. Where this much money is envolved, relatively tax-free, there will always be an element interested in taking advantage of the situation. Several precautions have been instituted to keep questionable practices to a minimum, but ticket sellers do not check the bettors credentials and there is always a race to the windows just before they close. This mask of confusion serves to protect the professional gambler. They wait until last minute to place large bets that will affect the odds some depending on how much they bet and how much is being wagered on this particular race. In any event the bet is placed too late to show up on the board and give the general public time to buy a ticket. For this reason the management of racetracks make every effort to keep known gamblers barred from the tracks. This is also one of the reason all of the telephones are padlocked prior to the start of the racing program for the day. While these efforts are commendable they are not entirely successful. Even if a bigtime gambler is not allowed to go to the track and place a bet himself there is little to keep him from sending any number of his trusted envoys to do the job in precisely the same manner.

Post Position Fixing

Whether the horses start on the rail (inside post position) or on the outside may be one of the biggest determining factors in the outcome of a race. This is especially true if it is a short race or if the horse in question is a slow starter, as many are. The shortest distance around the track is next to the rail and this is where they all head for as soon as possible. Obviously the horse starting from the inside position has a momentary advantage which is all that may be necessary to win the race. For this reason, everything else being equal, the number one

179

horse will be picked over the rest. This advantage is easily overcome in longer races and if another horse can beat the number one horse out of the gate as often happens. In fact several may charge out of the gate and go to the top leaving a slow starter far behind. However, the post position is considered enough advantage that it is normally assigned to the horses by a drawing. To keep this on the up and up a representative of the racehorse owners must be present along with commission personel. Fixing post positions by this method gives everyone the same chance.

There are handicap races where the racing secretary assigns post positions. This is done to even up a race where horses of various abilities are going to compete in the same race. It is an effort to equalize a field of horses that might not otherwise be a good race. This is practiced more with harness horses than thoroughbreds. The runners are more often handicapped with some additional weight. Addition of weight to sulky horses makes very little diference in the outcome. Deliberate fixing of post positions to make a better race is accomplished by starting with the horse least apt to win the race. With this one assigned to the rail, the others are assigned positions according to their ability with the outside position going to the best horse in the race in the opinion of the racing secretary.

Fixing The Horse

You likely have surmized by now that trainers in general and some in particular like to have a hand in anything that can be fixed. Most horses can't talk to voice their objections so they really get fixed. Now, mind you, some of this is necessary, but a lot of fixing our equine friends are subjected to is unnecessary, not conducive to good racing, and has ruined a lot of horses that might otherwise have been in the hall of fame and not have been deprived of their ability to reproduce. If his sounds unfair, I think it is—for the horse.

To cover the subject of fixing the horse properly, it becomes necessary to start with one part of his anatomy and go full circle because very little gets left out. His entire body including all systems (i.e., blood, vascular, nervous, etc.) come in for more than their fair share of fixing.

With his head properly extended to poke his nose across the finish line first, the horse's upper lip gets there first so we will use this as a point of beginning. No, they don't paint a filly's lips, but they do fix them in other ways. To start with the upper lip is tattoed for indentification purposes. This is done so the number can be checked before a race to be certain some unscrupulous person is not running in a substitute (with a lot more ability). After all there are a lot of horses about the same size, shape and color. By giving each a different tatoo number in the lip that can not be changed, positive identification is possible. In addition to this bit of horse fixing trainers have other lip fixing paraphenalia. For horses that are difficult to control while moving, a lip cord is used with considerable success. A twitch is used on the upper lip to restrain them in a standing position. A twitch consists of a wooden handle, usually two to three feet long with a hole bored in one end large enough for a loop of quarter inch rope or chain of comparable size. This loop of rope or chain 10 to 12 inches in diameter is placed over the upper lip and the handle twisted until the lip is secure within the loop. It has a quieting effect on the most cantankerous horses. The twitch can also be used on the ear with about the same effectiveness. Thinking he is punishing himself if he moves, the horse stands perfectly still.

The wolf teeth can be pulled and the rest filed or "floated" with a rasp so they do not cut into his tongue and cheeks. Usually when a horse bears in or out while racing, it can be corrected by correcting the teeth unless he is hurting somewhere else. This is often overlooked. Horses under five years of age should have their teeth checked at least twice a year and once a year for older horses.

The trainer will often tie a horses tongue to his lower jaw when saddling prior to a race. This is a good precaution to keep the horse from "swallowing his tongue". They can partially swallow their tongue while making a great effort coming down the stretch. This cuts off their wind and they stop or slow down. A piece of gauze or strip of muslin is used to tie the tongue.

181

Blinkers, blinder, and shadow rolls are used to change the horse's view of the surroundings. All of these things have their purpose and many have to be tried to see if they are helpful. There are a number of different bits used from a very mild to some that are very severe. It has been my experience the simpler the better and when horses are pulling very hard on severe bits they can often be corrected simply by using a milder bit and a little understanding. This about takes care of all that happens to the head.

If we travel down to the front legs the horse can get shoe boil or capped elbow, splints, wind-puffs, ringbones, contracted tendons, cocked ankles, sidebones and bowed tendons. He may also get navicular disease, bucked shins or sesmoid trouble. He may have to be fired, blistered, have splint bones removed or nerved to relieve these conditions and he most certainly will have to be shod every two or three weeks. In addition to those conditions mentioned the front feet are subject to quarter cracks founder or laminitis, thrush and scratches with any of these capable of fixing a race or the horses racing career.

The rear legs may be stifled, stringholt, windgalled, have ringbones or contracted tendons. The hocks may be involved with thoroughpin, blood spavin, bog spavin, bone spavin or jacks, capped hocks, curbs and quittor. On the hind feet we may get quarter cracks, founder, thrush or scratches.

In addition to these unsoundnesses we may get tumors of the skin (especially in white horses, hernias, roaring, heaves, asthma, or broken wind.

With so many conditions that fix the horse and fixes races it is good to know how to proceed to look for these conditions without overlooking any, so we will include a section on examination of the horse.

The following pages taken from the "Horsemen's Veterinary Adviser" will point out a great many conditions that may be minor from the standpoint of the horse's over-all health, but they can fix any given race. While this is not a treatment manual, it may be of general interest to racing fans to know some of the simple First Aid Treatments, so they are included here.

EXAMINATION OF A
SICK HORSE

In the examination of a sick horse it is important to have a method or system. If a definite plan of examination is followed one may feel reasonably sure when the examination is finished that no important point has been overlooked and that the examiner is in a position to arrive at an opinion that is as accurate as is possible for him. Of course, an experienced eye can see, and a trained hand can feel, slight alterations or variations from the normal that are not perceptible to the unskilled observer. A thorough knowledge of the conditions that exist in health is of the highest importance, because it is only by knowledge of what is right that one can surely detect a condition that is wrong. A knowledge of anatomy, or of the structure of the body, and of physiology, or the functions and activities of the body, lie at the bottom of accuracy of diagnosis. It is important to recognize animals of different races or families may react differently under the influence of the same disease process. In other words, in sickness as in health, Thoroughbreds, Standardbreds, Quarterhorses, or any others will show individual symptoms and responses to treatment.

The following order of examination is easy to follow and will be sufficiently thorough for most practical situations.

History

It is important to know, first of all, something of the origin and development of the disease, therefore the cause should be looked for. The cause of a disease is important, not only in connection with diagnosis, but also in connection with treatment. The character of food that the horse has had, the use to which he has been put, and the kind of care he has received should all be inquired into closely. It is important to know whether the particular horse that is under examination is the only one in the stable or on the premises that is similarly afflicted. It is most important to know any previous treatment.

Before beginning the special examination, attention should be paid to the attitude and general condition of the animal. Sometimes horses assume positions that are characteristic of a certain disease. For example, in tetanus, or lockjaw, the muscles of the face, neck, and shoulders are stiff and rigid, as well as the muscles of the jaw. This condition produces a peculiar attitude, that once seen is subsequently recognized as rather characteristic of this disease. A horse with tetanus stands with his muscles tense and his legs in a somewhat bracing position, as though he were gathered to repel a shock. The neck is stiff and hard, the head is slightly extended upon it, the face is drawn, and the nostrils are dilated. The tail is usually held up a little and when pressed down against the thighs it springs back to its previous position. In inflammation of the throat, as in pharyngolaryngitis, the head is extended upon the neck, and the angle between the jaw and the lower border of the neck is opened as far as possible to relieve the pressure that otherwise would fall upon the throat. In dumminess, or immobility, the hanging position of the head and the stupid expression are rather characteristic. In pleuisy, peritonitis, and some other painful diseases of the internal organs, the rigid position of the body denotes an effort of the animal to avoid pressures upon and to protect the inflamed sensitive region.

The horse may be down in the stall and unable to rise. This condition may result from paraplegia, from azoturia, from forage poisoning, from tetanus, or from painful conditions of the bones or feet, such as osteoporosis or founder. Lying down at unusual times or in unusual positions may indicate disease. The first symptom of colic may be a desire on the part of the horse to lie down at a time or place that is unusual or inappropriate. Sometimes disinclination to lie down is an indication of disease. Where there is difficulty in breathing, the horse knows that he can manage himself better upon his feet than upon his breast or side. It happens, therefore, that in nearly all serious disease of the respiratory tract, the horse stands persistently, day and night, until recovery has commenced and breathing is easier, or until the animal falls from sheer exhaustion. Where there is stiffness and soreness of the muscles, as in rheumatism, inflammation of the muscles from overwork, or of the bones in osteoporosis, or of the feet in founder, or where the muscles are stiff and beyond control of the animal, as in tetanus, a standing positio is maintained, because the horse seems to realize that when he lies down he will be unable to rise.

Abnormal attitudes are assumed in painful diseases of the digestive organs (colic). A horse with colic may sit upon his haunches, like a dog, or may stand upon his hind feet and fest upon his knees in front or may endeavor to balance himself upon his back, with all four feet in the air. These positions are assumed because they give relief from pain by lessening pressure, or tension upon the sensitive structures.

Under the general condition of the animal it may be necessary to observe the condition, or state, of nutrition; the conformation, so far as it may indicate the constitution and the temperament. By observing the condition of nutrition one may be able to determine to a great extent the effect that the disease has already had upon the animal and to estimate the amount of strength that remains and that will be available for the repair of the diseased tissues. A good condition of nutrition is shown by the rotundity of the body, the pliability and softness of the skin, and the tone of the hair. If the subcutaneous fat has disappeared and the muscles are wasted, allowing the bony prominences to stand out; if the skin is tight and inelastic and the coat dry and harsh, we have evidence of a low state of nutrition. This may have resulted from a severe and long-continued disease or from lack of proper food and care. Where an animal is emaciated—that is, becomes thin—there is first a loss of fat and later the muscles shrink. By observing the amount of shrinkage in the muscles

185

one has some indication as to the duration of the unfavorable conditions that the animal has lived under.

By constitution we understand the innate ability of the animal to withstand disease or unfavorable conditions of life. The constitution depends largely upon the conformation. The type of construction that usually accompanies the best constitution is a deep, broad chest, allowing plenty of room for the lungs and heart, indicating that these vital organs are well developed; capacious abdomen, allowing sufficient space for well-developed organs of digestion; the loins should be short—that is, the space should be short between the last rib and the point of the hip; the head and neck should be well molded, without superfluous or useless tissues; this gives a clear-cut throat. The ears, eyes, and face should have an expression of alertness and good breeding. The muscular development should be good; the shoulders, forearms, croup, and thighs must have the appearance of strength. The withers are sharp, which means that they are not loaded with useless, superfluous tissue; the legs are straight and their axes are parallel; the knees and hock are low, which means that the forearms and thighs are long and cannons relatively short. The cannons are broad from in front to behind, and relatively thin from side to side. This means that the bony and tendinous structures of the legs are well developed and well placed. The hoofs are compact, tense, firm structures, and their soles are concave and frogs large. Such a horse is likely to have a good constitution and to be able to resist hard work, fatigue, and disease to a maximum degree. On the other hand, a poor constitution is indicated by a shallow, narrow chest, small bones, long loins, course neck and head, with a thick throat, small bony, and muscular developments, Short thighs and forearms, small joints, long round cannons, and hoofs of open texture with flat soles.

The temperament is indicated by the manner in which the horse responds to external stimuli. When the horse is spoken to, or when he sees or feels anything that stimulates or gives alarm, if he responds actively, quickly, and intelligently, he is said to be of lively, or nervous, temperament. On the other hand, if he responds in a slow, sluggish manner, he is said to have a sluggish, or lymphatic, temperament. The temperament is indicated by the gait, by the expression of the face, and by carriage of the head and ears. The nature of the temperament should be taken into consideration in an endeavor to ascertain the severity of a given case of illness, because the general expression of an animal in disease as well as in health depends to a large extent on the temperament.

The Skin and The Visible Mucous Membranes

The condition of the skin is a fair index to the condition of the animal. The effect of disease and emaciation upon the pliability of the skin have been referred to above. There is no part of the body that loses its elasticity and tone as a result of disease sooner than the skin. The practical herdsman or flockmaster can gain a great deal of information as to the condition of an animal merely by grasping the coat and looking at and feeling the skin. Similarly, the condition of the animal is shown to a certain extent by the appearance of the mucous membranes. For example, when the horse is anemic as a result of disease or of inappropriate food the mucous membranes become pale. This change in the mucous membranes can be seen most readily in the lining of the eyelids and in the lining of the nostril. For convenience of examination the eyelids can readily be everted. Paleness means weak circulation or poor blood. Increased redness occurs physiologically in painful conditions, excitement, and following severe exertion. Under such conditions the increase of circulation is transitory. In fevers there is an increased redness in the mucous membrane, and this continues so long as the fever lasts. In some diseases red spots or streaks form in the mucous membrane. This usually indicates an infectious disease of considerable severity, and occurs in blood poisoning, purpura hemorrhagica, hemorrhagic septicemia, and in urticaria. When the liver is deranged and does not operate, or when the red-blood corpuscles are broken down, as in serious cases of influenza, there is a yellowish discoloration of the mucous membrane. The mucous membranes become bluish or blue when the blood is imperfectly oxidized and contains an excess of carbon dioxide. This condition exists in any serious disease of the respiratory tract, as pneumonia, and in heart failure.

The temperature of the skin varies with the temperature of the body. If there is fever the temperature of the skin is likely to be increased. Sometimes, however, as a result of poor circulation and irregular distribution of the blood, the body may be warmer than normal, while the extremities (the legs and ears) may be cold. Where the general surface of the body becomes cold it is evident that the small blood vessels in the skin have contracted and are keeping the blood away, as during a chill, or that the heart is weak and is unable to pump the blood to the surface, and that the animal is on the verge of collapse.

The skin is moist, to a certain degree, at all times in a healthy horse. This moisture is not in the form of a perceptible sweat, but it is enough to keep the skin pliable and to cause the hair to have a soft, healthy feel. In some chronic diseased conditions and in fever, the skin becomes dry. In this case the hair has a harsh feel that is quite different from the condition observed in health, and from the fact of its being so dry the individual hairs do not adhere to one another, they stand apart, and the animal has what is known as "a staring coat." When, during a fever, sweating occurs, it is usually an indication that the crisis is passed. Sometimes sweating is an indication of pain. A horse with tetanus or azoturia sweats profusely. Horses sweat freely when there is a serious impediment to respiration; they sweat under excitement, and, of course, from the well-known physiological causes of heat and work. Local sweating, or sweating of a restricted area of the body, denotes some kind of nerve interference.

Swellings of the skin usually come from wounds or other external causes and have no special connection with the diagnosis of internal diseases. There are, however, a number of conditions in which the swelling of the skin is a symptom of a derangement of some other part of the body. For example, there is the well-known "stocking," or swelling of the legs about the fetlock joints, in influenza. There is the soft swelling of the hind legs that occurs so often in draft horses when standing still and that comes from previous inflammation (lymphangitis) or from insufficient heart power. Dropsy, or edema of the skin, may occur beneath the chest or abdomen from heart insufficiency or from chronic collection of fluid in the chest or abdomen (hydrothorax, ascites, or anemia). In anasarca or purpura hemorrhagica large soft swellings appear on any part of the skin, but usually on the legs, side of the body, and about the head.

Gas collects under the skin in some instances. This comes from a local inoculation with an organism which produces a fermentation beneath the skin and causes the liberation of gas which inflates the skin, or the gas may be air that enters through a wound penetrating some air-containing organ, as the lungs. The condition here described is known as emphysema. Emphysema may follow the fracture of a rib when the end of a bone is forced inward and caused to penetrate the lung, or it may occur, when, as a result of an ulcerating process, an organ containing air is perforated. This accident is more common in cattle than it is in horses. Emphysema is recognized by the fact that the swelling that it causes is not hot or sensitive on pressure. It emits a peculiar crackling sound when it is stroked or pressed upon.

Wounds of the skin may be of importance in the diagnosis of internal disease. Wounds over the bony prominence, as the point of the hip, the point of the shoulder, and the greatest convexity of the ribs, occurs when a horse is unable to stand for a long time and, through continually lying upon his side, has shut off the circulation to the portion of the skin that covers parts of the body that carry the greatest weight, and in this way has caused them to mortify. Little, round, soft, dough-like swellings occur on the skin and may be scattered freely over the surface of the body when the horse is afflicted with urticaria. Similar eruptions, but distributed less generally, about the size of a silver dollar, may occur as a symptom of dourine, or colt distemper. Hard lumps, from which radiate welt-like swellings of the lymphatics, occur in gland-

189

ers, and blisterlike eruptions occur around the mouth and pasterns in horsepox.

Temperature

The temperature of the horse is determined roughly by placing the fingers in the mouth or between the thighs or by allowing the horse to exhale against the cheek or back of the hand. In accurate examination, however, these means of determining temperature are not relied upon, but recourse is had to the use of thermometer. The thermometer used for taking the temperature of a horse is a self-registering clinical thermometer, similar to that used by physicians, but larger, being from 5 to 6 inches long. The temperature of the animal is measured in the rectum.

The normal temperature of the horse varies somewhat under different conditions. It is higher in the young animal than in the old, and is higher in hot weather than in cold. The weather and exercise decidedly influence the temperature physiologically. The normal temperature varies from 99.5° to 101°F. If the temperature rises to 102.5° the horse is said to have a low fever; if the temperature reaches 104° the fever is moderate; if it reaches 106° it is high, and above this point it is regarded as very high. In some diseases, such as tetanus or sunstroke, the temperature goes as high as 108° or 110°. In the ordinary infectious diseases it does not often exceed 106°. A temperature of 107.5° and above is very dangerous and must be reduced promptly if the horse is to be saved.

The Organs of Circulation

The first item in this portion of the examination consists in taking the pulse. The pulse may be counted and its character may be determined at any point where a large artery occupies a situation close to the skin and above a hard tissue, such as a bone, cartilage, or tendon. The most convenient place for taking the pulse of the horse is at the jaw. The external maxillary artery runs from between the jaws, around the lower border of the jawbone and up on the outside of the jawbone to the face. It is located immediately in front of the heavy muscles of the cheek. Its throb can be felt most distinctly just before it turns around the lower border of the jawbone. The balls of the first and second or of the second and third fingers should be pressed lightly on the skin over this artery when its pulsations are to be studied.

The normal pulse of the healthy horse varies in frequency as follows:

Stallion . . . . 28 to 32 beats per minute.
Gelding . . . . 33 to 38 beats per minute.
Mare . . . . 34 to 40 beats per minute.
Foal 2 to 3 years old . . . . 40 to 50 beats per minute.
Foal 6 to 12 months old . . 45 to 60 beats per minute.
Foal 2 to 4 weeks old . . . . 70 to 90 beats per minute.

The pulse is accelerated by the digestion of rich food, by hot weather, exercise, excitement, and alarm. It is slightly more rapid in the evening than it is in the morning. Well-bred horses have a slightly more rapid pulse than sluggish, cold-blooded horses. The pulse should be regular; that is, the separate beats should follow each other after intervals of equal length, and the beats should be of equal fullness, or volume.

In disease, the pulse may become slower or more rapid than in health. Slowing of the pulse may be caused by old age, great exhaustion, or excessive cold. It may be due to depression of the central nervous system, as in dumminess, or be the result of the administration of drugs, such as digitalis or strophantus. A rapid pulse is almost always found in fever, and the more severe the infection and the weaker the heart, the more rapid is the pulse. Under these conditions, the beats may rise to 80, 90, or even 120 per minute. When the pulse is above 100 per minute the outlook for recovery is not promising, and especially if this symptom accompanies high temperature or occurs late in an infectious disease. In nearly all of the diseases of the heart and in anemia the pulse becomes rapid.

The pulse is irregular in diseases of the heart, and especi-

191

ally where the valves are affected. The irregularity may consist in varying intervals between the beats or the dropping of one or more beats at regular or irregular intervals. The latter condition sometimes occurs in chronic diseases of the brain. The pulse is said to be weak, or soft, when the beats are indistinct, because little blood is forced through the artery by each contraction of the heart. This condition occurs when there is a constriction of the vessels leading from the heart and it occurs in certain infectious and febrile diseases, and is an indication of heart weakness.

In examining the heart itself it is necessary to recall that it lies in the anterior portion of the chest slightly to the left of the median line and that it extends from the third to the sixth rib. It extends almost to the breastbone, and a little more than half of the distance between the breastbone and the backbone. In contracting, it rotates slightly on its axis, so that the point of the heart, which lies below, is pressed against the left chest wall at a place immediately above the point of the elbow. The heart has in it four chambers—two in the left and two in the right side. The upper chamber of the left side (left auricle) receives the blood as it comes from the lungs, passes it to the lower chamber of the left side (left ventricle), and from here it is sent with great force (for this chamber has very strong, thick walls) through the aorta and its branches (the arteries) to all parts of the body. The blood returns through the veins to the upper chamber of the right side (right auricle), passes then to the lower chamber of the right side (right ventricle), and from this chamber is forced into the lungs to be oxidized. The openings between the chambers of each side and into the aorta are guarded by valves.

If the horse is not too fat, one may feel the impact of the apex of the heart against the chest wall with each contraction of the heart, by placing the hand on the left side back of the fifth rib and above the point of the elbow. The thinner and the better bred the horse is the more distinctly this impact is felt. If the animal is excited, or if he has just been exercised, the impact is stronger than when the horse is at rest. If the horse is weak, the impact is reduced in force.

The examination of the heart with the ear is an important matter in this connection. Certain sounds are produced by each contraction of the normal heart. It is customary to divide these into two, and to call them the first and second sounds. These two sounds are heard during each pulsation and any deviation of the normal indicates some alteration in the structure or the functions of the heart. In making this examination, one may apply the left ear over the heavy muscles of the shoulder back of the shoulder joint, and just above the point of the elbow, or, if the sounds are not heard distinctly, the left fore leg may be drawn forward by an assistant and the right ear placed against the lower portion of the chest wall that is exposed in this manner.

The first sound of the heart occurs while the heart muscle is contracting and while the blood is being forced from the heart and the valves are rendered taut to prevent the return of the blood from the lower to the upper chambers. The second sound follows quickly after the first and occurs during rebound of blood in the arteries, causing pressure in the aorta and tensions of the valves guarding its opening into the left ventricle. The first sound is of a high pitch and is longer and more distinct than the second. Under the influence of disease these sounds may be altered in various ways. It is not profitable, in a work such as this, to describe the details of these alterations. Those who are interested will find this subject fully discussed in the veterinary textbooks.

The Organs of Respiration

In examining this system of organs and their functions it is customary to begin by noticing the frequency of the respiratory movements. This point can be determined by observing the motions of the nostrils or of the flanks; on a cold day one can see the condensation of the moisture of the warm air as it comes from the lungs. The normal rate of respiration for a healthy horse at rest is from 8 to 16 per minute. The rate is faster in young animals than in old, and is increased by work, hot weather, overfilling of the stomach, pregnancy, lying upon the side, etc. Acceleration of the respiratory rate where no physiological cause operates is due to a variety of conditions. Among these is fever; restricted area of active lung tissue, from filling of portions of the lungs with inflammatory exudate, as in pneumonia; compression of the lungs or loss of elasticity; pain in the muscles controlling the respiratory movements; excess of carbon-dioxide in the blood; and constriction of the air passages leading to the lungs.

Difficult or labored respiration is known as dyspnea. It occurs when it is difficult, for any reason, for the animal to obtain the amount of oxygen that it requires. This may be due to filling of the lungs, as in pneumonia; to painful movements of the chest, as in rheumatism or pleurisy; to tumors of the nose and paralysis of the throat, swellings of the throat, foreign bodies, or weakness of the respiratory passages, fluid in the chest cavity, adhesions between the lungs and chest walls, loss of elasticity of the lungs, etc. Where the difficulty is great the accessory muscles of respiration are brought into play. In great dyspnea the horse stnads with his front feet apart, with his neck straight out, and his head extended upon his neck. The nostrils are widely dilated, the face has an anxious expression, the eyeballs protrude, the up-and-down motion of the larynx is aggravated, the amplitude of the movement of the chest walls increased, and the flanks heave.

The expired air is of about the temperature of the body. It contains considerable moisture, and it should come with equal force from each nostril and should not have an unpleasant odor. If the stream of air from one nostril is stronger than from the other, there is an indication of an obstruction in a nasal chamber. If the air possesses a bad odor, it is usually an indication of putrefaction of a tissue or secretion in some part of the respiratory tract. A bad odor is found where there is necrosis of the bone in the nasal passages or in chronic catarrh. An ulcerating tumor of the nose or throat may cause the breath to have an offensive odor. The most offensive breath occurs where there is necrosis, or gangrene, of the lungs.

In some diseases there is a discharge from the nose. In order to determine the significance of the discharge it should be examined closely. One should ascertain whether it comes from one or both nostrils. If but from one nostril, it probably originates in the head. The color should be noted. A thin, watery discharge may be composed of serum, and it occurs in the earlier stages of coryza or nasal catarrh. An opalescent, slightly tinted discharge is composed of mucous and indicates a little more severe irritation. If the discharge is sticky and pus-like, a deeper difficulty or more advanced irritation is indicated. If the discharge contains flakes and clumps of more or less dried, agglutinated particles, it is probable that it originates within a cavity of the head, as the sinuses or guttural pouches. The discharge of glanders is of a peculiar sticky nature and adheres tenaciously to the wings of the nostrils. The discharge of pneumonia is of a somewhat red or reddish brown color, and, on this account, has been described as a prune-juice discharge. The discharge may contain blood. If the blood appears as clots or as streaks in the discharge, it probably originates at some point in the upper part of the respiratory tract. If the blood is in the form of a fine froth, it comes from the lungs.

In examining the interior of the nasal pasage one should remember that the normal color of the mucous membrane is a rosy pink and that its surface is smooth. If ulcers, nodules, swellings, or tumors are found, these indicate disease. The ulcer that is characteristic of glanders is described fully in connection with the discussion of that disease.

Between the lower jaws there are several clusters of lymphatic glands. These glands are so small and so soft that it is difficult to find them by feeling through the skin, but when a suppurative disease exists in the upper part of the respiratory tract these glands become swollen and easy to feel. They may become soft and break down and discharge as abscesses; this is seen constantly in strangles. On the other hand, they may become indurated and hard from the proliferation of connective tissue and attach themselves to the jawbone, to the tongue, or to the skin. This is seen in chronic glanders. If the glands are swollen and tender to pressure, it indicates that the disease causing the enlargement is acute; if they are

195

hard and insensitive, the disease causing the enlargement is chronic.

The manner in which the horse coughs is of importance in diagnosis. The cough is a forced expiration, following immediately upon a forcible separation of the vocal cords. The purpose of the cough is to remove some irritant substance from the respiratory passages, and it occurs when irritant gases, such as smoke, ammonia, sulphur vapor, or dust, have been inhaled. It occurs from inhalation of cold air if the respiratory passages are sensitive from disease. In laryngitis, bronchitis, and pneumonia, cough is very easily excited, and occurs merely from accumulation of mucus and inflammatory product upon the irritated respiratory mucous membrane. If one wishes to determine the character of the cough, it can easily be excited by pressing upon the larynx with the thumb and finger. The larynx should be pressed from side to side and the pressure removed the moment the horse commences to cough. A painful cough occurs in pleurisy, also in laryngitis, bronchitis, and bronchial pneumonia. Pain is shown by the effort the animal exerts to repress the cough. The cough is not painful, as a rule, in the chronic diseases of the respiratory tract. The force of the cough is considerable when it is not especially painful and when the lungs are not seriously involved. When the lungs are so diseased that they cannot be filled with a large volume of air, and in heaves, the cough is weak, as it is also in weak, debilitated animals. If mucus or pus is coughed out, or if the cough is accompanied by a gurgling sound, it is said to be moist; it is dry when these characteristics are not present—that is, when the air in passing out passes over surface not loaded with secretion.

In the examination of the chest we resort to percussion and auscultation. When a cask or other structure containing air is tapped upon, or percussed, a hollow sound is given forth. If the cask contains fluid, the sound is of a dull and of quite a differnt character. Similarly, the amount of air contained in the lungs can be estimated by tapping upon, or percussing, the walls of the chest. Percussion is practiced with the fingers alone or with the aid of a special percussion hammer and an object to strike upon known as a pleximeter. If the fingers are used, the middle finger of the left hand should be pressed firmly against the side of the horse and should be struck with the ends of the fingers of the right hand bent at a right angle so as to form a hammer. The percussion hammer sold by instrument makers is made of rubber or has a rubber tip, so that when the pleximeter, which is placed against the side, is struck the impact will not be accompanied by a noise. After experience in this method of examination one can determine with a considerable degree of accuracy whether the lung contains a normal amount of air or not. If, as in pneumonia, air has been displaced by inflammatory product occupying the air space, or if fluid collects in the lower part of the chest, the percussion sound becomes dull. If, as in emphysema or in pneumothorax, there is an excess of air in the chest cavity, the percussion sound becomes abnormally loud and clear.

Auscultation consists in the examination of the lungs with the ear applied closely to the chest wall. As the air goes in and out of the lungs a certain soft sound is made which can be heard distinctly, especially upon inspiration. This sound is intensified by anything that accelerates the rate of respiration, such as exercise. This soft, rustling sound is known as vesicular murmur, and wherever it is heard it signifies that the lung contains air and is functionally active. The vesicular murmur is weakened when there is an inflammatory infiltration of the lung tissue or when the lungs are compressed by fluid in the chest cavity. The vesicular murmur disappears when air is excluded by the accumulation of inflammatory product, as in pneumonia, and when the lungs are compressed by fluid in the chest cavity. The vesicular murmur becomes rough and harsh in the early stages of inflammation of the lungs, and this is often the first sign of the beginning of pneumonia.

By applying the ear over the lower part of the windpipe in front of the breastbone a somewhat harsh, blowing sound may be heard. This is known as the bronchial murmur and is heard in normal conditions near the lower part of the trachea and to a limited extent in the anterior portions of the lungs after sharp exercise. When the bronchial murmur is heard over other portions of the lungs, it may signify that the lungs are more or less solidified by disease and the blowing, bronchial murmur is transmitted through this solid lung to the ear from a distant part of the chest. The bronchial murmur in an abnormal place signifies that there exists pneumonia or that the lungs are compressed by fluid in the chest cavity.

Additional sounds are heard in the lungs in some diseased conditions. For example, when fluid collects in the air passages and the air is forced through it or is caused to pass through tubes containing secretions or pus. Such sounds are of a gurgling or bubbling nature and are known as mucous rales. Mucous rales are spoken of as being large or small as they are distinct or indistinct, depending upon the quantity of fluid that is present and the size of the tube in which this sound is produced. Mucous rales occur in pneumonia after the solidified parts begin to break down at the end of the disease. They occur in bronchitis and in tuberculosis, where there is an excess of secretion.

Sometimes a shrill sound is heard, like the note of a whistle, fife, or flute. This is due to a dry constriction of the bronchial tubes and it is heard in chronic bronchitis and in tuberculosis.

A friction sound is heard in pleurisy. This is due to the rubbing together of roughened surfaces, and the sound produced is similar to a dry rubbing sound that is caused by rubbing the hands together or by rubbing upon each other two dry rough pieces of leather.

The Examination of the Digestive Tract

The first point in connection with the examination of the organs of digestion is the appetite and the manner of taking food and drink. A healthy animal has a good appetite. Loss of appetite does not point to a special diseased condition, but comes from a variety of causes. Some of these causes, indeed, may be looked upon as being physiological. Excitement, strange surroundings, fatigue, and hot weather may all cause

198

loss of appetite. Where there is cerebral depression, fever, profound weakness, disorder of the stomach, or mechanical difficulty in chewing or swallowing, the appetite is diminished or destroyed. Sometimes there is an appetite or desire to eat abnormal things, such as dirty bedding, roots of grass, soil, etc. This desire usually comes from a chronic disturbance of nutrition.

Thirst is diminished in a good many mild diseases unaccompanied by distinct fever. It is seen where there is great exhaustion or depression or profound brain disturbance. Thirst in increased after profuse sweating, in diabetes, diarrhea, in fever, at the crisis of infectious diseases, and when the mouth is dry and hot.

Some diseases of the mouth or throat make it difficult for the horse to chew or swallow his food. Where difficulty in this respect is experienced, the following-named conditions should be borne in mind and carefully looked for: Diseases of the teeth, consisting in decay, fracture, abscess formation, or overgrowth; inflammatory conditions, or wounds or tumors of the tongue, cheeks, or lips; paralysis of the muscles of chewing or swallowing; foreign bodies in upper part of the mouth between the molar teeth; inflammation of throat. Difficulty in swallowing is sometimes shown by the symptom known as "quidding." Quidding consists in dropping from the mouth well-chewed and insalivated boluses of food. A mouthful of hay, for example, after being ground and masticated, is carried to the back part of the mouth. The horse then finds that from tenderness of the throat, or from some other cause, swallowing is difficult or painful, and the bolus is then dropped from the mouth. Another quantity of hay is similarly prepared, only to be dropped in turn. Sometimes quidding is due to a painful tooth, the bolus being dropped from the mouth when this tooth is struck and during the pang that follows. Quidding may be practiced so persistently that a considerable pile of boluses of food accumulate in the mnager or on the floor of the stall. In pharyngitis one of the symptoms is a return through the nose of fluid that the horse attempts to swallow.

In some brain diseases, and particularly in chronic internal hydrocephalus, the horse has a most peculiar manner of swallowing and of taking food. A similar condition is seen in hyperemia of the brain. In eating the horse will sink his muzzle into the grain in the feed box and eat for a while without raising the head. Long pauses are made while the food is in the mouth. Sometimes the horse will eat very rapidly for a little while and then slowly; the jaws may be brought together so forcibly that the teeth gnash. In eating hay the horse will stop at times with hay protruding from the mouth and stand stupidly, as though he has forgotten what he was about.

In examining the mouth one should first look for swellings or for evidence of abnormal conditions upon the exterior; that is the front and sides of the face, the jaws, and about the muzzle. By this means wounds, fractures, tumors, abscesses, and disease accommpanied by eruptions about the muzzle may be detected. The interior of the mouth is examined by holding the head up and inserting the fingers through the interdental space in such a way as to cause the mouth to open. The mucous membrane should be clean and of a light-pink color, excepting on the back of the tongue, where the color is a yellowish gray. As abnormalities of this region, the chief are diffuse inflammation, characterized by redness and catarrhal discharge; local inflammation, as from eruptions, ulcers, or wounds; necrosis of the lower jawbone in front of the first back tooth; and swellings. Foreign bodies are sometimes found embedded in the mucous-membrane lining of the mouth or lodged between the teeth.

The examination of the pharynx and of the esophagus is made chiefly by pressing upon the skin covering these organs in the region of the throat and along the left side of the neck in the jugular gutter. Sometimes, when a more careful examination is necessary, an esophageal tube or probang is passed through the nose or mouth down the esophagus to the stomach.

Vomiting is an act consisting in the expulsion of all or part of the contents of the stomach through the mouth or nose. This act is more difficult for the horse than for most of the other domestic animals, because the stomach of the horse is small and does not lie on the floor of the abdominal cavity, so that the abdominal walls in contracting do not bring pressure to bear upon it so directly and forcibly, as is the case in many other animals. Beside this, there is a loose fold of mucous membrane at the point where the esophagus enters the stomach, and this forms a sort of valve which does not interfere with the passage of food into the stomach, but does interfere with the exit of food through the esophageal opening. Still, vomiting is a symptom that is occasionally seen in the horse. It occurs when the stomach is very much distended with food or with gas. Distention stretches the mucous membrane and eradicates the valvular fold referred to, and also makes it possible for more pressure to be exerted upon the stomach through the contraction of the abdominal muscles. Since the distention to permit vomiting must be extreme, it not infrequently happens that it leads to rupture of the stomach walls. This has caused the impression in the minds of some that vomiting cannot occur in the horse without rupture of the stomach, but this is incorrect, since many horses vomit and afterwards become entirely sound. After rupture of the stomach has occurred vomiting is impossible.

In examination of the abdomen one should remember that its size depends largely upon the breed, sex, and conformation of the animal, and also upon the manner in which the animal has been fed and the use to which it has been put. A pendulous abdomen may be the result of an abdominal tumor or of an accumultaion of fluid in the abdominal cavity; or, on the other hand, it may merely be an indication of pregnancy, or of the fact that the horse has been fed for a long time on bulky and innutritious food. Pendulous abdomen occurring in a work horse kept on a concentrated diet is an abnormal condition. The abdomen may increase suddenly in volume from accumulation of gas in tympanic colic. The abdomen becomes small and the horse is said to be "tucked up" from long-continued poor appetite, as in disease of the digestive tract and in fever. This condition also occurs in tetanus from the contraction of the abdominal walls and in diarrhea from emptiness.

In applying the ear to the flank, on either the right or left side, certain bubbling sounds may be heard that are known as peristaltic sounds, because they are produced by peristalsis, or worm-like contraction of the intestines. These sounds are a little louder on the right side than on the left on account of the fact that the large intestines lie in the right flank. Absence of peristaltic sounds is always an indication of disease, and suggests exhaustion or paralysis of the intestines. This may occur in certain kinds of colic and is an unfavorable symptom. Increased sounds are heard where the intestines are contracted more violently than in health, as in spasmodic colic, and also where there is an excess of fluid or gas in the intestinal canal.

The feces show, to a certain extent, the thoroughness of digestion. They should show that the food has been well ground, and should, in the horse, be free from offensive odor or coatings of mucus. A coating of mucus shows intestinal catarrh. Blood on the feces indicates severe inflammation. Very light color and bad odor may come from inactive liver. Parasites are sometimes in the dung.

Rectal examination consits in examination of the organs of the pelvic cavity and posterior portion of the abdominal cavity by the hand inserted into the rectum. This examination should be attempted by a veterinarian only, and is useless except to one who has a good knowledge of the anatomy of the parts concerned.

The Examination of the Nervous System

The great brain, or cerebrum, is the seat of intelligence, and it contains the centers that control motion in many parts of the body. The front portion of the brain is believed to be the region that is most important in governing the intelligence. The central and posterior portions of the cerebrum contain the centers for the voluntary motions of the face and of the front and hind legs. The growth of a tumor or an inflammatory change in the region of a center governing the motion of a certain part of the body has the effect of disturbing motion in that part by causing excessive contraction known as cramps, or inability of the muscles to contract, constituting the condition known as paralysis. The nerve paths from the cerebrum, and hence from these centers to the spinal cord and thence to the muscles, pass beneath the small brain, or the cerebellum, and through the medulla oblongata to the spinal cord. Interference with these paths has the effect of disturbing motion of the parts reached by them. If all of the paths on one side are interfered with, the result is paralysis of one side of the body.

The small brain, or cerebellum, governs the regularity, or coordination, of movements. Disturbances of the cerebellum cause a tottering, uncertain gait. In the medulla oblongata, which lies between the spinal cord and the cerebellum, are the centers governing the circulation and breathing.

The spinal cord carries sensory messages to the brain and motor impressions from the brain. The anterior portions of the cord contain the motor paths, and the posterior portions of the cord contain the sensory paths.

Paralysis of a single member or a single group of muscles is known as monoplegia and results from injury to the motor center or to a nerve trunk leading to the part that is involved. Paralysis of one-half of the body is known as hemiplegia and results from destruction or severe disturbances of the cerebral hemisphere of the opposite side of the body or from interference with nerve paths between the cerebellum, or small brain, and the spinal cord. Paralysis of the posterior half of the body is known as paraplegia and results from derangement of the spinal cord. If the cord is pressed upon, cut, or injured, messages cannot be transmitted beyond that point, and so the posterior part becomes paralyzed. This is seen when the back is fractured.

Abnormal mental excitement may be due to congestion of the brain or to inflammation. The animal so afflicted becomes vicious, pays no attention to commands, cries, runs about in a circle, stamps with the feet, strikes, kicks, etc. This condition is usually followed by a dull, stupid state, in which the animal stands with his head down, dull and irresponsive to external stimuli. Cerebral depression also occurs in the severe febrile infectious diseases, in chronic hydrocephalus, in chronic

203

diseases of the liver, in poisoning with a narcotic substance, and with chronic catarrh of the stomach and intestines.

Fainting is a symptom that is not often seen in horses. When it occurs it is shown by unsteadiness of gait, tottering, and, finally, inability to stand. The cause usually lies in a defect of the small brain, or cerebellum. This defect may be merely in respect of the blood supply, to congestion, or to anemia, and in this case it is likely to pass away and may never return, or it may be due to some permanent cause, as a tumor or an abscess, or it may result from a hemorrhage, from a defect of the valves of the heart, or from poisoning.

Loss of consciousness is known as coma. It is caused by hemorrhage in the brain, by profound exhaustion, or may result from a saturation of the system with the poison of some disease. Coma may follow upon cerebral depression, which occurs as a secondary state of inflammation of the brain.

Where the sensibility of a part is increased the condition is known as hyperasthesia, and where it is lost—that is, where there is no feeling or knowledge of pain—the condition is known as anasthesia. The former usually accompanies some chronic diseases of the spinal cord or the earlier stages of irritation of a nerve trunk. Hyperasthesia is difficult to detect in a nervous, irritable animal, and sometimes even in a horse of less sensitive temperament. An irritable, sensitive spot may be found surrounded by skin that is not sensitive to pressure. This is sometimes a symptom of beginning of inflammation of the brain. Anasthesia occurs in connection with cerebral and spinal paralysis, section of a nerve trunk leading to a part, in severe mental depression, and in narcotic poisoning.

Urinary and Sexual Organs

In considering the examination of the urinary and sexual organs we may consider, at the beginning, a false impression that prevails to an astonishing extent. Many horsemen are in the habit of pressing upon the back of a horse over the loins or of sliding the ends of the fingers along on either side of the median line of this region. If the horse depresses his back it is at once said "his kidneys are weak." Nothing could be more absurd or further from the truth. Any healthy horse —any horse with normal sensation and with a normally flexible back—will cause it to sink when manipulated in this way. If the kidneys are inflamed and sensitive, the back is held more rigidly and is not depressed under this pressure.

To examine the kidneys by pressure the pressure should be brought to bear over these organs. The kidneys lie beneath the ends of the transverse processes of the vertebrae of the loins and beneath the hindmost ribs. If the kidneys are acutely inflamed and especially sensitive, pressure or light blows applied here may cause the horse to shrink.

The physical examination of the sexual and generative organs is made in large part through the rectum, and this portion of the examination should be carried out by a veterinarian only. By this means it is possible to discover or locate cysts of the kidneys, urinary calculi in the ureters, bladder, or upper urethra, malformations, and acute inflammations accompanied by pain. The external genital organs are swollen, discolored, or show a discharge as a result of local disease or from disease higher in the tract.

The manner of urinating is sometimes of considerable diagnostic importance. Painful urination is shown by frequent attempts, during which but a small quantity of urine is passed; by groaning, by constrained attitude, etc. This condition comes from inflammation of the bladder or urethra, urinary calculi (stones of the bladder or urethra), hemorrhage, tumors, bruises, etc. The urine is retained from spasms of the muscle at the neck of the bladder, from calculi, inflammatory growths, tumors, and paralysis of the bladder.

The urine dribbles without control when the neck of the bladder is weakened or paralyzed. This condition is seen after the bladder is weakened from long-continued retention and where there is a partial paralysis of the hind quarters.

Horses usually void urine five to seven times a day, and pass from 4 to 7 quarts. Disease may be shown by increase in the number of voidings or of the quantity. Frequent urination indicates an irritable or painful condition of the bladder or urethra or that the quantity is excessive. In one form of chronic inflammation of the kidneys (interstitial nephritis) and in polyuria the quantity may be increased to 20 or 30 quarts daily. Diminution in the quantity of urine comes from profuse sweating, diarrhea, high fever, weak heart, diseased and non-secreting kidneys, or an obstruction to the flow.

The urine of the healthy horse is a pale or at times a slightly reddish yellow. The color is less intense when the quantity is large, and is more intense when the quantity is diminished. Dark-brown urine is seen in azoturia and in severe acute muscular rheumatism. A brownish green color is seen in jaundice. Red color indicates a mixture of blood from a bleeding point at some part of the urinary tract.

The urine of the healthy horse is not clear and transparent. It contains mucous which causes it to be slightly thick and stringy, and a certain amount of undissolved carbonate, causing it to be cloudy. A sediment collects when the urine is allowed to stand. The urine of the horse is normally alkaline. If it becomes acid the bodies in suspension are dissolved and the urine is made clear. The urine may be unusually cloudy from the addition of abnormal constituents, but to determine their character a chemical or microscopic examination is necessary. Red or reddish flakes or clumps in the urine are always abnormal, and denote a hemorrhage or suppuration in the urinary tract.

The normal specific gravity of the urine of the horse is about 1.040. It is increased when the urine is scanty and decreased when the quantity is excessive.

Acid reaction of the urine occurs in chronic intestinal catarrh, in high fever, and during starvation. Chemical and microscopic tests and examinations are often of great importance in diganosis, but require special apparatus and skill.

Other points in the examination of a sick horse require more discussion than can be afforded in this connection, and require special training on the part of the examiner. Among such points may be mentioned the examination of the organs of special sense, the examination of the blood, bacteriological examinations of the secretions, excretions, and tissues, specific reaction test, and diagnostic inoculation.

MINOR AILMENTS
OF HORSES

In order to prevent complications of disease arising out of apparently simple ailments or injuries, all animals affected should be treated as early as possible. If a veterinarian is not available considerable care can be given by the average horseman if he is able to recognize the symptoms. Following are some of the most common ailments encountered and the first aid treatments recommended. If an improved condition is not readily evident after first aid treatments call a veterinarian immediately.

Heat Exhaustion

Overheating and sunstroke. These are noncommunicable disturbances of the nervous system due to heat.

1. *Cause:* Caused by long continued hard or fast work during very humid wether, especially among animals not in good condition or having heavy coats.

2. *Prevention:* Do not overtax the strength of the animal. Watch animals for early symptoms. Clip animals that have heavy coats. Water frequently on hot days and give the horse an ample supply of salt.

3. *Symptoms:* Thumps, a condition described in a later paragraph, often precedes overheating. The animal that has been sweating freely will cease to sweat and will be dull and the gait is staggering or wobbly, especially in the hindquarters. If halted, the animal stands with the legs spraddled; breathing very rapidly and shallow; nostrils dilated; expression drawn and anxious: nasal membranes bluish red in color; and trembling of body muscles. The body feels hot to the

207

Plate IV

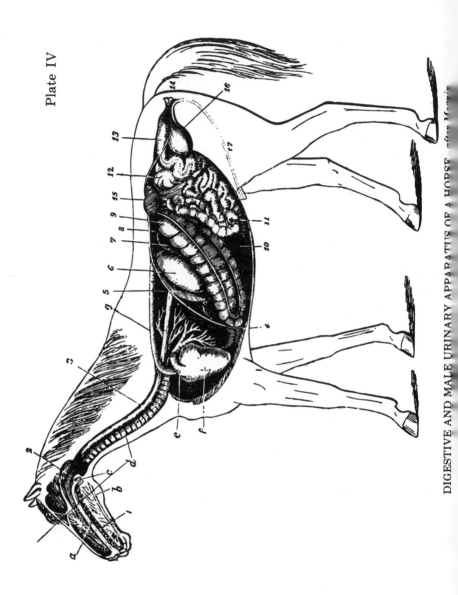

DIGESTIVE AND MALE URINARY APPARATUS OF A HORSE. after Morris

EXPLANATION OF PLATE IV.

Digestive Apparatus of the Horse.

1. Mouth.
2. Pharynx.
3. Esophagus.
4. Diaphragm.
5. Spleen.
6. Stomach (left sac).
7. Duodenum.
8. Liver (upper extremity).
9. Great colon.
10. Caecum.

11. Small intestine.
12. Floating colon.
13. Rectum.
14. Anus.
15. Left kidney and ureter.
16. Bladder.
17. Urethra.
A. Hard palate.
B. Tongue.
C. Soft palate.

D. Trachea.
E. Pulmonary artery (divided).
F. Heart.
G. Posterior aorta.

hand and the temperature will be from 103 to 109 degrees F.

4. *Nursing and First-aid Treatment:* Prompt first-aid treatment is of utmost importance. Stop the animal at once in the shade if any is nearby. Remove the equipment and apply large quantities of cold water to all parts of the body but especially to the head, sides of the neck, groins, and flanks. Wash out the mouth and nostrils with cold water. Give the animal three or four swallows of water every few minutes. Under this treatment the temperature will drop quite rapidly, and as improvement is noted move the animal about very slowly and rub the body to prevent chilling. As soon as the temperature is near normal, the animal may be moved slowly into the barn. The use of cold water in rectum prohibits obtaining of correct temperature readings which are very important. If temperatures lowered too much, the animal is apt to die of shock.

Thumps

Thumps are spasms of the diaphragm.

(1) *Cause:* Overwork or fast work during hot weather especially among animals not properly conditioned.

(2) *Symptoms:* General symptoms of fatigue with spasmodic jerking noticeable in the belly and flanks; frequently a distinct thumping sound will be heard.

(3) *Nursing and First-aid Treatment:* If riding away from the stable, halt the animal and if the temperature is elevated, reduce it by sponging the body with cold water and then have the animal ridden or led into the stable at the walk.

Exhaustion

(1) *Causes:* Over exertion; excessive or prolonged heavy work; lack of condition.

(2) *Symptoms:* After the animal arrives in stable, he may lie down and refuse his feed, especially his grain, yet drink considerable quantities of water. The temperature may be

slightly elevated and the pulse may be weak and thready. Sweating may be quite noticeable and possibly patchy, yet the body feels cold and clammy.

(3) *Nursing and First-aid Treatment:* Make a comfortable place for the animal to lie. Cover the body with a blanket to prevent chilling. Hand rub the legs. Give small amounts of water frequently. A period of rest is all that is needed to recuperate from excessive fatigue.

Colic

A general term applied to abdominal pain caused by digestive disturbance either spasmodic and flatulent or gas colic.

(1) *Causes:* The causes of both types of colic are very similar, but gas colic is more frequently caused by foods fermenting in the digestive tract. General causes are indigestible or spoiled feed, sudden changes in feed, overeating, eating while fatigued, working too soon after feeding, watering while exhausted or hot bolting the feed, overeating of green feed, and watering too soon after feeding. Windsucking or "cribbing" is frequently a cause of gas colic. Collections of sand in the bowel may result in repeated attacks of colic.

(2) *Prevention:* Close attention to the principles of feeding and watering will prevent most cases of colic.

(3) *Symptoms:* Pain as indicated by restlessness, pawing, stamping of the feet, looking around at the flanks, kicking at the abdomen, lying down, rolling, sweating, and frequent attempts to defecate usually resulting in the passage of but a few pellets of dung or a discharge of gas. In spasmodic form, the attacks are often intermittent with short periods of a few minutes of apparent freedom from pain. In the gas type of colic, the digestive tract is filled with gas, the belly is distended, and breathing is difficult.

(4) *Nursing and First-aid Treatment:* Place the animal in a well-bedded box stall. Get a veterinarian at once, if possible. Do not attempt to keep the animal from rolling, etc., unless he is throwing himself to the ground so violently that it is evident he may rupture some organ. Give frequent

rectal injections of 2 or 3 gallons of warm soapy water. Wring blankets out of hot water and wrap around the belly and flanks as hot as can be borne without burning the hands or animal. Water may be given in small amounts. Withhold all feed until at least 12 hours after all pain has disappeared and then feed lightly for 2 or 3 days.

Diarrhea

(1) *Causes:* Spoiled feed, overfeeding, of "washy" feeds, sudden changes of diet; and nervousness.

(2) *Prevention:* Careful attention to kind, quality, and quantity of feed and methods of feeding. Exclude "washy" feeds from the diet of animals which tend to scour.

(3) *Symptoms:* The droppings are frequent and of semi-fluid nature. If the condition continues long, the animal looses flesh and appetite is wanting.

(4) *Nursing and First-aid Treatment:* Correction of diet in mild cases will be sufficient. A veterinarian should be called in cases that do not show immediate results.

Azoturia

(1) *Cause:* Caused by violent exercise following idleness and heavy feeding.

(2) *Prevention:* When conditioned animals accustomed to regular work are given a period of complete rest for longer than a day, reduce the grain ration by at least one-half. When animals are exercised after a period of rest, they should be walked for at least 20 minutes after leaving the stables and not called upon to do more than a very small amount of fast work the first day.

(3) *Symptoms:* Increased excitability, profuse sweating, and rapid breathing are the first symptoms. Very soon the animal begins to stiffen in his hindquarters, drag the hind legs and knuckles over in the hind fetlocks. If continued in work the animal will become completely incapable of sup-

porting weight on the hind legs and fall to the ground, and in such cases the chances of recovery are remote. The urine is scanty and red or coffee-colored.

(4) *Nursing and First-aid Treatment:* Stop the animal immediately when the first symptoms are noticed. Remove the saddle or harness and cover with three or four blankets. Keep the animal standing, if possible; if not, provide a good bed. Heat some oats or common salt, place in a sack and spread over the loins to relieve the pain. If hot water is available, a hot blanket wrung out, placed over the back and loins, and covered with dry blankets is very beneficial. After a few hours the average case can be moved slowly to the stable, provided the distance is not too great. At this time he should be given a purgative which may be obtained from a veterinarian and be fed on bran mashes, grass, and hay for a few days.

Laminitis (Founder)

(1) *Causes:* Overeating grain, eating improper or spoiled feeds, colic, exhaustion, overexertion, long continued work on hard-surfaced roads, and drinking cold water while sweating.

(2) *Symptoms:* Intense lameness, which appears quickly. In mild cases the animal moves stiffly, taking short, rapid steps with the forefeet and with the hind legs carried well forward under the body to relieve the forefeet from the weight of the body. Usually only the forefeet are affected and the affected feet are very hot. The pulse and respiration are greatly accelerated and temperature may reach 105 degrees F.

(3) *Nursing and First-aid Treatment:* Remove the shoes from the affected feet and place the animal in a well-bedded box stall. Cover the affected feet and legs as high as the knees and hocks with several layers of burlap and keep saturated with cold water. (In this case the shoes need not be removed.) Laxative diet is indicated. Feed bran mashes and a little hay. Early treatment is an important factor. Cases

that are not cured in 4 or 5 days are likely to develop into chronic laminitis which is practically incurable. As soon as the acute pain has diminished, moderate walking exercise each day is beneficial. Following the attack, shoe with a bar shoe over a leather pad covering a tar and oakum pack. The horse should be induced to lie down. Moisture can be applied to the feet by packs as soon as the fever in the feet is noticed.

Scratches

An inflammation in the back of the pasten region.

(1) *Causes:* Wet muddy, and filthy surroundings; failure to dry legs that have become wet from slush, rain, or wash ing; pasterns not thoroughly cleaned while grooming; short clipping of hair on the back of the pastern. Most prevalent during wet, cold weather.

(2) *Symptoms:* Redness, heat, pain and swelling of the skin on the back of the pastern. Later the surface of the skin becomes moist and raw, and dust and dirt dry with the secretions to form a scabby mass sticking to the skin and hair. The skin may crack. Usually there is lameness.

(3) *Nursing and First-aid Treatment:* With soap and warm water carefully soak off all accumulated dirt and dried secretion. Rinse with clean, warm water and dry. Apply a white lotion pack under a bandage twice daily. Rest the animal on clean, dry standings and feed laxative feeds. After the moistness of the skin has decreased apply dry powdered boric acid or tamic acid held in place by cotton in a loose bandage. Avoid the use of water after the first cleansing.

Thrush

(1) *Causes:* Failure to clean out the depths of the commissures and cleft of the frog, lack of frog pressure, filthy standings, dryness of the feet, and cuts or tears in the horny frog are all contributing causes.

(2) *Prevention:* A hoof that is properly groomed once each day will not develop thrush. A thorough washing of the under surface of the hoof once a week will materially assist in prevention of this disease.

(3) *Symptoms:* Cracks, depressions, or fissures in the horn of the frog in which is found a thick, dark colored discharge with a very offensive odor. The cleft of the frog and the sides of the frog at the depths of the commissures are the parts usually diseased.

(4) *Nursing and First-aid Treatment:* Clean and wash the hoof. With a sharp hoof knife, trim away all diseased and torn horn and all ragged pieces. With cresolis solution (one and one-half teaspoonfuls to a cup of water) and stiff brush thoroughly scrub the horn. After it has dried, paint the area with iodine. Repeat the washing and iodine treatment daily until the horn begins to appear dry and then apply pine tar.

Tendonitis

Tendonitis is an inflammation of the large tendons on the back of the leg in the cannon region.

(1) *Causes:* A strain of these tendons; long toes and low heels; violent efforts and sudden checks, as in jumping or galloping over rocky, uneven ground; long-continued exertion in which the muscles tire and are more easily strained; lack of fit condition; tight bandaging.

(2) *Prevention:* Proper balance and shoeing of the feet. Have the animal in good, fit condition. Avoid other causes of the injury.

(3) *Symptoms:* Lameness; heat and swelling in the tendon, sensitiveness of the tendon to pressure. The tendons of the forelegs are far more frequently affected than are those of the hind legs. The tendons in the cannon region may be affected their entire length or only in a part of their length.

(4) *Nursing and First-aid Treatment:* Absolute rest is most essential. Shower the leg with cold water from a hose or apply cold or ice water packs throughout the day, and for the night apply a white lotion pack over the injured tendon.

After the acute swelling and tenderness have disappeared, bathe with hot water and massage, then rub the tendon briskly with tincture of iodine once daily.

Rope Burn

This is an injury usually occurring on the back of the pastern.

(1) *Causes:* Tying with the tie rope too long is the most frequent cause. Often caused by the animal getting his foot, usually a hind foot, over his own or an adjacent horse's tie rope or entangled in a picket line guy rope. An improperly made or improperly used side line of casting rope often results in rope burns.

(2) *Symptoms:* A simple chafe or abrasion of the skin. It may involve the underlying tendon. Lameness is usually a symptom.

(3) *Nursing and First-aid Treatment:* General methods of treatment same as for scratches (in a preceding paragraph) except that white lotion packs should not be used if the injury is more than a surface one.

Lameness

(1) Lameness may best be detected at the trot. When an animal is lame it takes as much weight as possible off the injured leg and places it on the opposite one. If lame in a foreleg, the animal will be seen to nod its head every time the sound foot comes to the ground. If lame behind, the hock of the sound leg comes higher and dips lower than that of the lame one, and the head may nod as the lame foot strikes the ground. Animals lame in both fore and hind legs take short strides with both; they idle along instead of striding out.

(2) Most cases of lameness occur at or below the knee and hock. The foot is the most common seat. Lameness in the shoulder is comparatively rare. In all cases where no apparent or sufficient cause can be detected the foot should be thoroughly examined.

216

Fractures

A fracture is a broken bone.

(1) *Causes:* Most fractures result from kicks inflicted by other animals. The bone forming the point of the hip may be fractured by falling on the side or by striking it against the side of a door.

(2) *Symptoms:* When any long supporting bone of the leg is completely fractured, the leg dangles helplessly and will bear no weight. When the bone forming the point of the hip is fractured the animal may show but few symptoms other than lameness, difficulty in advancing the hind leg on that side, tenderness and swelling over the seat of injury, and a noticeable lowering of the point of the hip on that side.

(3) *Nursing and First-aid Treatment:* Complete fractures of any of the supporting bones of the legs of horses or mules are generally considered incurable, and the destruction of the animal is usually advisable. Fracture of the bone forming the point of the hip will heal provided the animal is given a complete rest for a month or six weeks.

Sprains

A sprain is a joint injury usually without any break or injury of the overlying skin.

(1) *Causes:* Twisting or pulling of the joint or bending the joint beyond its normal range of action resulting in stretching or tearing of the ligaments.

(2) *Symptoms:* Marked lameness; heat and swelling over the joint; tenderness on pressure or manipulation.

(3) *Nursing and First-aid Treatment:* Treatment should be the same as outlined for Tendonitis.

Wounds

(1) *Classification:* Wounds are diveded into—
   a. Incised wounds or cuts.

b. Lacerated wounds or tears.

c. Punctured wounds or holes.

(2) *Treatment:*

a. Cleanliness of the wound itself, of the dressing and the dresser is of the greatest importance.

b. To stop bleeding: Stoppage of bleeding is the first point to be attended to. Tight bandaging above and below the wound or a pad on the wound is usually sufficient to control the flow. If a large blood vessel is cut and the end exposed, it should be tied around with clean thread which has been soaked in antiseptic.

c. *To clean:* Cut the hair from the edges of the wound and remove all dirt, clots of blood, splinters, and foreign bodies of all kinds. This may be done by carefully syringing the parts with clean warm water or a warm antiseptic solution.

d. *To close:* Sutures and bandages are used for this purpose, but no wound that has been dirty must ever be entirely closed. Sutures may be used in parts where there is little flesh, such as around the forehead, eyelids, and nose. They are less useful in the fleshy parts, because the movements of the muscles and swelling cause them to pull out.

e. *Drainage:* Drainage at the lowert part of the wound is necessary for the removal of pus. In horizontal wounds a small vertical opening must be made below the line of the stitches.

f. *Dressing:* Wounds should be dried carefully with gauze or cotton, treated with an antiseptic, covered with dry gauze or cotton, and a bandage applied; or cotton soaked in antiseptic may be put on and held in position by a bandage, care being taken to avoid undue pressure. If the location will not permit bandaging, the injured parts may be treated with an antiseptic and covered with a clean piece of cloth or gunny sack, the inside of which may be lined with a piece of gauze large enough to cover the wound. Bandaging for too long a period may prevent the area from covering itself with skin, resulting in proud flesh. After a wound has begun to granulate (fill in with repair tissue), it will often heal much better if no dressing or bandage is placed in contact with the wound, provided it is not irritated by flies.

g. *Rest and Restraint:* If the injury is slight, the animal may continue at work; otherwise he may be kept in a box stall, cross-tied, or subjected to some other form of restraint.

h. *After Care:* All wounds should be kept dry and dressings should be changed only often enough to keep the wound clean. As little washing as possible should be done, and the parts should be sopped instead of rubbed.

i. *Flies:* The healing of wounds that cannot be covered is sometimes retarded by the presence of flies. The edges of such wounds, and also the surface if not too moist, may be covered lightly with pine tar.

j. *Pround Flesh (Excessive Granulations):* In sluggish, slow-healing wounds small, rounded fleshly masses are called proud flesh. The growth may be kept down by removing with scissors to the level of the skin and treated with boric acid, tincture of iodine, powered burned alum or by searing to the level of the skin with a heated iron, care being taken to see that the surrounding skin is not burned. Inoculation for Tetanus (lockjaw) should be considered in any case where there is chance of infection.

Contusions (Bruises)

A contusion is an injury of a part without breaking the overlying skin.

(1) *Causes:* Blow from a blunt object. Being kicked is a common cause.

(2) *Symptoms:* When over a muscle, they produce soreness and lameness and, if severe, may rupture a blood vessel which will result in a fluctuating swelling caused by an accumulation of blood usually just under the skin. Such injuries are most common on the thigh and buttocks. Contusions over a joint may be mistaken for a sprain of the joint.

(3) *Nursing and First-aid Treatment:* Rest and general method of treatment as outlined for tendonitis. In bruises where a fluctuating swelling results that does not reduce in a week or ten days, the swelling may be opened with a knife

at its lowest point to allow the fluid contents to escape. After opening, the external parts should be kept clean and the external wound painted with iodine once daily.

Eye Injuries

(1) *Cause:* Apparently due to the effects of irritation of an ordinary wound by flies. They invariably occur during hot weather when flies are most prevalent.

(2) *Prevention:* Protect all wounds from flies by appropriate dressings or medicinal application.

(3) *Symptoms:* The wound tends to form proud flesh rapidly, and the surface of the area is porous and expels a considerable amount of thin discharge. Near the surface of the proud flesh and in its depths may often be found small, hard, grayish or yellowish bodies having much the appearance of cracked corn.

(4) *Nursing and First-aid Treatment:* Remove pronounced growth of proud flesh. Thereafter treat as other wounds with special protection from flies.

Summer Sores

(1) *Causes:* Eye injuries are usually due to blows, scratches, or punctures from brush, forage, etc., and to small objects lodging on the front of the eyeball or under the lids.

(2) *Symptoms:* Watery eye, flow of tears from the eye, reddened membranes, and partial or complete closing of the eye are symptoms of all forms of injury. If the cornea or clear part of the eyeball itself is injuried, the cut or wound may be visible, and surrounding it the eye will become milky white in color. Ordinarily foreign matter merely lodged behind the lids does not cause the eyeball to become milky in color.

(3) *Nursing and First-aid Treatment:* If there is any foreign body under the lids, flood it out with clean water using a syringe, or remove by the careful use of a tightly rolled

swab of cotton or gauze. Then flood the eye several times daily with boric acid solution prepared by dissolving two level teaspoons of boric acid in a cupful of warm water. Use an eye dropper for this purpose. Cover the eye with a pad of cotton about 6 inches square covered with gauze, and hold in position with strings tied about the head and to the halter, or sew the pad on the inside of an improvised head bandage made from a grain sack. In bad cases, soak the pad in boric acid solution before applying. Keep the animal in a dark place.

Treads and Overreaching

(1) *Causes:* Treads are injuries or wounds in the coronet on the front or sides of the feet which may be self-inflicted or inflicted by the shoes of other animals. They are caused frequently by animals crowding in stables, through doors, and in shipment. Overreaching wounds are selfinflicted and are injuries to the bulbs of heels, pastern, or fetlock, caused by the animal's hind foot striking the part. Those injuries are most frequently inflicted when landing after jumping an obstacle, at the extended trot, and at times at the gallop. Wounds similar to overreaching wounds are often caused on the heels of the hind feet by another horse crowding up on the animals from the rear.

(2) *Prevention:* The nature of some cases suggests the means of prevention. Shoeing with rocker-toed and high heels which speed up the action of the forefeet is often beneficial. Jumping horses, in which the injury cannot be prevented otherwise, should be jumped with bell boots.

(3) *Symptoms:* Treads wounds usually are in the coronet and the skin, and often some of the horn at the top of the hoof is torn. There is usually heat and swelling in the part. Most overreaching wounds occur at the bulbs of the heel; the skin above the horn is more bruised and scraped than cut; and the horn at the heel is torn loose and may be separated from the sensitive tissues, or the wound becomes infected.

221

(4) *Nursing and First-aid Treatment:* For either injury clip the hair around the wound and clean thoroughly with cresolis solution, removing all foreign material. With scissors cut off all loose flaps of skin or tissue and, with a hoof knife or rasp, thin somewhat the horn in the region of the injury. Saturate a small piece of cotton with iodine and bandage tightly over the injury. Dress in this manner daily. When the wound appears dry and is healing, cover with tar and a small pad of oakum and bandage tightly.

Interfering Wounds

Interfering wounds are self-inflicted wounds made on some part of the inside of the leg, usually the fetlock, by being struck by the hoof or shoe of the opposite leg.

(1) *Causes:* Defective conformation, such as toeing out, cow-hocked, and narrow breasted; defective shoeing; and traveling over uneven footing. Fatigued animals are more likely to interfere behind.

(2) *Prevention:* Corrective shoeing, etc. If not correctable, use leather or felt interfering boots, or pad the part with oakum held in place with a bandage.

(3) *Symptoms:* The injury may vary from a slight roughing of the hair at the coronet or inside of the fetlock to a deep wound causing marked lameness. At the moment of interfering, an animal will often carry the leg for a few steps without putting weight on it, then go very lame for a few steps and soon proceed without lameness.

(4) *Nursing and First-aid Treatment:* Treat the same as other wounds. Apply a thick, padded dressing to avoid further injury.

Penetrating Wounds Of The Foot

(1) *Causes:* Most penetrating wounds of the foot are caused by the animal stepping on nails or screws or by a misdirected shoeing nail.

(2) *Nursing and First-aid Treatment:* If the nail is still imbedded in the horn, clean all dirt from the bottom of the foot by washing and then wash with cresolis solution before removing it. Remove the nail or other object, and with a knife, thin the horn over a fair-sized area surrounding the penetration and make a final opening about ⅛ to ¼ inch in diameter through the horn to the sensitive tissue. Saturate a rather small piece of cotton with tincture of iodine and place it on the wound. Over this place a pad of oakum covering part of all of the bottom of the hoof and hold in place with strips of tin or light sheet metal of such length and width that their ends can be engaged between the hoof and the shoe on the inside and entirely around the shoe. Do not probe the wound in the sensitive tissue and do not compress the dressing so tightly that the secretions are dammed back into the wound. Dress daily with iodine until the wound appears to be dry and healing and then apply a tar dressing under an oakum pack about every 3 days until no further dressing is necessary. Inoculate for tetanus (lockjaw) in any case of penetrating wound.

Dry Feet

(1) *Causes:* Lack of frog pressure, lack of exercise, dry weather, allowing the shoes to remain on the feet too long, and a loss of the wax-like horny covering (periople) of the horny wall.

(2) *Prevention:* Make provision for frog pressure and exercise and animal regularly. During dry weather, pack the bottom of the hoof with wet clay, or turn horse on pasture.

(3) *Symptoms:* The first symptom is the hardness and drying of the horny frog. While dryness in itself may not cause lameness, it is an active cause of contracted heels, corns, thrush, etc.

(4) *Nursing and First-aid Treatment:* The first stop should be to correct errors in shoeing and the second to restore and maintain the normal moisture content of the horn. Moisture may be restored to the horn by packing the feet daily with

wet clay, by standing the animal in a shallow clay mud bath, by wet packs on the feet, or by standing in a foot bath. Turning on grass which is wet or has dew on is helpful, too. Treatment for Quarter Crack: Soften the horn of the wall by wet packs, bran poultices, or standing the animal in water for a few days. After this clean out the crack and cut away the overlapping edges of the horn. For an inch or more on each side of the crack and for 1½ inches or more downward from the coronary band, rasp the wall as thin as possible without injuring the "quick" or drawing blood. For a quarter crack, trim away the bearing surface of the wall from a point ½ inch in front of the crack back to and including the buttress so that the affected quarter does not come in contact with the shoe. Shoe with a bar shoe, with good frog pressure, over a leather pad with tar and oakum. Keep the wall soft with daily application of tar, especially over the crack. A little tar rubbed vigorously into the coronary band once a week will stimulate the growth of horn.

Sore Backs

Sore Backs are probably the greatest cause of disability among riding horses.

(1) *Causes:* Improper saddling, poorly fitted saddles, dirty or improperly folded saddle blankets, careless riding such as lounging in the saddle, unevenly placed loads, and poor conformation.

(2) *Prevention:*

a. The individual rider must be very careful that the adjustment of his saddle is correct and that his blanket is clean and accurately folded. Riders must sit erect in the saddle at all times. Riding on the cantle or standing in one stirrup is sure to bring saddle sores.

b. Intelligent application of the principles of correct saddling can usually overcome poor conformation or poorly fitted saddles. Small pads made from old blankets or strips of felt tacked on the bars of the saddle take the place of lack of flesh.

(3) *Treatment:*

a. Ascertain and remove the cause. In fresh cases where the skin is not broken it is sometimes beneficial to apply cold water baths with gentle hand rubbing. This should be followed by the application of wet packs saturated with cold water and held in position by means of a surcingle or bandage.

b. Injuries to the withers and ridge of the spine should be irrigated or bathed with cold water but without pressure and without massage.

c. Slight galls, chafes, or abrasions are treated with white lotion or powered boric acid.

d. "Sitfasts" are patches of dry dead skin and may involve deeper tissues. They are caused by continuous pressure of the saddle, cinch, or collar. When sitfasts appear, apply warm baths or warm poultices until the dead skin becomes loose. Then remove all dead and bruised tissue with forceps and a knife and treat with iodine and boric acid.

e. If it is necessary to continue to ride an animal with a sore back, means must be devised to relieve pressure from the affected part.

Prevention and Control Of Communicable Diseases

(1) *General Health:* Maintain animals in good condition, feed well, groom well, keep in clean surroundings, do not overwork, protect from undue exposure, and they will resist many forms of infection. Animals in rundown condition are very susceptible to disease.

(2) *Segregation:* Animals should be divided into three groups; affected, suspected, and healthy. The suspected animals include all those which have been in contact with the diseased. Attendants, watering and feeding arrangements, and all equipment should be included in the separation and should be kept separate until the outbreak is over. Once an animal is placed in the affected group it should remain there until all danger is over.

(3) *Disinfection:* Strict cleanliness of stalls, equipment,

225

water troughs, feed boxes, and feed bags is a good safeguard against the spread of disease. Stables, equipment, etc., which have been in contact with diseased animals should be disinfected with cresolis solution. Articles that can be boiled may be thoroughly disinfected in this manner.

Influenza

This is a very communicable disease, also known as shipping fever, affecting chiefly the respiratory system. It is spread by both direct and indirect contact.

(1) *Cause:* Influenza is caused by the animal's eating or breathing some of the body discharges of a diseased animal, particularly the nasal and bowel discharges.

(3) *Prevention:* Cleanliness of surroundings and good condition of animals. Quarantine of newly acquired animals for 21 days. Segregation of diseased animals. Disinfection of stall and equipment.

(3) *Symptoms:* The first symptoms noticed are depression, great weakness, loss of appetite, rapid breathing, hacking cough, and possibly a slight watery nasal discharge. At this stage the temperature is elevated (101.5 degreees to 106 degrees F.), and the mucous membrane of the eyelid will have a brick red color tinged with yellow. Later the nasal discharge becomes more profuse and usually thick and yellow. Pneumonia is often a complication. Young animals frequently develop strangles at the same time they have influenza.

(4) *Nursing and First-aid Treatment:* Isolate the diseased animal. Absolute rest and good nursing are very important. Allow plenty of sunshine and fresh air but protect the body from drafts. Keep the animals warm with blankets and leg bandages during cold weather. Induce the animal to eat, as the disease is very wasting and it is important to maintain the strength with feed. Give plenty of water. Do not give cathartics. Preventative vaccines should be given prior to exposure. These are usually given in a series within the last 2 weeks before exposure.

Strangles And Distemper

This is a communicable disease most often seen in your animals, affecting chiefly the glands in the regions of the throat. It is spread by both direct and indirect contact.

(1) *Cause:* This disease is caused by the infections (nasal, abscess, or other body discharges of a diseased animal) coming in contact with the nasal membranes or the digestive tract.

(2) *Prevention:* The instruction given for prevention of influenza applies also to this disease. The greatest danger of spread is by infected watering and feeding utensils. One attack usually renders the animal immune. There is a fairly effective vaccine available.

(3) *Symptoms:* Early symptoms are loss of appetite, increased temperature, pronounced moist cough, profuse watery nasal discharge which later becomes thick and yellow, head and neck extended stiffly, and a hot and painful swelling between the jaws. The swelling usually develops after about a week into an abscess containing very thick yellow pus. In more serious cases abscesses develop in other parts of the body.

(4) *Nursing and First-aid Treatment:* Segratate sick animals and see that they have absolute rest. Clothe the body according to the weather and prevent drafts but provide plenty of fresh air. Paint the swelling between the jaws with tincture of iodine once daily. Tempt the appetite and provide feed that is easily chewed. Clean the discharge from the nostrils two or three times daily with cresolis solution of strength for washing wounds, and after abscess opens, clean two or three times daily with same solution.

Coughs and Colds

Animals suffer from coughs and colds quite similar to the same conditions in man. They are mildly infectious inflammations of the membranes of the nose and throat.

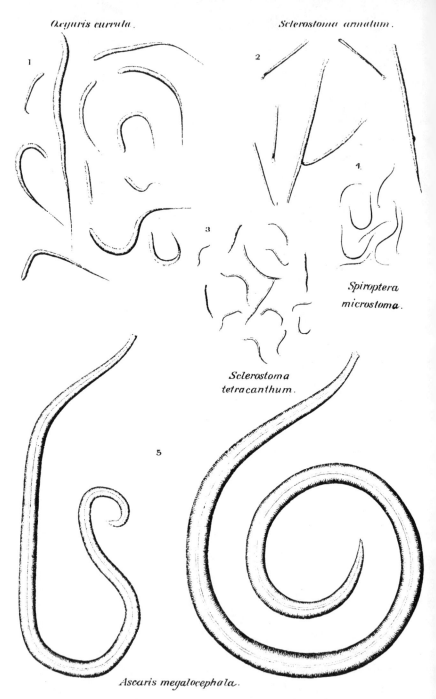

Oxyuris curvula.

Sclerostoma armatum.

1

2

4

3

Spiroptera microstoma.

Sclerostoma tetracanthum.

5

Ascaris megalocephala.

INTESTINAL WORMS.

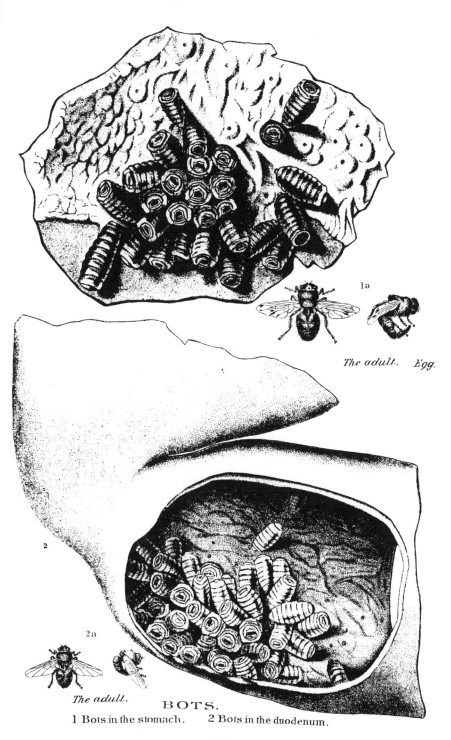

1a

The adult.   Egg.

2

2a

The adult.   BOTS.

1 Bots in the stomach.   2 Bots in the duodenum.

229

(1) *Causes:* Exposure to wet or cold, particularly when tired or heated; damp or poorly ventilated stables; sudden changes in weather.

(2) *Symptoms:* Dryness and redness of the nasal membranes followed by a watery discharge which in a day or so becomes grayish and thickened. (Normally with the mature horse the temperature should be 99-100 degrees, the pulse about 38 beats per minute, and the respiration rate about 15 per minute.) If the throat is affected, the cough is at first dry and later moist. The nasal discharge is odorless. In the early stages the animal is somewhat listless and may run a slight temperature, 100 to 102 degrees F.

(3) *Nursing and First-aid Treatment:* From early symptoms it is difficult to tell whether the condition is a simple cold or the beginning of influenza or possibly strangles. For this reason the animal should be handled as if he had influenza. Simple colds will usually respond to rest and a mild, laxative diet. The animal must be protected from cold and drafts or overheating.

Lice

Horses may be infested with three species of lice that bite and suck blood from the animal causing much discomfort. The horse itches severely and continual rubbing against solid objects causes a loss of hair. The lice avoid sunlight and seek the darker colored portions of the body. They are readily seen on tufts of hair pulled out of the coat. Treatment consists of thorough grooming and washing in 4 or 5 percent creolin solution. Baths can only be given during favorable weather and often it is advisable to clip lousy horses in the spring.

Mange

Mange resembles lousiness but it is caused by a mite that cannot be seen by the naked eye. Mange is also accompanied by more or less change in the texture of the hide. It becomes thick and scaly. Mange yields readily to treatment of lime sulphur dip.

Internal Parasites

There are many kinds of internal parasites or worms that infest horse. The commonest are the round worms, red or blood worms, and bots. Round worms are very large, from 6 to 8 inches in length. They live in the intestines of the horse and sometimes may be seen in the manure where they have passed out.

The red worms are very small and can barely be seen. They spend part of their life in the intestines, and part in the blood stream. They are particularly dangerous because in many cases they locate in the large blood vessels and cause a partial stoppage. They do this frequently in the arteries supplying the intestines, and the reduced blood supply is a frequent cause of colic. Horses may go lame from plugged arteries.

Bots

Bots are located in the stomach. The bot fly deposits its eggs on the long hair of the horse. From here they enter the mouth and then reach the stomach as bots.

The symptoms of internal parasites are unthriftiness, lack of condition, weakness, and paleness of the eyes. The hair is long and rough and colts become pot bellied. Young horses and colts are more affected than older ones.

The treatment of internal parasites is a serious question. Any drug that will kill the parasites is also poisonous to the horse. A dose may be given that will destroy the parasites and not injure the horse. This may vary from horse to horse. Also the proper time of year must be chosen in many cases, or the drug may be ineffective. Many horses have been severely damaged and even killed by improper treatment for worms.

For this reason the safest way is to have a diagnosis made and treatment prescribed by your veterinarian who is trained in the proper procedure. There is nothing that will pay bigger dividends to the horseman than having his horses properly treated for parasites. The horses will do better on less feed, there will be fewer attacks of colic, and they will have more endurance and vigor.

Symptoms of Disease

The most common indications of disease are partial or complete loss of appetite; abdominal temperature; accelerated breathing; increased pulse rate; listlessness; dejected countenance; profuse sweating; stiffness; nasal discharge; cough; diarrhea; constipation; pawing; rolling; lameness; inflamed membranes; unhealthy coat of hair; loss of hair; itching; or unnatural heat or swelling in any part of the body.

Nursing in General

The chief points to consider in nursing are:

a. *Ventilation* — Allow plenty of fresh air but protect from drafts. Avoid extremes of temperature and in the field provide shelter from wind and rain. Utilize grass plots and corrals whenever possible.

b. *Clothing* — The amount of clothing must be regulated by the climate. In winter woolen bandages on the legs are useful, and as many as three or four covers may be used. In summer fly sheets are extremely comforting.

c. *Bedding* — A good clean bed induces an animal to rest more and produces a soft springing surface for foot cases. It should be shaken up several times daily and be kept free of urine-soaked straw.

d. *Stalls* — A roomy box stall, well beded, should be used whenever possible. Keep a bucket of water in the stall and change the water frequently.

e. *Shoes* - The shoes may be removed and the feet leveled

232

if the animal is to remain in a stall for more than a few days.

f. *Exercise* — Convalescent patients should receive just as much exercise as each individual case permits. However, absolute rest is one of the very best treatments.

g. *Grooming*   (1) Animals that are weak and depressed should not be worried with unnecessary grooming. Such animals should be carefully hand-rubbed at least once a day, and their eyes, nostrils, and docks should be wiped out with a sponge or soft cloth. The feet should be cleaned. (2) Animals that are only slightly indisposed should be groomed in the usual way. (3) Animals with tetanus should not be cleaned at all.

h. *Feed* — Some sick animals retain a good appetite. The principal things to observe in their cases are that they are not overfed, that droppings are kept soft, and that they have plenty of water. Sick animals with impaired appetites require special attention. They often relish a change of diet, such as a bran mash, steamed oats, chopped alfalfa, grass, roots, and apples. Feed small amounts often; do not allow uneaten portions to remain in front of them; keep mangers and feed boxes clean; sprinkle a little sweetened water over the hay and grain.

HEALTH OF THE COLT

Mare and Foal

Pregnant mares should be given more care than the average horse receives in order to assure one of the best possible foals for the time, money, and effort spent. Such animals should be handled with judgment and patience as many of them tend to slow up and become, as is often termed "logy". Mares in foal should be given plenty of exercise in light work or turned in pasture when not at work. Mares should not be worked where there is danger of slips and overstrains. Stalls for pregnant mares should be amply large enough to allow the mare to lie down or get up with ease, and these should not be located near that of a vigorous tormenting stallion. The ration of the mare should be adequate to keep her in good flesh. If internal treatment for worms and other parasites is necessary it should be done in the late fall or early winter.

Care at Foaling Time

The commonly accepted gestation period of the mare is 330 to 340 days. As the foaling time approaches the mare should be kept in a clean, well bedded box stall at night. In warm weather a pasture lot free from other livestock is ideal. If a storm should threaten, the mare must be taken inside. If a night watch is kept it is well to see the mare every hour.

Shortly before parturition the mare will become restless and uneasy. She will repeatedly lie down and get up again.

234

When actual labor starts the mare will usually lie down stretched out on her side and strain. Sometimes they keep on their feet the entire time. Labor should normally last but a few minutes and if help is necessary a competent veterinarian should be called early in order to save the life of the foal. Foals seldom live more than three hours after the first contractions begin.

Colts may be born with the fetal membranes covering the body. This is sometimes called being born with a veil. If such happens, this should be quickly removed from the nostrils and breathing stimulated by brisk rubbing or artificial respiration.

As soon as the mare rises and takes possession of the foal, it is well to leave the stall and allow her full charge unless extra attention is necessary. Sometimes nervous mares or those with their first foal need some help to start the colt nursing. Soiled straw and membranes should be taken immediately from the stall. Retained membranes should be removed within 8 to 12 hours after foaling. The mare is very susceptible to infection in any manipulation. Removal of retained membranes should only be attempted by one who is trained in anatomy and can secure surgical cleanliness.

Care of Foal For The First Few Days

The umbilical cord should break normally at birth or when the mare rises. In case the stump remains too long or the cord fails to rupture it may be pinched off with clean fingers about two inches from the belly wall. No time should be lost in applying tincture of iodine to the umbilical stump. It is well to apply this once daily until the stump is dried up. The tincture of iodine may be placed in a short wide-mouthed bottle such as a vaseline bottle, and this held over the stump of the cord.

Bowel movement should take place in the foal within 6 to 8 hours after birth. If bowel movements are not normal it will be necessary to treat the baby colt by rectal injections and medicine by way of the mouth. Coals with an obstructed bowel are very sick and need quick relief.

To hold a colt, it should be grasped with one arm around the chest and the other around the rump. This is the most practical method and affords the least pressure on the delicate bones and joints.

Foals are much easier to handle than three year olds and they should be broken to halter, feet picked up, and taught to lead or stand. These lessons well learned by the foal are never forgotten, and breaking two years later is made much easier. Allow the colts to run with mares on clean grass pastures as much as possible.

Navel Ill

Navel ill is a bacterial or germ infection in the blood stream that may be present before birth or be obtained through an open navel after birth. It is a disease of the new born and is especially prevalent in colts kept in dirty stalls or colts born in fly season.

This condition affects the entire body but tends to localize in the navel and joints. It is a serious disease and demands preventive or immediate attention. Even with the best of care recovered animals may be left with a leg weakness as shown by enlarged hocks, etc.

Navel ill may sometimes be prevented by vaccinating the mare two or three times before foaling. This is usually done at 6 weeks, 4 weeks, and 2 weeks before foaling. If the mare has not been vaccinated, it may be wise to vaccinate the colt with two or three injections. If the foal becomes dumpy or stiff, your veterinarian should be called at once. Certain drugs or sometimes blood from the mare can be injected into the blood stream, and frequently are of great value, but they must be used early to be of benefit.

Scours or Diarrhea in Colts

The digestive tract of the new born is very sensitive and

easily disturbed. Scours may be caused by an infection from the mare's udder or improper composition of the milk. The first milk the mare gives to the colt is thought to be benficial in preventing scours. Too much milk per feeding—usually in hand fed colts—will cause scours. Navel infection sometimes leads to scours. Try to determine the causes and eliminate these, as the first step in treatment. A medium dose of mineral oil followed by bismuth subnitrate is generally effective for simple cases of diarrhea. In persistant cases the colt becomes weak and professional help in the early stages will pay big dividends.

LAMENESS

Lameness is any irregularity in gait which results from moving with pain or difficulty because of some defect. Severe lameness may make a horse worthless; any lameness lowers his value.

Severe lameness may often be detected by examining the horse in the standing position. If the lameness is severe enough, he will refuse to place any weight whatsoever on the affected limb. "Pointing," or placing the limb in an unnatural position indicates that pain exists in that limb.

Most lameness may be detected at the walk, although the symptoms are usually accentuated at the trot. Since the individual is forced to carry most or all of his weight on the sound limb, there is always a sinking or "nodding" of the hip or head as the sound limb strikes the ground. When the lameness is in the left fore leg, for example, the head will "nod" as the right foot is planted on the ground but will jerk up as the left or lame leg touches the ground. Lameness in the rear limbs may be detected in the same manner by observing the motion of the hips. The hip opposite the lame leg always drops as the sound foot hits the ground. Always observe the horse carefully from in front, from behind and from the side.

Lameness in both front legs is indicated by stiff stilted action and short stride, which often gives the impression of stiffness in the shoulders. The head is carried higher than usual without "nodding." The hind feet are lifted high while the front feet scarcely leave the ground as the horse moves. When at rest, the weight of the body is constantly shifted from one foot to the other and the hind feet may be cramped under the body in an attempt to relieve the pain in the front feet. Such symptoms are characteristic of navicular disease.

238

Symptoms of lameness in both hind limbs are short stride, awkward gait and lowered head. The front feet are raised higher than usual as the horse walks. It is very difficult or impossible to back a horse that is lame in both hind legs. When at rest the horse is very uneasy and constantly shifts his weight from one leg to another.

A swinging leg lameness is a symptom of pain resulting from advancing the limb. This type of lameness usually results from inflammation occurring above the knee or hock. A supporting leg lameness is characterized by pain when weight is put upon the limb. The source of this lameness is usually located below the knee or hock.

Shoulder lameness occurs occasionally but is less frequent than most horsemen believe. As the affected limb is advanced, pain is produced, resulting in a short stride and dragging of the toe of that limb.

The exact location of the lameness is usually more difficult to determine. Many common unsoundnesses of the limb may be observed by carefully comparing the general outline of the opposite legs. Swellings or bony growths can usually be detected in this manner. Inflammatory areas can usually be detected by pressing the region firmly with the fingers. Many cases require the services of a veterinarian for a correct diagnosis.

Unscrupulous dealers often resort to many methods of relieving symptoms of lammeness. If the lameness is slight, the sound foot is sometimes made equally lame by cutting the hoof to the sensitive portion in order to make the gait appear normal. Drugs are sometimes injected to deaden the nerves of the foot in order to relieve the pain which causes the animal to limp. Holding the rein close to the head when leading may prevent "nodding."

The possible causes of lameness in horses have never been numbered.

An exhaustive treatise upon the one subject of lameness would probably require an entire book larger than this one.

As to the prevalence of lameness, it has been said that half of the average veterinarian's income is derived from treating ailments at or below the knees and hocks of horses. Granting

239

that this may be an exaggeration, it still serves to illustrate the importance of the subject.

Though the possible causes of lameness are many, the probably or common causes are comparatively few, and these are spoken of separately farther on.

Locating Lameness

Lameness being of many kinds and due to many causes, it is somtimes difficult to tell in what part the trouble is located.

We offer the following suggestions for what help they may afford, and not as a set of infallible rules for determining the location of lameness.

Observe how the horse stands as well as how he travels.

Note his mammer of standing when he is quiet in his own stall where the floor is level and there are no exciting influences.

If one fore foot is advanced eight or ten inches in front of the other, and the animal shows a tendency to retain this position, or assumes it again shortly after having been induced to shift, there is apt to be soreness or tenderness in the heel, or in the back part of the limb somewhere a little higher up.

If the animal stands with knee and fetlock bent, resting the foot on the toe without advancing it in front of the other, the lameness is probably in the shoulder or elbow joint.

Where a horse stands with both front feet forward throwing the weight on the heels, and the hind feet are advanced farther under the body than they naturally would be, there may be soreness in the front part of the feet.

If there is a tendency to rest one limb more than the opposite one, there is probably something wrong with the limb that is being favored.

When a lame animal rests on all four limbs, the pastern of the lame limb is apt to have a more upright position than the other.

In exercise, the lameness is apt to be most apparent at a

slow trot. Make your observations when the animal has been at rest rather than when warmed up; or, as is sometimes best, warm him up pretty well, then let him stand perfectly quiet for a half hour or so to cool off.

Have a man lead him, allowing plenty of free rein instead of holding close to the bit. Some horsese will not carry the head in a natural manner when being led, so let the leader take first one side, then the other, in order that this may not deceive you.

If there is lameness in one limb, the animal will throw less weight upon it, and will lift the foot of the lame leg from the ground as quickly as possible. The sound may be a help in detecting this, as the lame foot strikes the ground with less force.

If the lameness is in a fore leg the head and fore part of the body will likely show a quick upward motion when the lame foot comes in contact with the ground, with a corresponding drop when the sound foot strikes the ground and takes the weight. At the instant when the lame foot takes the ground and the head is thrown upward, a tendency to droop the hip on the opposite side may be noticed, but this would not indicate lameness behind.

Where there is lameness in both fore limbs the animal steps short, strikes the ground lightly and makes the interval that the feet are on the ground as short as possible. The shoulders keep a rather stiff and upright appearance and the head is apt to be carried high. In endeavoring to make the hind feet carry more of the weight, they are brought well forward under the body, which arches the loins somewhat and gives the croup or rump a drooping appearance.

Lameness in one hind limb is accompanied by a greater rising and falling motion of the hip on the lame side when the animal travels.

If there is lameness in both hind limbs the animal will be reluctant about backing, the head will be carried low with a probable tendency to poke the nose forward, and the fore feet will be kept rather backward and under the body instead of reaching forward. The impact of the hind feet upon the ground will be light, and the interval of contact will be short.

241

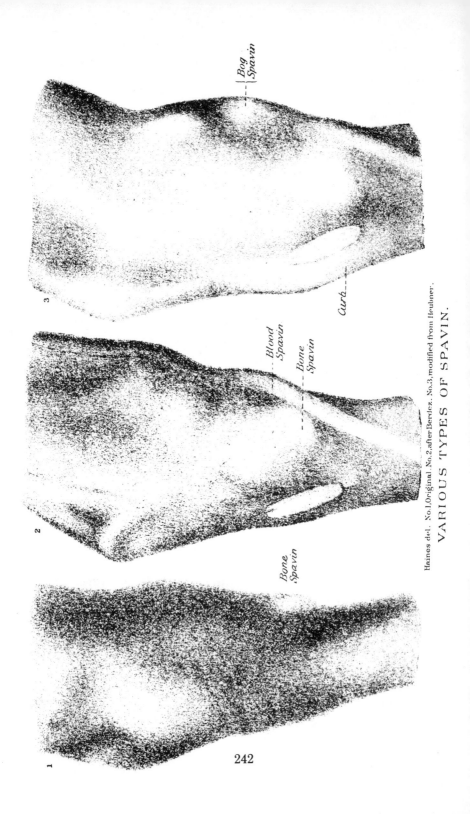

Bog
Spavin

Curb

Blood
Spavin

Bone
Spavin

Bone
Spavin

3

2

1

Haines del. No.1,Original. No.2,after Berdez. No.3,modified from Heubner.

VARIOUS TYPES OF SPAVIN.

242

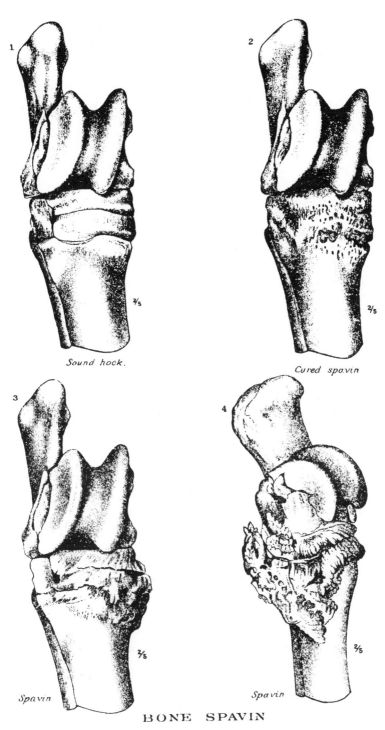

1

2

3

4

Sound hock.

Cured spavin

Spavin

Spavin

²⁄₅

²⁄₅

²⁄₅

²⁄₅

BONE SPAVIN

Lameness in front an behind on the same side produces a swaying, ambling gait.

Lameness in front and behind on opposite sides causes the horse to travel somewhat as he would if only one of the legs were lame, though the defect in gait is more marked.

When a horse is lame in two legs, he is usually more disposed to avoid trotting than where but one leg is lame.

Bone Spavin

Bone or "Jack" Spavin is a disease of the small flat bones at the lower part of the hock joint, and is marked by lameness and the formation of a bony deposit. It is a prevalent ailment and probably ruins many horses.

The part affected is the inner side of the hock, rather low down and a little forward of the center of the leg, at about the point shown in the drawing. The true hock joint is not  usually involved, but may be in some of the very bad cases. The somewhat characteristic lameness is apt to be present in some degree before the enlargement becomes noticeable, though often the development of the blemish is observed before lameness is apparent, and some little time may elapse before it becomes troublesome. Sometimes, too, there may be the external appearance of Bone Spavin without lameness developing, and we advise letting these cases alone.

A sprain, often very slight, is the usual beginning of Bone Spavin. Inflammation and the throwing out of the bony substance follows. Any horse is liable to develop a spavin, but some are rather predisposed to bony blemishes, and it is said that such a tendency is more or less hereditary. This being accepted as correct, Bone Spavin and Ringbone will become less prevalent only when the common practice of using blemished animals for breeding purposes is discontinued.

When an animal having Bone Spavin is made to move over in the stall, he will likely move the lame leg in a stiff manner, throwing the weight mostly on the toe, and may make a quick hitch with the sound leg. When taken out of the stall the same stiff limping is observed, but often for a few steps only. If allowed to stand for a half hour, the lameness occurs again in starting. If made to turn quickly in a short circle, the animal flinches and may even hop on three legs a little distance. as the case develops the lameness does not work off so readily, and finally exercise may aggravate instead of diminish it, the horse sometimes becoming entirely unfit for service, or even too lame to get about in grazing.

The enlargement is hard on bony, usually shaped like the bowl of a spoon, and may attain the size of a hulled walnut.

Treating Recent Bone Spavin

Taken in the very start, an application of strong blister will completely overcome the lameness, and will usually cause the bunch to be absorbed as well. No scar results and the limb in left as clean as before the blemish appeared.

Even if the trouble is of three to six months' standing, we would advise using this remedy if the animal is young, or if especially desirous of avoiding a scar. Keep the horse as quiet as possible in the stable for four weeks or more, making the first application rather toward the forward edge of the enlargement, then after the proper interval apply again, just back of where you did before so that you reach the back edge of the formation. After that, if further treatment is needed, apply a little higher or a little lower than the center of the bunch, as may seem best, no particular location being especially essential. Cover only a small surface each time; ordinarily in such a case we would advise that each treatment cover a spot about the size of a one-cent piece.

Treating the Older Cases

When Bone Spavin is well developed and has become firmly established, use Ringbone Paste. We would consider a case well developed and the Paste the proper treatment if either the lameness or the enlargement has been observed for six months or more. If the horse is old or the lameness quite severe, it is well to use the Paste even if the case is of less than six months' duration.

Rest is essential in connection with this treatment, and the horse should remain quiet in the stable. The time required varies in different cases, but is usually four to six weeks.

Most cases of Bone Spavin are cured with one treatment, though the lameness may hang on for several weeks after the outward effects of the remedy have passed off. A few cases require a second treatment, and an occasional one may even need a third, but do not attempt to rush matters by applying again at once if the lameness does not seem to be improved by the time the part is fully healed. Wait a few weeks and you will likely find that the lameness is subsiding, and that no more of the remedy will be required. If the lameness passes off and the bunch remains, let well enough alone, for it is usually considered well enough and all that can reasonably be expected is when an animal is made serviceably sound.

Occult Spavin

In Occult or Blind Spavin the characteristic bone spavin lameness is present, but no enlargement or bony deposit is to be observed. If in doubt as to whether the lameness is located in the hock, lift the foot so as to bend the hock joint as far as it will go, hold it in that position a minute or two, then let it down and start the horse quickly. If the trouble is there he will show a more decided lameness for a few steps.

Occult Spavin is apt to be tedious and rather difficult to cure, as the trouble is deep seated, usually affecting the surfaces between the flat bones of the lower part of the hock.

Splint

This is a bony deposit on the inside of the fore leg below the knee, the distance from the knee varying in different

246

cases. It may occur upon the outside of the leg as well, but such cases are quite rare. If the enlargement is not high up against the knee, and is well forward and out of the way of the tendons, it is not apt to give much trouble. Sometimes the animal will show no lameness on soft ground, but become very lame upon a hard road, and carry the head in a drooping fashion.

Old cases that are causing no lameness should be let alone, as the bunch is apt to be too thoroughly hardened to be absorbed away. If there is a lameness, or if you want to remove a recent growth, note whether the part is feverish. If it is, use the sedative lotion (formula given)  for a few days to reduce the heat, then apply a Blister, repeating it a time or two if required. This will almost invariably remove the lameness, and, except in the old cases, cause the bunch to be absorbed as well. No scar remains.

Ringbone

Ringbone is a bony formation, sometimes just above the hoof, and sometimes higher up and on the upper pastern bone. The enlargement may extend nearly around the part, or may be in front or upon the side only. Lameness sometimes appears before an enlargement is noticed, while in other cases the enlargement exists some little time before causing lameness. Some regard Ringbone upon the fore foot more difficult to cure than when upon a hind foot, for the reason that the pasterns are more upright and the fore legs carry nearly two-thirds of the animal's weight.

We will not dispute that there may be some truth in this, though our own observations do not tend to confirm such a theory.

To enter fully into the treatment of Ringbone would be to repeat much that we have said concerning the treatment of Bone Spavin. If there is merely an enlargement and no lameness, let it alone. There are a few

247

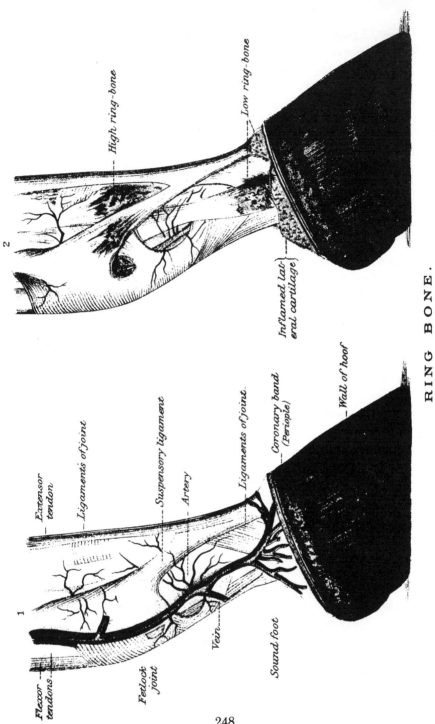

Flexor tendons
Extensor tendon
Ligaments of joint
Suspensory ligament
Artery
Ligaments of joint
Coronary band (Periople)
Wall of hoof
Vein
Sound foot
Fetlock joint
1

High ring-bone
Low ring-bone
Inflamed lateral cartilage
2

RING BONE.

cases that never cause trouble so treat these cases early.

Where Ringbone is just developing on a colt or young horse and is accompanied by lameness, blister and rest.

The cases that are pretty well established and causing lameness should be treated with Ringbone Paste. This remedy seldom fails even in the very old cases that have been fired or unsuccessfully treated in various other ways. Do not apply it all over the enlargement, but upon one small spot. One treatment in this way is often sufficient to cure, even though the blemish extends well around the foot. Use your own judgment in selecting the spot. If the enlargement is principally in one place, cover a surface only the size of a dime as advised for Bone Spavin. If the bunch is longer than it is wide, extending around the foot partially or entirely, it will be all right to place the paste in an oblong position, narrower than the dime and enough longer to involve about a third more surface. Keep the horse quiet and after the part is healed repeat on a different surface if necessary. If the animal has more than one Ringbone, treat only one at a time.

Sidebone

Sidebone is practically the same formation as Ringbone, though some authorities make a slight distinction. All agree, however, that the same treatment is required. In appearance it differs from Ringbone in that the enlargements are upon the sides of the foot and do not meet in front, and sometimes only one side is enlarged. Where the animal is not lame no treatment is advised. If it is a very recent case on a young horse, showing little lameness and slight development, use the Blister, treating alternately one side then the other, if both sides are affected, at intervals of a week or so. If well developed and lameness is quite marked, use the Ringbone Paste, treating one side first, then the other after the first has fully healed. Too much treatment at one time may make the horse shift too much weight to the other legs with bad effects.

Sedative Lotion

The formula here given is a valuable remedy to have about the stable. It is inexpensive and can be prepared by any druggest. For recent sprains, feverish joints, hot swellings, etc., it is the best possible application.

Muriate of Ammonia .... 2 ounces
Acetic Acid .... 1 ounce
Nitrate of Potash .... ½ ounce
Alcohol .... 2 ounces
Water sufficient to make one pint.

In this form the lotion is too concentrated to use, and should be diluted with eight parts of soft water. Apply freely two to four times a day until the temperature of the part is reduced to normal. Do not attempt to rub it in, but simply saturate the hair thoroughly.

Curb

 This is an enlargement of the ligament at the back part of the hock, due to sprains, kicks, etc. It occurs rather low down, and in the beginning is usually accompanied by heat and tenderness. In some cases there is lameness only in the earlier stages, while in other the blemish may continue troublesome. Where an old curb does not lame the horse we do not advise treatment of any kind, as after a time the enlargement becomes solid and permanently fixed.

In the early stages, notice whether there is heat in the part, and if there is use the sedative lotion to reduce it. Then apply a Blister. If there is little or no heat, it will not be necessary to use the lotion. In the fairly recent cases, this treatment will overcome the lameness and reduce the enlargement completely, but where the blemish has become well set the appearance of the part may not be improved. Allow rest until the horse recovers. The hocks of some animals have rather a curby appearance that is entirely natural,

and must be regarded as a slight deformity rather than unsoundness.

Sprains and Swellings

In cases of ordinary sprains and swelling accompanied by
heat and soreness, we would direct your attention to what is
said under the heading of "Sedative Lotion." If, after all inflammation has been removed from the part, the lameness
or enlargement does not disappear within a week or so,
Blister in the manner directed for ordinary blemishes, repeating the applications as may be required. Steroid therapy
is beneficial.

Bog Spavin

This is a soft, yielding, bulging enlargement occurring in front and a little to the
inside of the true hock joint, and is formed
by excessive secretion of the lubricating
fluid or joint oil. From the feeling of the
bunch some are led to inquire whether it

should not be opened, but to open it would be to risk ruining
the animal.

There are two wrong ideas concerning Bog Spavin that
have some prevalence. One is that the blemish never lames
a horse; the other is that it is necessarily permanent and incurable. These theories, however, may readily be accounted
for where one's observations have been limited to a few cases.

In order to make the matter clear, we will say that
Bog Spavin occurs in two forms, and will speak of each
in the light of our own experience and observations. The first
form is merely an excessive secretion of fluid or a dropsical
condition of the part, producing no lameness and objection-
able only on account of its ugly appearance and the conse-
quent disadvantage when the horse is offered for sale. The
second form is just the same in appearance, but involves act-

ual disease or inflammation of the joint, and is accompanied by lameness that may be only moderate or very severe.

In cases like the first mentioned we do not urge treatment, owing to the uncertainty of removing the blemish. Nevertheless, a large percentage of them can be removed, and our estimate is that a good Blister is effective about three times out of four in such cases, but we cannot say in advance which will yield and which will not. Ordinarily, we would discourage treatment if the animal is of the large-boned type, or if the blemish is so small as to be of little consequence.

It is not uncommon for boggy bunches to appear on young colts. We do not advise treating these, as they usually disappear later on of their own accord. A little brisk rubbing with the hand occasionally is said to be benefical.

In cases of the laming type, keep the animal quiet and use the sedative lotion if there is heat in the part. After a few days when the heat has been removed, or at once if there is little or no excess of heat, apply a Blister. By this treatment the lameness will be overcome, and the blemish will usually be reduced or removed entirely, the latter being more probably in cases of this type than in those where there is no lameness except in some of the older cases where the bunch has become quite hard.

Wind Galls

Every horseman is familiar with the bulging enlargements called Wind Galls or Wind Puffs. They are quite common and appear on either side of the tendons above the fetlock joint. As they are usually harmless and frequently obstinate, we do not strongly advise treatment unless the horse in lame. If there is lameness, treat with Iodine or a Blister.

Blood Spavin

Most of the so-called cases of Blood Spavin are Bog Spavin. Blood Spavin is seldom very conspicuous, and is both harmless and incurable. It is merely a dilation of the vein that passes over the part where spavin occurs.

Capped Hock

This blemish appears on the point of the hock and is caused by kicks and bruises. Treat the same as Crub, first using the sedative lotion if there is heat in the part, then applying a Blister. Repeat the treatment a time or two if required. Would not advise treating old case not attended by lameness, as removel of the blemish would be very doubtful.

Thoroughpin

Read what is said concerning Bog Spavin, which may apply to Thoroughpin as well, the two blemishes being practically the same in character, but differently situated. It is not uncommon for both Bog Spavin and Thorough- pin to occur on the same hock, and such cases are apt to be rather tedious, so much of the hock being affected.

The seat of Thoroughpin is at the upper and back part of the hock, as shown in the drawing, and the enlargement may appear upon one or both sides. Often by pressing upon one side the accumulation of fluid may be forced through to the other. In treating Thoroughpin Blister on one side, then after a week or ten days treat the other side in the same manner, alternating in this way a few times if necessary. Where Bog Spavin is present as well, rotate the applications, applying to one enlargement at a time and allowing a week or so to elapse before treating another. Any condition envolving the hock xoint will require a great deal of patience to be effective because there are so many moving structures in close proximity.

Stifle Lameness

Lameness may develop in the stifle joint from a kick, sprain or injury of any kind. Usually the animal stands with the leg in a half bent position, the foot resting on the toe. The lameness is not alike in all cases. The leg may be brought forward with a sudden jerk, or the motion may be a stiff, awkward swing. Often a swelling or enlargement forms, either at the point of the stifle or a little farther back.

Rest is essential in overcoming this difficulty. Keep the animal as quiet as possible, and apply a good Blister, either in front or upon the outside of the part as may seem best, repeating the treatment at intervals of ten days or so. It is not necessary to apply to any exact or particular spot, as the effect of the remedy is somewhat distributed, but keep within the vicinity of the seat of trouble. Some of these cases may prove a little tedious, but sufficient rest and some perseverance will usually bring them out all right. If there should be considerable heat in the part, it would be well to begin the treatment by using the sedative lotion for a few days.

Dislocated Patella

Dislocation of the patella or knee-cap is sometimes an accident attending a slip when a horse is rising in his stall. The animal stands with the leg extended backward and is unable to bring it to its natural position. Fasten a rope about the fetlock, pass the other end through a collar or strap around the horse's neck, and while a strong man or two draws the foot forward by means of the rope, stand behind the horse, with one hand on the inside of the stifle joint and the other on the outside, pressing the patella into its place. If dislocation occurs frequently, treat the same as stifle lameness or inject a blister.

Sometimes a young animal will be troubled with the patella slipping out and in with a snapping sound at every step. This is due to a weak or relaxed state of the muscles that should hold this bone in place. Keep the animal quiet in the stable and treat as for stifle lameness, which will have a stimulating and strengthening effect upon the muscles.

Inflammation of the Hock Joint

A kick or sprain is apt to set up violent inflammation in the hock joint, accompanied by great swelling and lameness. If not relieved the result may be serious, and as such accidents are always liable to occur, it will be well to know what to do. The treatment should be directed toward keeping down the inflammation. Put the animal in a comfortable stall and pack the joint loosely with cotton batting, then keep the cotton constantly wet with the sedative lotion. If after three days the condition is not improved, discontinue the lotion and apply hot poultices. If matter should form, let it break of its own accord, then wash the opening with a solution of chloride of zinc, one dram to a pint of water. After the part heals, if lameness yet remains, apply a blister. Steroids and antibiotics are the best professional treatment, better if applied in the early stages.

Sprained Tendons

Drawing heavy loads is a common cause. The horse digs his toes into the ground and throws great stress upon the back tendons of the legs. Sprain of the tendons is indicated by swelling, heat and lameness. Kicks and bruises may also produce the same effect, and should be treated in the same manner. Sometimes the swelling is so light as to hardly be detected, yet there is considerable lameness. Pressure causes flinching, however, and in this way the injury may be located.

If heat and swelling are present, use the sedative lotion, applying freely three or four times a day. If the lameness hangs on, or if the case is an old and chronic one, apply a blister, repeating the treatment upon a different spot at intervals of two or three weeks, meanwhile allowing rest. In severe cases a high-heeled shoe is advisable.

255

Callous Enlargements

Frequently a callous enlargement or thickening of the skin follows barb wire cut or other injury. These blemishes may in most instances be reduced by applying a smart blister each time, repeating the applications as often as may be required. Should it fail to take hold actively enough, rub it in with a little friction. There is nothing that will grow hair on an old and bare scar.

Collar Boil

This name is often applied to hard lumps forming under the skin of the shoulder where the collar rests. A blister is successful in most cases of the kind, causing the bunches to disappear by absorption. Apply to a small surface, repeating on different spots as may be necessary. This should be done at same time when the animal is not required for work, or else used only in brest harness that exerts no pressure upon the part. The same applies to saddle sores.

Shoe Boil

 Shoe Boil or Capped Elbow is a growth or tumor at the point of the elbow joint, caused by pressure upon the heel of the shoe when the animal lies cow-fashion with his legs bent under him. This manner of lying is sometimes induced by the stall being too narrow. If it is, widen it and he will likely assume a different position. Shortening the heel of the shoe, especially on the inner side, will sometimes be sufficient to remove the cause, or it may be necessary to pad the foot each night. Treat the bunch with a blister at intervals of two weeks or so until reduced. The primary object is to remove the cause and most of these will heal up of their own accord without treatment.

Construction of the Foot

Before entering upon the common causes of lameness in the foot, it will be well to consider, at least in a superficial way, the general structure of this part.

The foot is not the dead and insensitive thing that its external appearance suggests. Within the horny box that we call the hoof are bones, ligaments, tissues, blood vessels and nerves that are as much alive and just as sensitive as those that go to make up other parts of the horse. First, let us think of the coronary band around the top of the hoof, from which continually grows the wall of the foot. If any part of this band becomes injured in a permanent way so as to interfere with its formation, the wall of the foot will always be weak below that point.

The wall of the foot, a fibrous horny substance, is hardest upon the surface, and provided with a thin varnish-like coating to prevent both the escape of moisture from within and the absorption of moisture from without, and it is evident from this that rasping high up on the surface of the wall should be avoided by the smith in shoeing.

Beneath the wall is the quick or sensitive laminae, in which inflammation from disease, a shoe-nail prick or other injury, may cause intense pain and lameness.

The horny sole is produced from the sensitive sole beneath it, the process being continuous to provide for wear. It is composed of numerous horny layers that become harder as they approach the surface. Stone bruises or punctures may injure the sensitive sole.

The frog is a V-shaped yielding formation with a horny surface, extending forward from the heel, with cavities, called clefts, at either side, and a third and smaller one dividing it at the back part. The purpose of the frog is to act as a cushion, and in order to do this it must bear a little weight when the foot is upon the ground, which is to be considered in shoeing. Beneath the horny frog is the sensitive frog, subject to disease or injury.

Finally, let us remember that inflammation of the sensitive interior of the foot is apt to be especially painful, owing to

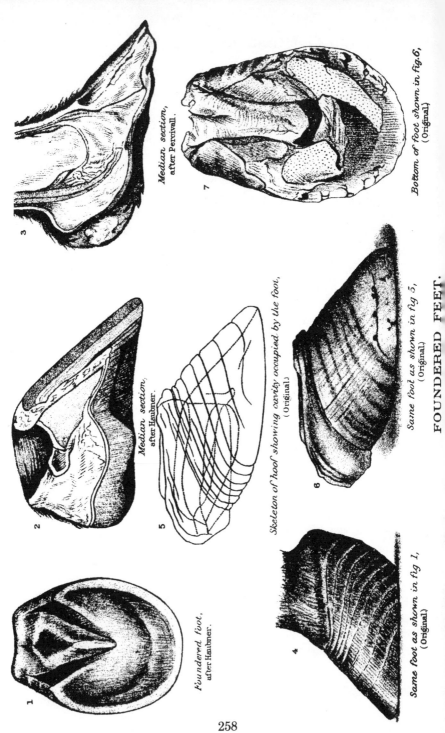

3

Median section,
after Percivall.

7

Bottom of foot shown in fig. 6,
(Original)

2

Median section,
after Haubner.

5

Skeleton of hoof showing cavity occupied by the foot,
(Original)

6

Same foot as shown in fig 5,
(Original)

1

Foundered foot,
after Haubner.

4

Same foot as shown in fig 1,
(Original)

FOUNDERED FEET.

258

pressure of the almost unyielding hoof that resists swelling.

Acute Founder or Laminitis

This disease is an inflammation of the sensitive laminae and sensitive sole, or may in bad cases involve still other parts of the internal foot. Some animals, especially those having badly formed feet, seem rather predisposed to this ailment. It may arise from a great variety of causes, and in consequence it is one of the common ailments. Eating wheat or rye, even in moderate quantity, will sometimes produce it or it may be due to eating too much of any kind of food, drinking cold water when heated, over-exertion on hard roads, bruises, punctures, shoe-nail pricks, badly fitted shoes, etc., or it may appear without any special cause being apparent.

Laminitis occurs most frequently in one or both feet, though the hind feet are sometimes affected. Some cases recover completely, while in others the foot is permanently injured and becomes badly deformed.

Where both fore feet are affected the animal extends them forward, resting the weight upon the heels, and brings the hind feet well forward under the body. If both hind feet are affected, they will have a forward position to get the weight upon the heels, and the fore feet will be placed backward and made to support as much of the weight as possible. Where only one foot is affected, the animal will relieve it of weight. The breathing is fast and heavy, with nostrils dilated, and the pulse is usually rapid and strong. If made to move the horse will groan and sway and finally slide his feet, though very reluctantly. The hoofs of the affected feet are hot, and if tapped lightly the animal will evince great pain.

Sometimes the horse will be found lying down instead of standing. Do not make him get up. If he is standing, induce him to lie down if possible. Give him a nice bed of straw, and if he still persists in standing, take a rope or strap and pass one end under him, then a man at each side raises the rope tightly against his belly, as though to carry a part of his weight. Gradually the animal takes advantage of the help given, and tries to rest on the rope. At the proper time let the rope go and he is apt to drop down. Feeling the relief that lying down affords, he is apt to remain down quite a while, and thereafter no encouragement with the rope will be required.

Ordinarily it is better to begin treatment by removing the shoes as gently as possible. Then dip cloths in hot water and wrap them about the feet, changing them every ten or fifteen minutes for a half to three quarters of an hour, then for a like period use cold applications instead, alternating in this way for about four hours. Follow with hot poultices until the soreness passes off. After two to four weeks when the inflammation has subsided, use a blister lightly upon the coronets, covering a surface an inch or so long and repeating upon different surfaces at intervals of two or three weeks. This will overcome any remaining sensitiveness and tend to ward off Chronic Founder. Allow a long rest at pasture or in a roomy box stall with soft earth floor or plenty of straw.

Some stand the horse in a tub of hot or cold water instead of applying the wet cloths, but it is always advisable to get him off his feet while the inflammation and pain are so intense. Antihistamines are sometimes effective if used early.

Chronic Founder

Chronic Founder is apt to follow the acute attack, through slight inflammation remaining after a cure seems to have been effected, or as a result of injury done the internal structures of the foot by the excessive feverishness and congestion. There is usually more or less lameness, and the feet gradually shrink, sometimes becoming very much deformed. In a majority of cases a complete cure can never be effected, though by proper treatment and care the animal will be able to render good service. Note what is said about Contraction of the Feet and treat Chronic Founder accordingly. Keep the animal off the hard roads. Recently plastic casts are used with good results.

Contraction of the Feet

Contraction of the Feet may be due to anything that causes a shrinking or wasting away of the soft structures within the foot. Standing on hard floors, alternate soaking and drying of the hoofs, allowing the wall at the back part of the foot to become overgrown and turned in, too much paring about the sole and frog, bad shoeing, injuries, etc., tend to produce this condition.

In undertaking a cure the first thing essential is to remove the cause if possible. Remove the shoes and place the horse in a stall having a soft, moist earth floor. Apply a blister upon the coronet, covering a surface about an inch long, and repeating after two or three weeks upon a different surface. This will help through its stimulating effect, and the treatment may be prolonged as required. Several months' rest is advisable, especially in the bad cases. Put on a level bar shoe when the horse is ready for work.

In very bad cases precede this treatment by applying poultices for a couple of weeks, or allow the horse to stand twelve or fourteen hours a day with his feet in a pool of clay mud.

Navicular Disease

Another name that is sometimes applied to this disease is Coffinjoint lameness. The part affected is the Navicular Bone and its surrounding tissues, and anything that may tend to set up inflammation in the back part of the foot may produce it. It is most common among fast road horses that have good action and strike the road hard with the feet.

Usually the first symptoms observed is that the horse when quiet in his stall will place one fore foot forward about eight or ten inches with the heel slightly raised; or, if both feet are affected, he will advance first one then the other. In traveling there may as yet be no lameness apparent, but the horse does not reach out as he should and is liable to stumble frequently. Gradually lameness develops, at first disappearing with exercise and only returning after the animal has been standing a time. Later on the lameness is more aggravated, the heel may contract, and the muscles of the shoulder or chest may waste away, producing Sweeny or what some call "Chest Founder." Upon examination heat in the back part of the foot is usually detected, and the animal flinches from pressure in the hollow of the heel, or when the wall in the region of the quarter, or the sole at each side of the frog, is tapped with a hammer.

Treatment, except in some of the recent cases, is usually unsatisfactory. Remove the shoe. If inflammation is quite marked, stand the horse in wet clay or poultice the foot until it is reduced. If there is little or no heat, or after you have reduced it as above, apply a good blister on the heel freely enough to blister. At intervals of about two weeks repeat on different spots about the heel or sides of the pastern. Some cases are apparently cured in this manner, but we cannot promise definite results. Even though the lameness is entirely relieved, a return of the trouble is always probable. Rest for a year is the best cure.

Corns

Ninety-nine corns in every hundred are due to faulty shoeing, and the remedy is to remove the cause. Corns occur on the fore feet and are indicated by lameness, the animal placing the affected foot forward and resting it on the toe when standing. Examining the foot you will find heat on the inside of the hoof at the heel and on pressing or striking the part the animal will flinch. Remove the shoe and pare off a little of the sole at that point, and you will find a red spot. In bad cases where matter forms, there is great lameness, and the matter may find its way out at the top of the hoof. In long-standing cases the result is usually contraction of the heel.

After removing the shoe poultice the foot to soften the hoof, overcome the inflammation and take out the soreness. Rasp the wall of the hoof level and put on a level bar shoe, rasping away a little of the wall at the corn to relieve it from pressure. Pare the corn very little, if at all, and do not apply caustic or strong medicine of any kind. Use the bar shoe until the sole of the foot becomes strengthened, then use a flat shoe and do not pare the sole, and you will have no more trouble with corns.

Seedy Toe

Sometimes the wall at the front part of the foot separates from the sensitive laminae, producing a hollow space. Such a condition is called Seedy Toe. It rarely causes lameness, and when lameness occurs it is probably due to sand or dirt getting into the cavity and causing irritation.

Treatment is seldom effective in uniting the parts. Put on a shoe having a broad toe clip, and fill in between the clip and separation with tar and oakum. Keep the hoof soft by occasional poultices, and blister the coronet at intervals to stimulate the growth of horn.

Quittor

Quittor is the name given to a fistulous disease of the foot resulting from bruises, pricks in shoeing, pebbles working up into the clefts of the frog, or any injury causing suppuration within the foot. It is marked by swelling upon the coronet, lameness, and finally fistulous openings upon the heel or at the top of the hoof. If there is considerable inflammation and soreness, apply poultices for a few days until relieved. Treat with antibiotics and a good wound dressing, meanwhile keeping the horse quiet.

Quarter Crack

Quarter Crack or False Quarter is due to derangement of that portion of the coronary band just above it. For instance, an injury to the coronary band may destroy its power to produce healthy horn, and at that point the wall of the foot is weak and imperfect. These cracks are usually widest at the bottom, as shown in the illustration.

If there is lameness, poultice the foot to reduce the inflam-mation, then put on a bar shoe so fitted that there will be no pressure upon the wall at the affected part. Apply a blister upon the coronet above the crack, which in many cases will stimulate the production of healthy horn, the exceptions being those in which the functions of the coronary band are permanently impaired.

Sand Crack

Sand Crack is a split in the upper part of the hoof where the wall is thin, due to a dry and brittle condition of the horny substance. It may appear suddenly, and usually occurs on the front or inside quarter of the foot. When weight is thrown upon the foot the crack may spread and the sensitive tissue bulging into the opening, may be caught and pinched when the foot is raised and the crack closes. This causes inflammation and lameness.

Apply poultices to soften the hoof and take out any inflam-mation or soreness that may be present. Put on a bar shoe so fitted as to relieve that part of the wall from pressure. With a sharp knife cut out a piece of the hoof clear to the quick at the upper end of the crack, which is likely to be at the coronary band. Fill the place with tar to keep out the dirt. This cutting, if carefully and properly done, removes the pressure at that point and gives the new hoof a chance to grow out sound. Apply a blister to the coronet above the crack once a month.

Thrush of the Foot

Thrush is a diseased condition of the frog of the foot. It may be caused by injury, bad shoeing, filthy stables, and by long continued wet weather and mud, the feet scarcely getting a chance to dry. The disease is marked by a very foul-smelling discharge from the clefts of the frog. In bad cases the horny frog may even become detached from the sensitive frog.

Clean out the clefts. You will likely find them very deep and extending into the sensitive parts of the foot. If the case is a bad one or the horse is lame, apply a poultice for a few days.

Treat with a good fungicide and sanitation.

Canker

Canker affects the frog, and may sometimes spread to the sole of foot. It is accompanied by a thin and very foul-smelling discharge, and the frog becomes much enlarged, soft and spongy, there being rapid growth of a peculiar horny, fungus like substance that bleeds quite freely when it is pared. Canker probably results from causes similar to those that produce Thrush. The presence of some form of vegetable parasite being an added feature. It is a disease that is difficult to cure, but most cases will yield to the following treatment:

Apply poultices for two or three days, changing them twice daily, and adding a little carbolic acid to the water used in making the poultice, about a teaspoon to each pint. Then pare down the frog, cutting away all the unhealthy growth that you can without too much bleeding. After the bleeding has stopped apply terchloride of antimony, commonly called butter of antimony, covering all the diseased surfaces. Repeat about every other day, cleaning the part each time by scraping the surface carefully. When the unhealthy growth seems to have disappeared completely, discontinue the antimony and use tincture of iodine lightly, once daily or every other day, until the part assumes a healthy appearance. Keep the horse in a clean place, and if necessary in order to keep out the dirt and protect the sore, cover the part with cotton batting or oakum and fasten it on.

Nail Injuries in Shoeing

Sometimes in shoeing a nail is driven too close to the sensitive sole, causing pressure and soreness. Where lameness develops a few days after the animal has been shod and no other cause can be found, tap the heads of the nails or the wall at each nail lightly with a hammer. The offending nail may often be detected in this way, and ordinarily its removal will be all that is required.

Should the nail strike the sensitive sole the smith will observe it at the time, withdraw the nail and reset it, but the injury done may be sufficient to cause inflammation and sometimes suppuration. If this occurs, remove the shoe and apply poultices for a few days. Should the lameness fail to pass off, open the part by paring along the course of the nail to allow the matter to escape, then continue the poulticing until the soreness subsides. These injuries are most apt to occur in horses having thin and weak hoofs. Give penicillin and tetanus shot.

Punctured Wounds in the Foot

The treatment of wounds of this character should depend somewhat upon the nature and extent of the injury. Deep punctures especially should have the early attention of a veterinarian who can judge as to the probable damage done and treat accordingly, for if the bone, coffin joint or flexor tendon is injured, results more or less serious are apt to follow. Shallow punctures may also bring serious consequences, especially if caused by a rusty and dirty nail. In such cases it is well to enlarge the opening slightly by paring out a little of the sole, then if you have a Veterinary Healing Oil handy, a few drops injected or otherwise introduced will, if it reaches the bottom of the wound, destroy any germs that may have been implanted, and also tend to prevent inflammation. If there is apparent soreness or any sign of inflammation, poultice the foot and see that there is a sufficient opening for matter to escape. Give penicillin and tetanus shot.

Elephantitis or Milk Leg

Elephantitis and Milk Leg are names sometimes given to chronic enlargement of the leg from the hock down, resembling Lymphangitis in appearance, and usually being a result of that disease. The animal may not seem to suffer from the ailment, and the swelling remains about stationary, fluctuating but little if at all. Not much can be expected from treatment in such cases, as the lymphatics are permanently injured. Tincture of iodine applied to limited surfaces once or twice a week may prove helpful.

Lymphangitis or Water Farcy

This is an acute inflammation of the lmyphatics. It is most common among heavy draft horses, and most frequently follows a few days rest after having been at hard work on heavy feed. It may also be due to  over-feeding, sudden exposure, general disorder, etc. It often comes on in a night, and in the morning the animal will be found shivering, breathing heavily, and stiff in one or both hind legs. Soon a general fever comes on, the pulse is rapid, and the glands high up on the inside of the thigh are enlarged and tender. In a few hours the lymphatic vessels of the leg begin to swell, and the limb may become two or three times its natural size. If the inflammation is not relieved in a day or two, suppuration may occur in the glands and the animal may die of blood poisoning, or the lymphatic vessels will be so impaired thta the leg will remain permanently enlarged.

In very mild cases moderate exercise may throw off the attack. If more severe, and especially if due to heavy feeding and lack of exercise, dissolve an ounce of aloes and an ounce of ginger in half a pint of boiling water, add half a pint of cold water, and give as a drench. Give also twenty drops of tincture of aconite every two hours until the pulse approaches normal. Three time a day for two or three days, give a quarter ounce of nitrate of potash in drinking water. Bathe the swollen leg for an hour at a time with hot water at intervals of three or four hours, and after each bathing apply the sedative lotion (formula given on another page). After a day or so when the inflammation is well reduced, exercise the animal lightly for half an hour two or three times daily. Feed bran mashes or other easily digested foods.

Sweeny

Sweeny is a very common trouble, and is especially liable to occur in young horses that have but recently been put to work. The usual form of Sweeny results from a sprain of the muscle that fill the posterior cavity on the outside of the shoulder blade, and at first there may be heat, swelling and some lameness, followed by rapid wasting of the muscle. Very often this shrinking of the muscle is the first symptom observed, and in some bad cases the shoulder blade becomes so denuded that there appears to be no flesh at all between the skin and the bone. Sweeny should be treated early, as in old cases a fatty degeneration of the tissues may occur, rendering complete restoration of the muscle impossible.

A sweenied condition of the shoulder may also result from Ringbone, or any form of lameness that interferes with the natural activity of the shoulder muscles, and in such cases it is necessary to give attention to the cause. Hip Sweeny may likewise be due to lameness farther down, or to an injury, or it may result from an attach of Azoturia. Treat with internal blister.

Shoulder Lameness

Lameness in the shoulder is indicated by the animal carrying his head low, dragging the toe on the ground, swinging the foot outward in bringing it forward, or standing with the joints bent and heel raised, but without advancing the lame foot in front of the other. Such lameness may be of a rheumatic nature, or due to strain or injury of some sort. In cases where there are no outward signs, such as heat or swelling it is often very difficult to locate the seat of lameness.

If the part is hot and swollen, apply two or three times a day the sedative lotion, formula for which is given on another page. Where there is no heat or swelling, use the blister in the same manner, applying where, in your judgement, it is most needed. Complete rest must be given until all lameness has disappeared. Steroids are usually effective.

Broken Knees

This name is given to bruises or abrasions of the knees such as may occur in falling. Slight injuries of the kind require no treatment, but if the knee is considerably bruised and swelling follows, bandage the part loosely and keep it wet with a solution of acetate of lead, one ounce to about three pints of water. Tie the horse high so that he will not attempt to lie down. If the wound is deep, extending through the skin, bend the knee to the position it was in when injured, and if you see any dirt wash it away with a stream of tepid water or a soft, clean sponge. Do not probe the wound. Trim the hair from any loose flaps of skin, draw them together and fasten with strips of ahesive plaster. If swelling and inflammation follow, use the lead solution as above. In bad cases it may be advisable to put the animal in a sling. Such an injury may ruin a horse if severe enough to break bones, lacerate the tendons, or open the joint so that the lubricating fluid escapes.

Knee-Sprung

Some cases of Knee-Sprung are hereditary, even existing

from colthood up, and nothing can be done for them. Most cases are due to sprain or other injury, or to some over-exertion or continued hard usage, causing the back tendons of the leg to become contracted. It is first noticed that the animal is weak or unsteady at the knees, with a probable tendency to stumble. As the tendons become more contracted, it is readily seen that the knee is not brought up to its nat-ural position in standing, and in bad cases the animal stands with the knees bent forward to a very conspicuous extent.

It is only the reasonably favorable cases that we advise treating. Where the trouble is due to wire cut or any injury that may have lacerated the tendons, or if the horse is some-what advanced in age and has had hard usage, we would ad-vise letting the case alone. But if the subject is a young ani-mal and the trouble is just coming on, or has appeared within a year and is moderate only, treatment will as a general rule prove effective. Use Steroids.

Cocked Ankle

This is a knuckling over or breaking forward at the pastern, indicating some weakness of the ligaments. It is sometimes induced by overwork, or by allowing the foot to become over-grown so that it does not rest in a natural position upon the grund. If there is any apparent cause, correct it. If the foot has been growing long at the toe, shaping it up properly and putting on a shoe slightly elevated at the heel may be bene-ficial. Allow rest, and if there seems to be any heat in the part, apply a loose bandage for a few days and keep it wet with cold water. Follow with light applications of a blister at intervals of two or three weeks. Bent Ankle, sometimes seen in young foals, is of a different character. They usually straighten up with age.

Rheumatic Lameness

Rheumatic Lameness is most common in the shoulder, but

also affects other parts. It is apt to have a shifting tendency, changing from one leg to another, and may sometimes be accompanied by swelling. There may also be more or less general stiffness, dullness or lack of energy, all the symptoms being aggravated by exposure to cold and dampness.

Rheumatism is due to an irritating principle, causing inflammation of the joints and muscles. Stimulating liniments may afford some temporary relief, but a cure requires that the cause be eliminated.

It is well to first empty the bowels with a dose of physic, a pint and a half to two pints of raw linseed oil, then give aspirin, a dose each evening in bran mash for a week or ten days, then every other day for a couple of weeks to obtain a thorough action upon the system. Half ounce doses of nitrate of potash, given in drinking water once a day for several days, may also be helpful. Steroids help many cases.

Fractures of the Bones

This is a subject that we shall touch upon only briefly, because in the larger animals treatment is seldom advisable, except in cases of simple fracture, and if possible professional attention should be given them. By simple fracture is meant a single break and not a shattering of the bone, and without wounding or lacerating the flesh about the part.

If, for instance, the case is simple fracture of a horse's leg, the ends of the broken bone should be brought into proper position and secured as promptly as possible. Tear long strips of muslin about three or four inches wide, wet with starch and wrap smoothly around the part. After sevral layers have been put on, apply splints of thin wood or stiff leather, bandaging them firmly in place with the starched muslin. The bandage should extend clear down to the foot, otherwise there is apt to be a serious swelling and inflammation in the lower parts, and should also extend well above the fracture, holding all joints below and the first above in a fixed position if possible. If swelling exists before the bandage is applied, it

271

may be necessary after a few days to readjust the bandage, which should be done with the utmost care.

It is also necessary to put the animal in a sling and keep him there until the bones have united, which is apt to be six weeks, and the bandage should remain on about as long. After that, rest should be given for two or three months.

COMMON UNSOUNDNESSES

The horse buyer must be familiar with common unsoundnesses in order to evaluate a horse properly. The following discussions give a definite, description, and the usual causes of the most common unsoundnesses.

The subject of transmissible unsoundnesses is widely debated. Probably no disease is actually inherited, but the fact that individuals may inherit a predisposition to unsoundnesses through faulty conformation cannot be questioned. This predisposition to contact bone diseases is particularly marked; hence, breeding stock should be absolutely free from bone spavin, ringbone, sidebone and similar diseases.

Location of Common Unsoundnesses and Blemishes

I. Head:
   1. Defective eyes
   2. Poll-evil

II. Withers and shoulders:
   1. Fistula of the withers
   2. Sweeney

III. Front Limbs:
   1. Shoe boil or capped elbow
   2. Splint
   3. Wind-gall, wind-puff or road-puff
   4. Ringbone
   5. Contracted tendons, cocked ankle or knuckling.
   6. Sidebone

273

7. Quittor)
8. Quarter-crack or sand-crack)
9. Navicular disease) front feet
10. Founder or laminitis)
11. Thrush)
12. Scatches or grease heel)

IV. Rear Limbs:
1. Stifled
2. Stringhalt
3. Wind-gall, wind-puff or road-puff
4. Ringbone
5. Contracted tendons, cocked ankle or knuckling
6. Thoroughpin)
7. Blood spavin)
8. Bog spavin)
9. Bone spavin or jack) HOCKS
10. Capped hock)
11. Curb)
12. Quittor)
)
13. Quarter-crack or sand-crack)
14. Founder or laminitis) hind feet
15. Thrush)
16. Scratches or grease heel)

V. General:
1. White horse tumors, black pigment tumors or mela-
nomas
2. Hernia or rupture
3. Thick wind and roaring
4. Heaves, asthma or broken wind.

Defective Eyes

The eyes should always be examined very closely with a
flashlight in a darkened stall, or by standing the horse in an
open doorway. Cataracts and cloudiness of the cornea usu-

274

ally are easily detected. Other defects are not so easily observed, but the general expression of the head, with unnatural carriage of the ears, may indicate poor eyesight. The horse that is partially blind usually shies at objects, keeps his ears constantly moving, and stumbles frequently.

A pale blue or cloudy, watery eye is characteristic of periodic ophthalmia or "moon blindness." Since the eye may appear quite normal after recovery from the first few attacks, an examination of the interior of the eye by a veterinarian is necessary to determine if the horse is suffering from this disease. Repeated attacks of periodic ophthalmia usually produce permanent blindness in one or both eyes.

Sweeney

Sweeney is an atrophy or decrease in size of a single muscle or a group of muscles. The term is commonly applied to the extreme atrophy of the shoulder muscle. It is usually caused by a blow, ill-fitting collar or severe strain. Sweeney of the hip may follow difficulty in foaling or an attack of azoturia. Some cases of sweeney recover after a few months' rest. Blisters and subcutaneous irritants applied under the direction of a veterinarian may hasten recovery.

Splint

A splint is a bony enlargement usually found on the inside of the upper part of the front cannon bone of young horses. It may occasionally occur on the outside of the front cannon bone but is rarely seen on the rear cannon. Splints usually follow kicks, over-exertion or concussions produced by work ing on hard surfaces. The bony growth may result from irritation between the large cannon bone and small splint bone. Splints are easily seen if one stands directly in front of the horse and observes the outline of the cannon. Splints are very common blemishes of race horses. Aside from the slight lameness which rarely occurs during the first stages of formation, splints are of little importance since horse dealers and judges ignore them almost entirely. Splints can be reduced or removed by one or more applications of a strong blister. If the splint is near enough to the tendons to allow the tendon to rub on the rough surface of the splint, considerable damage may result. The leg will fill and the animal will become very lame. In these cases the splints should be removed and the horse rested until the tissues return to normal.

Shoe Boil or Capped Elbow

Capped elbow or shoe boil is a swelling at the point of the elbow. This condition is usually caused by constant irritation of the heel or shoe upon the point of the elbow when the horse lies with the front leg flexed underneath the body. Recovery usually follows proper treatment. Most important point of treatment is eliminating the cause. This usually means making another shoe slightly shorter to prevent the irritation. If the heel is causing the irritation, it can be bandaged when the horse is in the stall.

Wind-Gall, Road-Gall, Wind-Puff or Road Puff

Wind-galls are small, puffy swellings which usually occur on each side of the tendons just above the fetlock or knee. Wind-galls are much more common in the young, light-legged breeds of horses than in draft horses. They are formed by an excessive secretion of synovia which distends the sheaths surrounding the tendons. Severe strain, over-exertion or infectious disease may be predisposing factors. Wind-galls are not often considered serious since they usually disappear and cause no lameness unless pathological changes occur within them. Do not attempt to drain them. Bandaging will hasten recovery. Applications of cold water may be beneficial.

Ringbone

Ringbone is a bony growth on either or both of the bones of the pastern which may involve the joints. The ringbone may appear as a hard bony swelling on any part of the pastern. It may be so small that it escapes notice or as large as a walnut or even larger. The outlines of right and left pasterns should always be compared in cases of doubt. Small ringbones may be felt by carefully passing the hand over the pastern. Lameness usually develops gradually but may appear suddenly after severe strain. The lameness produced may not be proportionate to the size of the growth, since a small ringbone may sometimes produce a more serious lameness than a larger one. The location of the swelling is of most importance. Ringbone at the front or rear of the pastern usually produces severe lameness because it interferes with the free movement of the tendons. Ringbone on etiher side of the pastern is usually less serious. Severe chronic lameness always results if the joints become involved. There is no treatment known which will remove the bony enlargement, but firing or blistering may cause the bones of the diseased joints to grow together, thus relieveing the pain. Nerving is occasionally performed as a last resort.

Contracted Tendons,
Cocked Ankle or Knuckling

Contracted tendons, cocked ankle, or knuckling is a partial dislocation of the fetlock or pastern joint produced by the shortening of the tendons at the back part of the cannon. The tendons may contract as a result of over-exertion, founder, or a local inflammation of the tendons. Knuckling must always be regarded as very serious, although some cases may be cured by expert veterinary surgery. Colts usually have a better chance for recovery than mature horses.

277

Sidebones

Sidebone is an ossification of the lateral cartilage of the foot. The lateral cartilages extend upward above the margin of the hoof so that they may easily be felt under the skin. These cartilages are normally firm and elastic but yield to the pressure of the fingers. Depositions of mineral salts in these cartilages change them to bone so that they become very hard and unyielding to pressure, producing the condition known as sidebones. Sidebones usually occur on the front feet as a result of concussion or injury. They are common in draft horses more than two years old and vary greatly in size and severity. If lameness occurs, it is usually intermittent in character and rarely severe. Although sidebones are considered serious in show and breeding stock, they rarely produce lameness. Sidebones cannot be removed. "Nerving" is sometimes performed if the lameness is severe and persistent.

Quittor

Quittor is a decay of the lateral cartilage of the foot characterized by a discharge of pus through a fistulous tract extending from the cartilage to the coronet or hoof head. Quittor produces severe lameness and shows no tendency to heal. Quittor is more common in the front feet but sometimes occur in the hind feet. The degree of severity of this unsoundness is dependent upon the structures of the foot which are involved, although all cases must be considered serious. Many cases may be cured by an operation, but several months of rest are required for complete healing.

Quarter Crack or Sand Crack

Quarter-crack or sand-crack is a vertical split in the wall of the hoof which results from a dry or brittle hoof or improper shoeing. Proper treatment may hasten recovery, but lameness sometimes remains severe until the new hoof has formed. About 12 months are required for the growth of a new toe, while the heels grow in less than half that time. Treatment consists of taking pressure off that part of the hoof to prevent further splitting. Sometimes it becomes necessary to make a V-cut or burn a semi-circle into the hoof wall above the split to stop its progress. Recently plastic patches have produced good results in selected cases.

Navicular Disease

Navicular disease is an inflammation of the small navicular bone and bursa inside the hoof just behind the coffin bone and small pastern bone of the front foot. The symptoms of this condition are "pointing" when at rest and a short, stubby, painful stride which may give the impression that the horse is lame in the shoulders. Navicular disease is incurable. In selected cases, veterinarians sometimes perform a nerving operation that will relieve the lameness and increase the usefulness of the horse for a time.

Founder or Laminitis

Founder or laminitis is an inflammation of the sensitive leaves which attach the hoof to the fleshy portion of the foot. It is usually the result of over-feeding, infectious disease, long shipment or standing in a stall for long periods because of some other lameness. Founder may also follow foaling, as a result of infection and inflammation of the uterus. All the feet may be affected, but the front feet are more susceptible. If laminitis is properly treated as soon as it occurs, most cases will completely recover in a few days. If the disease is neglected, however, it will often become chronic, resulting in a dropping of the hoof soles and a turning-up of the toe walls (chronic deformities of the hoof that are incurable). A veterinarian should always be called immediately when founder or laminitis occurs.

Thrush

Thrush is a disease caused by decomposition of stable manure and other filth that is allowed to collect in the cleft of the horn frog, betwen the frog and the bars. Old, severe cases of thrush occasionally produce lameness, but most cases respond to cleanliness and proper treatment.

Stifled

A horse is said to be stifled when the patella of the stifle joint is displaced. If the patella is displaced toward the outside of the leg the condition is serious and usually incurable. If the displacement is in an upward direction, the reaction to a sudden fright that causes the horse to jump may throw the patella back to its normal position. Backing a horse uphill may accomplish the return to normal. However, this condition is likely to recur quite frequently. The stifles may be injected by the veterinarian with a good internal blister to tighten them, thus preventing further trouble.

Stringhalt

Stringhalt is a nervous disorder characterized by a sudden, involuntary flexion of one or both hocks in which the foot is jerked up much higher than normal. The symptoms are usually noticed as the horse is backing from his stall, turning on the affected leg, or when suddenly frightened. The exact cause is unknown, although many horsemen consider the disease hereditary. Stringhalt may be so mild that, the jerking is noticed only occasionally or so severe that the leg is jerked upward at each step. Some cases may be cured by surgery.

Scratches or Grease Heel

Scratches or grease heel is an inflammation of the posterior surfaces of the fetlocks characterized by extensive scab formation. Heavy, highly-fitted show horses seem most susceptible to this condition. Most cases respond to treatment. Brush and clean the area and apply zinc ointment or a healing powder. Keep the heals clean and dry.

Thoroughpin

Thoroughpin is a soft puffy swelling which occurs on each side of the gaskin just above the hock in the region known as the "hollow." Pressure exerted on one side decreases the swelling on that side but increases the swelling on the opposite side. Lameness does not usually occur, but the condition greatly decreases the sale value of a horse and renders him worthless as a show animal. Most thoroughpins are incurable.

Bog Spavin

Bob spavin is a large, soft, fluctuating swelling which usually occurs on the front and inside of the hock. This condition is fairly common in heavy highly-fitted horses with soft, meaty hocks. It results from an excess secretion of joint fluids which produces a distention of the joint capsule. A bog spavin is very easily seen and is much larger than a blood spavin. Although a bog spavin does not usually cause lameness, its presence indicates a lack of wearing qualities and is the object of very unfavorable comment among judges and horsemen. Treatment is usually unsuccessful.

Blood Spavin

Blood spavin is a swelling over the front and inside of the hock caused by the dilation of the large vein which crosses that region. Since lameness never occurs, this condition may be regarded as a blemish of very little significance. Very mild blisters with no rubbing may be attempted to reduce the swelling.

Bone Spavin or Jack

Bone spavin is a bony growth which may occur on any of the bones which form the hock, although it is usually found on the inside and lower portions. It is caused by an inflammation of the periosteum such as may be produced by strain or over-exertion. Since a predisposition to the disease may be hereditary, affected animals should not be used for breeding purposes. The spavin usually may be seen by one's standing directly behind or in front and a little to one side of the horse. In cases of doubt, lift the foot upward and forward in order to bend the hock as much as possible. After holding for two or three minutes, release the leg and start the horse at a brisk trot. A characteristic lameness will sometimes be noticed if the individual is affected. Bone spavin is one of the most serious unsoundnesses of the draft horse. Firing tends to make the bones unite and will often relieve lameness if only the flat bones of the hock are affected.

Curb

Curb is a hard, firm swelling on the back surface of the rear cannon, about a hand's breadth below the point of the hock. A large curb is easily seen by observing the hock and cannon directly from the side. A smaller one may help by passing the fingers over the region. Crooked or sickle hocks are most subject to this unsoundness since this faulty conformation throws a greater strain on the hock. A curb usually follows strain or over-exertion but may result from a kick or blow. The initial lameness disappears after the formation of the curb, but the condition must still be considered an unsoundness because an affected hock is thought to be less likely to endure severe strain.

Capped Hock

Capped hock is a firm swelling which occurs on the point of the hock. This blemish may be as large as an apple or so small that it escapes notice. Capped hock usually results from constant irritation, such as might be produced by rubbing or kicking the walls of the stable; hence it may be indicative of the horse's disposition.